LUTHER'S

TABLE TALK;

OR,

SOME CHOICE FRAGMENTS

FROM

THE FAMILIAR DISCOURSE OF THAT GODLY,

LEARNED MAN,

AND FAMOUS CHAMPION OF GOD'S TRUTH,

DR. MARTIN LUTHER.

LONDON:

PRINTED FOR LONGMAN, REES, ORME, BROWN, AND GREEN;
HATCHARD; SEELEY; AND RIVINGTONS: TIMMS, DUBLIN: W.
WHYTE AND CO., EDINBURGH: BELLERBY, YORK; AND FINLAY
AND CHARLTON, NEWCASTLE UPON TYNE.

1832.

PREFACE.

Reader,

You are here presented with a few fragments, gathered up from the conversations of that great and good man, Dr. Martin Luther, of Wittemberg, which, it is hoped, will afford you a comfortable and salutary repast.

The original volume of the "Table Talk," from which they are selected, is said to have been compiled by Dr. John Aurifaber, or Goldschmidt, from a vast collection of Luther's sayings, made by Dr. Antony Lauterbach. It was first published in the year 1571, by Mr. Henry Peter Rebenstock, minister of Eischenheim, and, having been translated into English by Captain Henry Bell, an English officer, who had served long in Germany, was printed in London, anno 1651, under the sanction of a committee * of Parliament.

* The two members to whom the committee referred this subject, delivered in their report in these words:—" To the Committee of the Honourable House of Commons concerning Printing.

" According to an order directed unto us by this honourable committee, we have perused so much of Mr. Henry

PREFACE.

It is but justice to inform you, that the authority of the book (taken as a whole) is questioned by the learned, inasmuch as it was published contrary to a strict injunction of Luther himself [*],

---

Bell's translation of the book, entitled 'Martin Luther's Divine Discourses,' as will enable us to give this testimony and judgment of the whole.

"We find many excellent divine things are contained in the book, worthy the light and public view: among which Luther professeth that he acknowledgeth his error, which he formerly held, touching the real presence,—'*Corporaliter in Coena Domini.*' But we find withal many impertinent things; some things which will require a grain or two of salt; and some things which will require a marginal note, or a preface.

         "CHARLES HERLE.
"Nov. 10. 1646.   "WILLIAM CORBET."

To the word "impertinent," the English editor attached the following note:—" And no marvel that among so much serious discourse on matters of religion, sometimes at table, some *impertinent* things might intermix themselves, and some things, *liberius dicta*, to recreate and refresh the company."

[*] Luther's language, addressed to his friends concerning some of his written papers which might fall into their hands, is this:—" I entreat them in the name of Christ, not to be ready to publish such things, either while I live, or after my death. From the times in which I live, and the part which I am obliged to act, it cannot be but that some strange thoughts should bubble up in my mind by night and by day, which the impossibility of otherwise retaining them obliges me to note down upon paper, like a confused chaos, in the fewest words possible, for future use. But to publish such things, however obtained, would be both ungrateful and inhuman. Not that they are wicked and bad, but because

and without the sanction of any respectable name but that of John Aurifaber. It contains, besides, many things which it is hardly reasonable to suppose that Luther would have spoken, even at those times of relaxation, when, to judge from the title of the book, the greater part of its contents were uttered.

Its authority, therefore, as an historical document, is very properly disallowed.

But, whatever may be the opinion of the learned on the respectability of the original publisher of the Table Talk, and the authenticity and correctness of the *whole* of its contents, this is certain, — that somebody, intimately acquainted with Luther, was at great pains to collect and commit to writing, partly from his own knowledge, and partly from the communications of others, every sentiment and sentence of Luther's which appeared to him at all worth recording. Luther seems, in short, to have had his Boswell, — some humble admirer, who, like the entertaining biographer of Johnson, thought every thing of value

---

many of them, when I am able to reflect coolly upon them, appear to myself foolish and objectionable. Wherefore I again entreat that no one of my friends will publish any thing of mine without my concurrence. If he does, he must take the whole responsibility upon himself. Charity and justice require it."

which fell, or might have fallen, from the lips of so great a man as Dr. Martin.

It will be a subject of regret with many, that a collection of sentiments, so intrinsically excellent as most of these sayings of Luther are, was not enlivened by some of those minute details of time, place, manner, and other circumstances, which render Mr. Boswell's book so peculiarly attractive; and every one will admit that such a narrative must needs have been peculiarly interesting and instructive. Luther's ordinary associates were, for the most part, men of the highest order for learning, talents, and piety; and his house was open to all the learned and the wise, who resorted from every quarter of Europe to the University, which the joint labours of himself and his colleagues had raised to great celebrity. It is highly probable that the Table Talk is mainly composed of recollections of Luther's share in conversations with men of this character.

In the absence of such desirable details, which would have served to explain many sayings of Luther, to which those who are unacquainted with his character are apt to give an unfavourable interpretation, it may be proper to remind the reader: that Dr. Martin was a man of strong sound sense, but, withal, of a native playful humour, which he did not always keep under sufficient restraint. A vein of jocularity, something similar to which appeared in our two worthy martyrs, Bishop Latimer and Dr. Rowland Taylor*, would mix itself with some of his

* The facetiousness of Father Latimer is well known. The reader, whether he have read it before or not, will not be displeased at the insertion here of the following anecdote of Dr. Taylor, as delivered by John Fox, in his Martyrology. " This good man, who was vicar of Hadley, in Suffolk, was condemned to be burned alive in his own parish. In pursuance of his sentence, he was delivered over to the sheriff of London, and, subsequently, to the sheriff of Essex, who was to escort him to the borders of Suffolk. With the sheriff of Essex, and his men, the good doctor held much cheerful and serious conversation, as they rode along, and so won their hearts, that at Chelmsford, where they supped, they all joined in earnest entreaties that he would save his life. ' You may do well yet,' said Mr. Sheriff, ' if you will but recant: doubt not but you shall find favour at the Queen's hands. I, and all these your friends, will be suitors for your pardon. This counsel I give you, Doctor, of a good heart and will towards you; and, thereupon, I drink to you.' In this joined all the rest, saying, ' Upon this condition, Doctor, we will all drink with you.'

" When the cup was handed to him, he stayed a little, as one studying what answer he might give. At last he said, ' Mr. Sheriff, and my masters all, I heartily thank you for your good will. I have attended to your words, and marked well your counsels. And, to be plain with you, I find that I have been deceived myself, and am like to deceive a great many at Hadley of their expectation.' With that word they all rejoiced. ' Yes, Doctor,' said the sheriff; ' God's blessing on your heart, hold you there still. It is the most comfortable word we have heard you speak yet.'

" Then continued Dr. Taylor, ' I will tell you how I have

most serious thoughts, and the most important events of his life.

This infirmity of Luther's mind has evidently been the occasion of introducing a few strange stories, and somewhat strange sentiments, into the original volume of the Table Talk. These, again, being recorded without any reference to the circumstances under which they were spoken, have been the means of disparaging Luther's judgment in the eyes of those who have no wish to think well of him. But whoever reads the following extracts with attention, will soon perceive, that the general strain of conversation between the great Reformer and his friends, though not unalloyed by human folly, was such as became men employed in so great a work as the Head of the Church had assigned them; and if, after long

---

been deceived, and, as I think, shall deceive a great many. I am, as you see, a man of a very large body, which I thought should have been laid in Hadley church-yard, had I died in my bed, as I hoped I should have done; but herein I was deceived: and there are a great many worms in Hadley church-yard, which would have had merry feeding upon me, but now we shall be deceived, both I and they; for this carcass must be burnt to ashes, and they shall lose their feast.'

"When the sheriff and his company heard him say so, they were amazed, and looking one on another, marvelled at his constant mind, who thus, without all fear, made but a jest at torment and death now prepared for him."

hours of study, and engagements which tend to fatigue the spirits, this great and good man carried the *dulce est desipere* beyond its proper bounds; every candid mind will make allowance for him, and every judicious one guard against the imitation of a worthy man's fault.

Should any one ask the Editor his reasons for publishing these extracts, he has only to say, he thinks the publication calculated to be useful.

It contains excellent sentiments, which may prove the more acceptable to some readers as coming from a famous man.

It may serve to show, better almost than any thing else, what sort of a man Martin Luther was; and to rescue a character valuable to Christendom from the calumnies of Romish writers, and the sneering misrepresentations of infidels.

It may help to remind Englishmen of the blessings of The Reformation, and of the thanks which we owe to God for raising up those mighty champions, who have been His instruments in conferring such benefits upon us.

There is in it much that is peculiarly suited to the present times, in which the increase of true religion in the land has been attended with circumstances very similar to those which drew forth many of Luther's remarks.

Some excellent hints and admonitions are here given to the Clergy on the subject of preaching, well calculated to check the rage for fine, *i. e.*

ostentatious, preaching; which, by the compliance of the clergy with the false taste of a portion of their hearers, in these days of ease and refinement, is so sadly gaining ground; and to reduce preaching to its primitive character,— that of a solemn, plain, affectionate address to the congregation, on the subject of their salvation through Christ.

It may be the means of recommending other works of Luther to the attention of many who would not otherwise be aware what wholesome, excellent, instructions may be found in the writings of this good man: especially to people with afflicted consciences, of whose cases Luther was particularly careful.

May it not be useful, also, as a *hint* (by way of example) to Bishops, Doctors of Divinity, and others placed in authority, or had in reputation for piety, what the fruits of *their* table talk and familiar conversations ought to be? while it may suggest to all the enquiry, whether our communications with one another are such as would bear to be written down.

For these, and other reasons, the Editor feels himself authorised, and almost obliged, to add one more to the many books which are every day issuing from the press.

In making the selection from the larger volume of the Table Talk, he has studiously endeavoured to admit only such passages as every reader, at all acquainted with Luther's history, character, sentiments, and style, would, at once, recognise as his. If, in other respects, he has admitted what the reader would have left out, or omitted what he would have introduced, the Editor counts upon the usual allowance made to difference of taste. It has been an object with him to make a selection likely to interest and inform readers generally; and while he has admitted much that exhibits Luther's views of Christian doctrine, he begs to refer the reader to the works of Luther (many of which have of late years been printed in England) for a further exposition of them.

If the reader object, which, without the imputation of fastidiousness, he may, to the antiquated style of the book, let him consider, whether it is not more in keeping with a work of this character than the modern: or let him excuse its uncouthness, on account of the Editor's want of time, perhaps, also, of skill, to improve it.

The arrangement of materials, somewhat different from that of Dr. Aurifaber, has been made with a two-fold design. First, to give an interest to the contents of the volume, by a close association with the interesting character of Luther, and the times in which he lived: and, secondly, for more convenient reference; for the book may prove *a help to profitable conversation,* an object much to be regarded in all Christian families.

Some notes and observations are here and there

interspersed, principally for the benefit of the less informed readers; and, in some instances, to obviate the misconceptions to which the productions of a mind like Luther's are peculiarly liable.

For an account of Luther's life, which every Protestant should read, and which no one can read (one would think) without advantage, the reader is referred to a short memoir prefixed to a volume containing thirty-four of his sermons, or Middleton's Evangelical Biography, vol. i., or to Milner's Church History, with Continuation by Scott; in which great and successful pains have been employed to draw the great Reformer to the life.

The Editor will conclude this preface by copying from the last of these works two characters of Luther, as given by two eminent partisans of Rome, and sworn enemies to the Reformer and his cause; the Jesuit Maimbourg, and the French historian Varillas; together with some notices of his character, motives, and pretensions, by the famous Erasmus of Rotterdam. To these he will subjoin a short sketch of him by one of his cotemporaries who knew him well. Having done this, he will leave the reader to profit (as he prays God he may) by the perusal of the little volume.

The Jesuit Maimbourg, in his History of Lutheranism, records many particulars of the learning and abilities of this celebrated heretic, as he calls him:—

"He possessed," says the Jesuit, "a quick and penetrating genius; he was indefatigable in his studies, and frequently so absorbed in them, as to abstain from meat whole days together. He acquired great knowledge of languages and of the Fathers. He was remarkably strong and healthy, and of a sanguine, bilious, temperament. His eyes were piercing and full of fire. His voice sweet, and vehement when once fully raised. He had a stern countenance; and, though most intrepid and high spirited, he could assume the appearance of modesty and humility whenever he pleased, which, however, was not often the case. In his breast was lodged plenty of fuel for pride and presumption; hence his indiscriminate contempt of whatever opposed his heresies: hence his brutal treatment of kings, emperors, the Pope, and of every thing in the world that is deemed most sacred and inviolable. Passionate, resentful, and domineering, he was continually aiming to distinguish himself by venting novel doctrines, and on no occasion could be induced to retract what he had once advanced. He maintained that Aristotle, Thomas Aquinas, Scotus, Bonaventura, and others, had undermined the foundations of true philosophy, and of Christian theology; and he endeavoured to raise up a system of his own upon the ruins of these very great geniuses. This is an exact portrait of Martin Luther, of whom it may be truly said, there was in the man a great mixture both of good and bad qualities,—the bad predominated; but he was abundantly more corrupt in his thoughts and sentiments than in his life and manners. He was always reckoned to live sufficiently blameless while he remained in the monastery, 'and till he absolutely ruined all his good qualities by his heresies."

Varillas, a celebrated French historian, in his diffuse history of various heresies, speaks of Luther in the following terms:—"This Augustine monk united, in his single person, all the good and all the bad qualities of the heresiarchs of his time. To the robustness, health, and industry, of a German, nature seems here to have added the spirit and vivacity of an Italian. Nobody exceeded him in philosophy and scholastic theology, nobody equalled him in the art of speaking. He had completely discovered where lay the strength and the weakness of the human mind; and, accordingly, he knew how to render his attacks successful. However various or discordant might be the passions of his audience, he could manage them to his own purposes; for he presently saw the ground on which he stood: and, even if the subject was too difficult for much argument, he carried his point by popular illustration and the use of figures. In ordinary conversation he displayed the same power over the affections, which he had so often demonstrated in the professor's chair, and in the pulpit. He rarely attempted to convince; his method was to inflame men's passions, and, afterwards, gradually to insinuate his opinions. No man, either of his own time or since, spoke or wrote the German language, or understood its niceties, better than Luther. Often, when he had made his first impressions by bold strokes of eloquence, or by a bewitching pleasantry of conversation, he completed his triumphs by the elegance of his German style. On the contrary, he was rude, satirical, ambitious, and ungrateful; disposed to anger on the slightest occasions, and, for the most part, implacable. He was much addicted to excesses at the table, and was capable of the usual concomitant vices, though his monastic life deprived him almost entirely of opportunities of indulging them."

Such is the character ascribed to Luther by two Roman Catholic adversaries. The reader, in the midst of much surmise and exaggeration, will perceive the admission, that this man, so much spoken against, was possessed of some remarkable excellences; a fact further confirmed by the testimony of the learned Erasmus, a man who (whether conscientiously or not may be doubted) remained to his death in communion with the church of Rome; and, at the instigation of the Pope, wrote several pamphlets against Luther. Erasmus, in various letters, and particularly in one to Cardinal Cajetan, opens his mind freely concerning Luther and his proceedings. He acknowledges that he possessed great natural talents, and that he had a genius particularly adapted to explain the difficult points of literature, and for rekindling the sparks of genuine Christian religion, which were almost extinguished by the trifling subtleties of the schools. He adds, that men of the very best character, of the soundest learning, and of the most religious principles, were much pleased with Luther's books: further, that in proportion as any person was remarkable for upright morals and gospel purity, he had the less objections to Luther's sentiments. "Besides," said he, "the life of the man is extolled, even by those who cannot bear his doctrines. Some, indeed, in hatred to his person, condemn what is true; pervert and misinterpret what is right, and make him pass for a heretic, for saying the same things which they allow to have been pious in Bernard and Austin. Truly, it grieves me that a man of such fine parts should be hunted and made desperate by the mad cries and bellowings of the monks. We ought," continues this sagacious writer, "to take notice of the source and spring of all this evil. *The world was burdened with human inventions* in the business of religion; loaded with opinions and doctrines of the schools, and oppressed with the tyranny of the monks and begging friars. I do not condemn them all, but many of them are so

men, that, for the sake of interest and rule, *they temper the consciences of men on purpose.* They lay aside Christ and modesty; they preach nothing but their own innovations, and oftentimes scandalous doctrines. They speak of *indulgences* after such a manner as is even insupportable to the laity. By these and such like methods the power of the Gospel is dwindled to nothing; and, it is to be feared, matters becoming continually worse, the little spark of Christian piety, by which the stifled spirit of charity might be rekindled, will be entirely quenched. The chief parts of religion are *lost in ceremonies* more than Judaical. Good men lament and weep for these things; and even divines, who are not monks, yea, and monks themselves, in their private conversations, acknowledge them to be true. These things, I believe, first put Luther upon the dangerous work of opposing some of the most intolerable and shameless abuses. For what can we think otherwise of a person who neither aims at worldly honour or riches? I do not consider the charges which they bring against the man. I speak only of the apparent grounds of their animosity towards him. Luther had the boldness to call in question the good of indulgences; but others had, first, spoken too much and too boldly for them. Luther has dared to speak indecently of the power of the Pope of Rome; but others had first exalted it too imdecently; and, in particular, three preaching friars, Alvarus, Silvester, and the Cardinal of St. Sixtus. He dared to despise the decrees of Thomas Aquinas; but the Dominicans had extolled them almost above the Gospel. He dared to disclose some doubts in the matter of confession; but the monks continually perplexed the consciences of men upon that head. He dared to reject the conclusions of the schools in part; but others ascribed too much to them, and yet disagreed with them as well as he, altering them often, and introducing new notions in the place of those they abolished. It was matter of grief to pious minds to hear almost nothing said in the schools of the doctrines of the Gospel, and that, in the sermons, little mention was made of Christ, but much of papal power, and the opinions of recent writers. Luther has written much that relishes more of imprudence than of irreligion. But the greatest offence he has given is, his want of respect for Thomas Aquinas; his lessening of the profits of indulgences; his despising of the mendicant friars; his preferring of the Gospel to the doctrines of the schools; his opposition of the sophistries of disputants: all these are intolerable heresies."

Thus wrote the learned Erasmus of Luther and his times, and of the origin of his movements against Popery. He was certainly a very competent witness of the facts to which he refers: and though his observations were made at a time when people of influence might speak their minds without peril of their lives; yet such sentiments would expose a man to suspicion of disaffection to the Romish church; and a person of Erasmus's timidity, to give utterance to them, must have been very deeply sensible of their truth.

And now, Reader, having shown you the judgment of three Roman Catholics concerning Luther, two of whom were his declared enemies, and the other not his friend, we will give you a small portrait of him from the hand of a Protestant who knew him well. "Martin," he writes to a friend, " is a man of a middle stature, hath a lean body, exhausted with cares and study, so that his bones may almost be numbered. He hath a clear and sharp wit; his learning and knowledge of the Scriptures is admirable, so that he seems to have them all by heart. He is already so good a Greek and Hebrew scholar, that he can make judgment upon interpreters.* He wants not eloquence; but hath matter and words at will. In his life and conversations he is affable and courteous, not stoical and supercilious; yea, he seems

* This remark shows that this was written in an early stage of Luther's career, for he became eventually an excellent Hebrew scholar.

to be (as once the Apostle) all things to all men. He is cheerful in his communications, and withal sufficiently smart and acute. Though his adversaries threaten cruel things, yet his countenance is always the same, — settled, serene, and fearless. It can scarcely be imagined that he should attempt such arduous enterprises without a call thereto from God; but that which is most condemned in him is, he is bitter and tart in his reproofs beyond what is meet in a theologue."

CONTENTS.

CHAPTER I.

PASSAGES RELATING TO THE LIFE AND CHARACTER OF LUTHER.—HIS VIEW OF THE ROMISH CORRUPTIONS OF CHRISTIAN RELIGION, AND THE GREAT REFORMATION EFFECTED PRINCIPALLY BY HIS MEANS.

	Page
Luther's Ignorance in Popery	1
The Bondage of Luther's Conscience under Popedom	3
Touching Martin Luther's Progress in the Work of Reformation	8
Luther's Interview with Cardinal Cajetan	15
Luther's Integrity and Disinterestedness	18
Luther's unfeigned Love to Jesus Christ our Saviour	20
Luther's Firmness and Decision	23
Luther's Confidence in dangerous Times	27
Luther's Domestic Character	30
Luther's Vehemence and Asperity	37
Luther's Constitutional Melancholy, and Attendant Tribulations	50
Luther's warm and humble Piety	60
LUTHER'S REMARKS ON SOME OF THE ERRORS AND ABOMINATIONS IN POPEDOM	65
The Book of the Birth and Generation of Antichrist, the Son of Hypocrisy, the Son of the Devil	65
Luther's Opposition to the Popish Doctrine	66
The Pope's Decrees	75
Of the Idolatry in Popedom	76
Idolatrous Religions encouraged in the World	80

to be (as once the Apostle) all things to all men. He is cheerful in his communications, and withal sufficiently smart and acute. Though his adversaries threaten cruel things, yet his countenance is always the same, — settled, serene, and fearless. It can scarcely be imagined that he should attempt such arduous enterprises without a call thereto from God; but that which is most condemned in him is, he is bitter and tart in his reproofs beyond what is meet in a theologue."

CONTENTS.

CHAPTER I.

PASSAGES RELATING TO THE LIFE AND CHARACTER OF LUTHER.—HIS VIEW OF THE ROMISH CORRUPTIONS OF CHRISTIAN RELIGION, AND THE GREAT REFORMATION EFFECTED PRINCIPALLY BY HIS MEANS.

	Page
Luther's Ignorance in Popery	1
The Bondage of Luther's Conscience under Popedom	3
Touching Martin Luther's Progress in the Work of Reformation	8
Luther's Interview with Cardinal Cajetan	15
Luther's Integrity and Disinterestedness	18
Luther's unfeigned Love to Jesus Christ our Saviour	20
Luther's Firmness and Decision	23
Luther's Confidence in dangerous Times	27
Luther's Domestic Character	30
Luther's Vehemence and Asperity	37
Luther's Constitutional Melancholy, and Attendant Tribulations	50
Luther's warm and humble Piety	60
LUTHER'S REMARKS ON SOME OF THE ERRORS AND ABOMINATIONS IN POPEDOM	65
The Book of the Birth and Generation of Antichrist, the Son of Hypocrisy, the Son of the Devil	65
Luther's Opposition to the Popish Doctrine	66
The Pope's Decrees	75
Of the Idolatry in Popedom	76
Idolatrous Religions encouraged in the World	80

CONTENTS.

	Page
The slavish Praying in Popedom	81
The Value of holy Places, and of Relics	81
A Friar at Compostella	82
Of Rome and Jerusalem	83
Celibacy in Popedom	83
The Social Life is the best	84
A Friar's Fast in Popedom	85
The People's Fasting	86
Auricular Confession	86
The Pope's Perversion of the Bible and Sacraments	88
The True Use and Understanding of the Sacrament	89
The Abomination of the Popish Mass	90
Of Purgatory	92
The Pope's Covetousness	93
A Lying Wonder	94
Self-righteousness of Popedom	94
A Popish Argument	96
ANECDOTES RELATIVE TO THE REFORMATION	96
Bishop of Mentz and the Bible	96
The World's Judgment of the Bible	97
Elector Frederick's Judgment	98
The sad End of one who trifled with God	98
A fearful Story	99
Prince George and his Son	100
Henry VIII. King of England	101
Sir T. More	102
A Prince turned Friar	103
A merry Tale of two Friars	103
A shrewd Decipherer	105
St. Bernard	105
Prince Henry of Saxony	106
The Landgrave of Hesse	106
John, Elector of Saxony	107
The Diet of Augsburg	110
Prince George's Reformation	114
Luther's Discourses on the Times	115
Luther's Prayer for a gracious Rain, and the Success thereof	125

CHAPTER II.

CONTAINING DIVERS WEIGHTY SENTENCES OF DR. MARTIN LUTHER TOUCHING THE HOLY SCRIPTURES, AND THE PROFITABLE STUDY THEREOF.

	Page
The Excellency of the Scriptures	127
On the Study of Divinity	137
Of the School Divines, and their vain speculating Divinity	139
How Luther learnt his Divinity	144

CHAPTER III.

SAYINGS OF DR. MARTIN LUTHER TOUCHING THE KNOWLEDGE OF GOD.

Of Man's Ignorance	148
The Trinity	149
How to find out God	151
Concerning the Attributes and Proceedings of the Almighty	153
Of Christ — God manifest in the Flesh	162
Of the Holy Ghost	181

CHAPTER IV.

TOUCHING CERTAIN PRINCIPAL DOCTRINES OF THE CHRISTIAN RELIGION.

Concerning Justification	186
Concerning the Law and the Gospel	191
Concerning Sins, and the Confession and Forgiveness of the same	207
The Character of God's People	209

CHAPTER V.

TOUCHING THE CHURCH, AND THE MINISTRY THEREOF; AND HEREIN CONCERNING PREACHING.

| Of the Church, and its Condition and Appearance in this World | 212 |

CONTENTS.

	Page
Of Excommunication	216
Of the Sacrament of the Lord's Supper	218
OF THE MINISTRY OF THE CHURCH, PREACHING, ETC.	221
Luther giving Orders	221
Prayer for Ministers	222
A Minister's Honour	223
A Minister's Spirit	224
The right Etymology of the Word "Bishop"	224
Scandalous Ministers	225
Concerning the due and honourable Maintenance of Church Ministers	225
A Minister's Learning	228
OF PREACHING	229
The best Preachers and best Hearers	229
Of powerful Preaching	229
Luther's Preparation of a Sermon	230
Long Sermons	231
Rambling Preachers	231
Preacher's Defects	232
Luther's Recommendation of Cellarius	232
Qualities of a good Preacher	232
A Preacher to please the World	233
How to preach before a Prince	233
Luther's Preaching	234
St. Paul a plain Preacher	234
Plain Preaching commended	234
Ambitious Preaching	235
How Luther would make a Preacher	237
Of the Children's Catechisms	238
Brentius a good Preacher	240
Arnsdorff, Osiander, &c.	241
Dr. Brucken	241
A Preacher (in Controversy more particularly) ought to keep to his Point	242
Ostentatious prating Preachers	243
A good Preacher	244
The Preacher's Burden and Strength	245
Luther's Admonition to Preachers	245

CONTENTS. XXV.

CHAPTER VI.

TOUCHING CHRISTIAN DUTIES.

	Page
Of Faith, and the Proof thereof	247
Of Prayer	249
Precatio Lutheri	255
Of Works of Charity, &c.	255
Of the Merit of Works	256
Luther's Exposition of Isaiah xxx. 16.	257
How necessary Patience is	258
On being good	258
On confessing Christ	258
Of brotherly Forgiveness	259
Of friendly, Christian-like, Reproof	260

CHAPTER VII.

MISCELLANEOUS REMARKS AND OBSERVATIONS OF DR. MARTIN LUTHER TOUCHING MATTERS IN DIVINITY, AND AFFLICTIONS OF THE HEART AND CONSCIENCE.

Sundry wholesome Counsels uttered by Dr. Luther for the helping and solacing of those who are troubled in Mind, and the Subjects of Spiritual Temptations	261
How those who are in Tribulation concerning Faith are to comforted	269
Of Adam's Fall	274
Adam's Judgment of Modern Luxury	275
Of Adam's Tribulations	276
Of David	277
Of Hezekiah	279
Of Jonah	279
Luther's Judgment concerning the Fathers	279
Sundry Similitudes	287
CONCERNING THE JEWS	289
Their Sufferings and continued Obstinacy	289
Condition of the Jews in Luther's Time	290

a

CONTENTS.

	Page
An Argument with the Jews	292
Of the Destruction of Jerusalem	293
What came of a Jew's visiting Rome	294
Of the miserable State of People's Lives	295
A few short Sayings	295
That Women must not have the Government	296
Dr. Luther's Thoughts on Domestic and Political Government	297
Difference between Parents and Magistrates	298
How Governors should be qualified	298
The false Reckonings of ungodly Princes	299
Concerning Pontius Pilate the Governor	299
The Prince's best Wealth	301
A Great Man's Example	301

CHAPTER VIII.

MISCELLANEOUS THOUGHTS ON POLITICS, LAW, LITERATURE, &c.

Dr. Luther's Judgment touching Resistance to Government, or constrained Defence	303
Luther's concluding Speech concerning forced Defence	308
Luther's Discourse of Lawyers	309
Of a strange Case at Law	313
Of Astronomy and Astrology	314
A Word of Advice to Students	318
OF SUNDRY LEARNED MEN	319
Of John Huss the Martyr	319
Of Livy, &c.	320
Of Bucer	321
Of Aristotle and Cicero	321

LUTHER'S TABLE-TALK.

CHAPTER I.

PASSAGES RELATING TO THE LIFE AND CHARACTER OF LUTHER. — HIS VIEW OF THE ROMISH CORRUPTIONS OF CHRISTIAN RELIGION, AND THE GREAT REFORMATION EFFECTED PRINCIPALLY BY HIS MEANS.

Luther's Ignorance in Popery.

" THIRTY years back," said Luther, " the Bible was unknown, the prophets were nameless, and held impossible to be understood: when I was thirty years old, I had seen no Bible, and thought there had been no epistles or gospels but those in the Postills.* At length, by accident, I found a Bible in the library at Erfurth,—the same I read oftentimes, to the great wondering of Dr. Staupitz.

" In such darkness," said Luther, " governed the Pope, with great superstition. I," said Luther, " should

---

* The Postills are the portions of Scripture appointed by the Roman Breviary, or Roman Catholic Prayer Book, to be read on particular days.

never have dared to fall upon the Pope's angelical shine and lustre, had not St. Paul, with clear and bright witnesses*, shown the future blindness of popedom; and also if Christ, the Son of God, with great thunderbolts had not beaten down the high majesty of the Pope, where he says, '*In vain do they worship me, teaching for doctrines the commandments of men.*' (Isaiah, xxix.) If Isaiah alone had written the same, and Christ himself had not repeated and alleged it against the Pharisees, it would have been utterly despised."

"In popedom," said Luther, "I was also a presumptuous worker of seeming holiness; when I celebrated that abominable idol, the mass, then I presumptuously trusted and relied thereupon. But at that time I saw not the knave that lay hid thereunder. I did not put my confidence in God, but in my own righteousness and good works. I rendered no thanks to God for the Sacrament, but God must be glad to give me thanks, in that I would vouchsafe to sacrifice and offer up his Son to him. This may justly be called blaspheming and deriding God, and when one went to say mass, he used this proverb:—'I will go and lift up a child to the Virgin.'"

"When I was in my monkery at Erfurth," said Luther, "I was, as St. Paul saith, (Romans, ix. 16.) a willer and a runner; but I ran the longer the farther from the true righteousness which availeth before God; therefore what I now have was not gotten by that race."

* 2 Thess. ii. 1, &c.   1 Tim. iv. 1, &c.   Col. ii. 16, &c.

The Bondage of Luther's Conscience under Popedom.

When Luther first began to celebrate mass, and to make the crossings, *mira gesticulatione digitorum*, and could not rightly hit the old customs, he would say, " Mary, God's mother, how am I plagued with the mass, and these crossings, which I can never hit aright. Ah! Lord God," said Luther, " we were in those times poor plagued people, and yet it was nothing but mere idolatry. They so terrified some with the words of consecration (specially those who were good and godly, and meant seriously *) that they trembled and quaked at the pronouncing of the words, ' *Hoc est corpus meum;*' for they were to pronounce them *sine ulla hesitatione.* He that stammered, or left out but one word, committed a great sin. Moreover, the words were to be spoken without any strange cogitations, and so that none of the standers by might hear him. Such an honest friar," said Luther, " was I for fifteen years together; the Lord forgive it me."

" When I was a young man at Isleben, I went with the rest in procession, on the day of Corpus Christi, and had on my priest's attire: it happened that I was in such sort affrighted before the Sacrament, which Dr. Staupitz carried, that I thought I should have fallen down stark dead. Now when the procession was ended, I confessed, and opened my grief to Dr. Staupitz. He said, ' O! your thoughts are not Christ's.' These were

* This was Luther's own case. He was always, like St. Paul, before his conversion, as well as afterwards, a strictly conscientious man.

good words; I received them with joy, and they were very comfortable to me."

"When I was a friar in the monastery at Erfurth," said Luther, "I wrote to Dr. Staupitz thus, '*O my sins, sins, sins!*' Whereupon he sent me this answer, 'Thou wouldest fain be without sins, and yet thou hast no right sins, as murdering of parents, public blasphemy, contemning of God, adultery, &c. Thou must have a register wherein are written, noted, right and true sins, if thou wilt have Christ to help thee: thou must not trouble thyself about such puppy sins, nor make out of every bombard a sin.' Was not this a comfortable priest?—fit for the devil!"

"The praying in popedom," said Luther, "is a mere tormenting of the conscience, only a prating and tongue threshing; not prayer, but a work of obedience. From thence proceeded a confused sea full of canonical hours * the howling and babbling in cells and monasteries, where they read and sang the Psalms and Collects, without any spiritual devotion; insomuch that they understood neither the words, nor sentences, nor meaning.

"How, before the Gospel came, I tormented myself," said Luther, "with those canonical hours (which, by reason of many businesses I often intermitted) I am not able to express. On the Saturdays I used to lock myself up in my cell, and accomplished what, during the week, I had neglected.† I was, afterwards, troubled

* Prayers to be repeated at particular hours of the day or night.
† Luther, on one occasion, brought on a painful nervous disorder, which almost deprived him of sleep for five weeks, by his anxious labour in making up the prescribed number of prayers.

with so many affairs, that I was fain, oftentimes, to omit also my Saturday's devotions; at length, when I saw that Amsdorff and others flouted such manner of devotions, then I left it quite off.

"It was, indeed, a great torment, from which we are now delivered by the Gospel. Although," said Luther, "I had done no more than this, namely, freed people from that torment of the conscience, they might well give me thanks. Many, innumerable, laws and works were taught and imposed upon the people, without the Spirit; as in the book *Rationale Divinorum*, many abominable things are written."

"Gabriel Biel wrote a book," said Luther, "upon the canon in the mass, which at that time I held for the best; my heart bled when I read therein. I still keep those books which in such sort tormented me."

"The power of God's word is great, that one brother and Christian cheereth up and comforteth another. In popedom," said Luther, "I was a poor perplexed friar. I was continually in the greatest labour and vexation. At last I received comfort through a few words of a brother, who said unto me 'Brother Martin, you must cheer up yourself and hope; our satisfaction and salvation is the faith on God in Christ,—why, then, should we not put our trust in God, who commandeth, and will have us to hope?' With these words was I so refreshed, that, for a time, I rested satisfied."

"The words, '*I am the Lord thy God; thou shalt have none other gods but me; thou shalt not take the name of the Lord thy God in vain;*'—I thought them," said Luther, "to be of no value, before the light of the Gospel came; yea, I thought them unprofitable and ridiculous words when I read them first. I thought with myself, 'Who knoweth not this?' But now (God be praised!) I see what they mean and require. Yea, they are far more wonderful than any creature can express or comprehend. The Pope and his shaven crew believe not these words, though they prate much about them.

"These words — justice, and righteousness," — said Luther, "were heretofore like a thunderclap in my conscience; I was sorely affrighted at hearing of them. Methought, 'If God be just, then surely he will punish me;' but when I began more diligently to consider those words, then came in my mind this sentence of Habakkuk, ' *The just shall live by his faith;*' also, ' *The righteousness of God without the law is manifested, — the righteousness of God by faith in Jesus Christ.*' Then I was of another mind, and presently thought, 'If the just shall live by faith, and the righteousness which is acceptable before God shall save those that believe, (Rom. iii.) then surely those words will not terrify poor sinners and sorrowful consciences, but rather will comfort them.' In such wise was I refreshed and strengthened, and was assured that God's righteousness is not that wherewith he punisheth as a stern judge, but wherewith he justifieth and saveth sinners which do repent. This art I received only of the Holy Ghost."

In ecclesia nemo potest absolvi, nisi promittat emendationem vitæ. "Faith in Christ," said Luther, "belongeth thereunto (*i. e.* to absolution) and amendment of life. My sins, which I do confess," said Luther, "are these, — I do not pray to God so much as I should; neither do I thank him so much as I ought; and sometimes I provoke him to anger in cursing George, Prince of Saxon.* The confession in former time was an abominable kind of torment; but what a precious life have we now in comparison!"

Dr. Antony Staupitz, complaining to Luther how much tribulation and vexation he endured by his preaching, was by Luther answered as follows: — " ' Loving friend, it hath gone even so with me likewise. I was as much afraid of the pulpit as you are; yet I was compelled to proceed; I was constrained to preach; and to begin at the Grape-gate, where I preached to the brethren.† But I mark your disease; you would fain be exquisite at an instant; you will be more learned than I, or others, who are exercised therein; perhaps you are seeking after honours, and therewith you are vexed. What you have to do is to preach Christ and the Catechism, and not regard what people do hold and censure. Such wisdom will exalt you beyond all human judgment, for the same is God's word, which is wiser than men. Do not expect from me any praise when I hear you preach. But you must know that you are called; Christ hath need of you for the praise of his name; thereupon stand fast.' When the Prince Elector of Saxony, through Dr. Staupitz‡ caused me to be called to the office of preaching, I had fifteen arguments with which I intended to

* George of Saxony was a great persecutor of the Protestants; more will be found relating to him in the sequel.
† The monks.
‡ This Dr. S. was vicar-general of the Augustin monks, probably some relation of Dr. Antony.

refuse my vocation; but they would not help. At last I said, 'Loving Dr. Staupitz, you will be the cause of bringing me to my death; I shall not be able to stand it.' Then said he, 'Well — on in God's name, he our Lord God hath many businesses. He hath need, even above in heaven, of wise people.'

"By the by," said Luther, "as this Dr. Staupitz was elected chief vicar in the whole province, three years together, he intended to accomplish every thing against the adversaries with his own counsel, head, and brain; but it would not forward.* The next three years he was chosen again; then he tried to fulfil the same through the assistance of the most ancient fathers, but failed again. The third three years he committed the work to God's power; but then it went less forward; wherefore he said, '*Mitte vadere sicut vadit, quia vult vadere ut vadit*. Let it go,' said he, 'as it goeth; for neither I nor the fathers can, nor God will, do any thing to alter it; there must be another three years' vicarship.' Then came I," said Luther, "and began another game."

Touching Martin Luther's Progress in the Work of Reformation.

"God, in wonderful wise," said Luther, "hath led us out of the darkness of the sophists, and cast me unwittingly into the game, wherein He hath kept me now more than twenty years. It went weakly forward

---

* Dr. S. appears to have been a conscientious man, and much more enlightened in religion than the ecclesiastics of his day. He had a sincere desire to reform the abuses which prevailed in the district placed under his jurisdiction; and, of course, met with many difficulties.

at first, anno 1517, when, after Allhallows' tide, we came to Kemburgh, where I first began to write against the gross errors touching indulgences. At that time Dr. Jerome withstood me, and said, 'What will you do?' they will not endure it.' Then said I, 'What, if they must endure it?' Soon after him came Silvester Sacripalacius * into the lists. He lightened and thundered against me with this syllogism:—
'Whosoever maketh doubt of any one act or decision of the Romish church, the same is a heretic; Martin Luther doubteth thereof; *ergo*, he is a heretic.' Then went it on."

"Tetzel wrote and taught," said Luther, "that the Pope's indulgences or pardons could remit even such sins as one intended, and was resolved to commit at a future time. He also affirmed that the cross of indulgence (which the Pope had set up and ordained) was of equal power and value with the cross of Christ. These and the like abominations," said Luther, "constrained me to oppose and write against the same †,

* Silvester Prierias (an officer of the Pope), master of the sacred palace.

† It is really affecting, to observe the gross misrepresentation which Hume, with the semblance of superior understanding, gives both of the Reformation itself, and of the character and motives of Luther, and the leading reformers. It never seems to have entered that vain man's mind, that *he* was almost entirely *ignorant of the subject in controversy*, while *they* — many of them men of the first rate talents, profound learning, various experience, and great moral worth, — had devoted a great part of their lives to the contemplation of it; and were so satisfied of its importance, as to venture all, even life itself, for the hopes which religion had imparted to them. Hume had never read the Scriptures seriously, and, therefore, was ignorant of the nature of the Christian re-

not for the sake of any one man, nor for the sake of any preferment, gain, or wealth."

" That I fell out with the Pope," said Luther, " this was the chiefest cause. The Pope boasted of himself that he was the head of the church, and condemned all that would not live under his power and authority; for he said, ' Although Christ be the head of the church, yet, notwithstanding, there must be a visible and corporeal head of the church on earth.' With

---

ligion, and, of course, insensible to its worth. How could such a man estimate the evil of its corruption by the church of Rome? or, the blessings of the Protestant reformation? Or, how could he judge of the character of such men as the Protestant reformers, when of the motives which actuate the true Christian, of the principles which direct, and of the hopes which support him, he was altogether ignorant? He could only measure their character by his own; and as he would have acted the part which they did, from no motives but those of self-interest, pride, envy, or ambition, — he, naturally enough, imputes the same to these worthy men.

They were, however, men of another spirit; and it is much to be lamented that the most popular writer of English history should be a person of such Epicurean sentiments, and that so many of our youth should receive their first impressions of this great event from the misrepresentations of one (in this respect) so ignorant; a man, who could only view the Reformation in a political light, and regarded the religious bearings of it as a proper subject of contempt; and why? because he, and some other wits, without any thing like a reasonable examination of evidence, had peremptorily decided that Christianity itself was a fable.

The story of Luther's pique against the Dominican Tetzel, because his order had supplanted the Augustine in vending the Pope's indulgences, is a fabrication of the Popish historians, carelessly, or maliciously, adopted by some Protestant writers. A candid reader of Luther's writings will perceive that petty feelings of that kind were completely alien from his character.

this," said Luther, "I could have been well content, in case he had but taught the Gospel pure and clearly, and had not brought forward human inventions and lies instead thereof. But what!" said Luther; "he usurped and took upon him power and authority over the Christian church, and over the Scriptures, God's holy word. No man must presume to expound the Scriptures, but only he; and the same also according to his ridiculous conceits; insomuch as therewith he made himself a lord over the church, and proclaimed the same to be a powerful mother, and an empress over the Scriptures, while we (forsooth) must all yield to her, and be obedient. The same was not to be endured," said Luther.

"Had I known at first," said Luther, "when I first began to write, what I now see and find, namely, that people had been such enemies to God's word, and so fiercely had bended themselves against the same, truly I had held my peace; for I never should have been so courageous as to have fallen upon the Pope, and angered him, and almost all the Christian world with him. I thought, at first, that people had sinned ignorantly, and through human weakness, and not wittingly, and of set purpose, to suppress God's word. But it pleased God to lead me on in the mouth of the cannon, like a war-horse that hath his eyes blinded, and seeth not who runneth upon him. Even so was I (as it were) tugged by the hair to the office of preaching. But had I known then, what I know now, methinks ten horses should hardly have drawn me to it. Moses and Jeremiah also did complain that they were deceived." Jer. xx. 7.

"I never thought," said Luther, "when the Gospel began to be preached, that the world had been so wicked as I now see it is; I rather hoped that every one would have leaped for joy, to have found themselves freed from the filth of the Pope, from his lamentable forcings and molestings of the poor troubled consciences, and insufferable oppressions; and to think that, through Christ, they now should obtain, by faith, the celestial treasure, which they sought before with innumerable costs, charges, labour, and travail, though all in vain. And, especially, I thought, that the bishops and universities with joy of heart would have received the same. But what followeth? Truly," said Luther, "even for the self-same cause that I preach and teach the Gospel, they now tread me under their feet. Neither have I greater enemies than the Popish bishops and universities, and those which are the most expert and chiefest people in the commonwealth. Well, be it so; we must learn to know the devil and his members by the Gospel, that he is God's enemy, and the world God's adversary."

"Truly," said Luther, "I would not take the wealth of the whole world that I should now have to begin the work against the Pope, which thus far I have wrought, by reason of the exceeding heavy care and anguish wherewith I have been burdened. Again, when I look upon Him that called me to it, so would I not, for the world's wealth, but that I had begun it."

"It is an office exceeding dangerous to preach Christ: had I," said Luther, "known so much before as now I know, I should never have been drawn thereunto, but with Moses I would have said, '*Send whom thou wilt send.*' The Bishop of Brandenburgh spoke truly unto me at Worms (meaning to dissuade me from writing against the Pope). 'Loving Sir Martin,' said he, 'I told you thus much before, and advised you to be silent, and not to enter on too far; you will bring much trouble upon you; for it toucheth the whole Christian church.' I ween, indeed," said Luther, " I have trouble enough thereby. I have loaded upon me the hatred of the whole world, when before I lived securely and at ease." *

" In what great darkness, and false-believing in the traditions and ordinances of men, we have lived," said Luther, " and with what manifold conflicts in the consciences we have been snared, confounded, and captivated in Popedom; the same is yet witnessed by the books of the Papists, and by many people now living. But for myself, I will declare," said Luther, " the superstitions and idolatries in Popedom were such horrible abominations, that if with mine own eyes I had not seen them, but only read thereof as written things, I should never have believed them. From all these snares and horrors we are now delivered by Jesus Christ and his Gospel, and are called to the true righteousness of faith. Now, at length, with good and peaceable consciences, we believe in God the Father, we trust in Him, and have just cause to boast that we have sure and certain remission of our sins, through the bitter passion and death of Christ Jesus, full dearly bought and purchased. Who is able to extol and sufficiently to praise these treasures of the conscience, which are every where sounded out, spread

---

* *i. e.* with respect to the world's treatment of him.

abroad, offered, and presented, merely by grace! We are now," said Luther, " conquerors of sin, of the law, of death, and the devil; we are now also freed and delivered from all human traditions. If we would think of and consider the tyranny and torments of the auricular confession alone (and this is but one of the least of our freedoms), we could not be sufficiently thankful for the Gospel, which has loosed us out of that one snare. In the time when Popedom stood and flourished among us, then every king would willingly have given 1,000,000 of guilders, a prince 100,000, a nobleman 1000, a gentleman 100, a citizen or countryman 20 or 10, that they might have been freed from that tyranny. But now, seeing such freedom is obtained for nothing, by grace, it is regarded by no man, neither give we so much as thanks to God for the same. The Gospel also," said Luther, " bringeth freedom to the Waldenses or Hussites (as they are called) in Bohemia and Moravia, but they abuse the same; they are unthankful, as we all be."

" It is a great wonder," said Luther, " that in this our time the majesty of the Pope is (for the most part) fallen. All monarchs, emperors, kings, and princes, heretofore, feared and quaked by reason of the Pope's majesty and power, who held them, with a wink, all at his bidding; none durst so much as mutter a word against him. This great god is now fallen. Even his own creatures (monks and friars) are his enemies: if they still hold to him, they do it for their gain's sake, otherwise they would oppose him more fiercely than we do."

" Next unto my just cause," said Luther, " the small

repute and mean aspect of my person, gave the blow to the Pope. For when I began to preach and write, the Pope scorned and contemned me: he thought, 'It is but one single poor friar; what can he do against me, who have defended this my doctrine in Popedom against many emperors, kings,' &c. But* if he had regarded me, he might easily have suppressed me in the beginning.

Luther's Interview with Cardinal Cajetan.

" In the year 1518, the 9th of July †," said Luther, " when I was cited and summoned, I came and appeared at Augsburg, before Cardinal Cajetan, the Pope's legate; Frederic, Prince Elector of Saxony, having appointed me a great and strong convoy and safe conduct. I was warned in any case not to have conversation with the Italians, nor to repose any trust or confidence in them. I was three whole days in Augsburg, without the Emperor's safe conduct. In the mean time an Italian came unto me, and conducted me to Cardinal Cajetan, earnestly persuading me, by the way, to revoke and recant. 'I should need,' said he, 'to speak only one word before the Cardinal, — the word *Revoco*, — that the Cardinal would then recommend me to the Pope's favour, so that I might return again with honour to my master, the Prince Elector.' After three days the Bishop of Triers came, who, in the Emperor's name, showed the Cardinal my safe conduct. Then I went unto him

---

* 1 Kings, xii. 15.
† About a twelvemonth after Luther had made his first protest against the Popish indulgences.

in all humility, falling, first down upon my knees; secondly, upon the ground all along; thirdly, when I had remained awhile so lying, then the Cardinal, three times bade me rise: whereupon I stood up. This pleased him well, hoping I would be advised, and better bethink myself.

"The next day, when I came before him again, and would revoke nothing at all, then he said unto me, 'What! thinkest thou that the Pope careth for Germany? or dost thou think that the princes will raise armies to defend thee? Where, then, wilt thou remain in safety?' I said, 'Under Heaven.'

"After this the Pope humbled himself, and wrote to our church. He wrote even to the Prince Elector's chaplain (Spalatine*), and to one of his counsellors (Pfeffinger), that they should give me up into his hands, and procure that his pleasure and command might be put in execution. The Pope wrote also to the Prince Elector himself, after this manner following:—'Although, as touching thy person, thou art to me unknown, yet I have seen thy father (Prince Ernestus) at Rome, who was altogether an obedient son to the church: he visited and frequented our religion with great devotion, and held the same in highest honour. I would that thy illustrious serenity would also tread in his footsteps†,' &c. But the Prince Elector

* This worthy man was private secretary, as well as chaplain, to the Elector, Frederic the Wise.

† The Elector Frederic had, in fact, imbibed much of his father's devotion to the Roman Catholic religion. So that, although a prince of sound sense and very superior political sagacity, he became a great collector of relics, and increased the number of masses to be said (and paid for) in the church at All Saints, Wittemberg to 1(\1\8) per annum. In a will, likewise, made so

well marked the Pope's unaccustomed humility, and his evil conscience. He was also acquainted with the power and operation of the Holy Scriptures; he, therefore, remained where he was, and returned thanks to the Pope for his affection towards him.

"My books and resolutions," said Luther, "in a short time went, yea flew, through all Europe (the third part of the world), therefore the Prince Elector was confirmed and strengthed, insomuch that he utterly refused to execute the Pope's command; but subjected himself under the acknowledgment of the Scriptures.

"If the Cardinal had handled me with more discretion at Augsburg, and had dealt kindly with me when I fell at his feet, then it had never come thus far, for at that time I saw very few of the Pope's errors which now I see. Had he been silent, so had I, probably, held my peace.

"The style and custom of the Romish court in dark and confused cases was this,—that the Pope said, 'We, by papal power, do take these causes unto us; we quench them out and destroy them.' I am persuaded," said Luther, "that the Pope would willingly give three Cardinals, on condition that things were still in that state wherein they were before he meddled with me."

---

late as the year 1517, he made provision for the saying of fifty masses daily, on his special account, for a month after his decease.

The curiosity of the reader may be excited, to know how these large orders for masses could be executed within the prescribed period, since no priest is allowed to say mass more than once a day. He must know, then, that, before the Reformation, there were eighty priests connected with All Saints' church alone: they were, therefore, in sufficient force to accomplish, without assistance, considerably more than the 10,000 regularly agreed for.

Luther's Integrity and Disinterestedness.

"I," said Luther, "could well be content to hold the Pope in suitable respect and honour, yet so far that he permitted me to have my conscience at liberty, and did not force me to offend my God, and to act against Him in any thing. But he will not do so; he peremptorily insists that I shall so honour and fear him, as to wound my conscience, and dishonour God's majesty, and provoke His displeasure. Now, therefore," said Luther, "seeing I must needs lose and forsake one of these two, either God or the Pope;—then away with that painted mask, to the end I may keep God Almighty. Otherwise I could well have borne with the Pope's glorious domineering. But forasmuch as he abuseth his power too, too much, and will force me directly to blaspheme and deny God,—whose word he over-rules,— it is by God's first commandment I am compelled to resist the Pope, seeing it is written, ' *We must obey God rather than men;*' and God our heavenly Father calleth down from Heaven, and saith, ' *This my well-beloved Son ye shall hear:*' what He saith and commandeth, thereafter shall ye do, and that alone is God's heart and will."

"If," said Luther, "the great pains and labour which I take, were not done by me for the sake of Him who died for me, the world could not give me money enough to write only one book, or to translate the Bible. I desire not to be paid or rewarded by the world for my work; the world is far too poor and simple to give me satisfaction. I have not desired the value of one penny of my master, the Prince Elector, so long as I have been in this place."

"Philip Melancthon and myself," said Luther, "have justly deserved so much riches in this world, at God's hands, as any cardinal possesseth; for we have done more in His business than one hundred cardinals. But God saith unto us, 'Be ye contented that ye have Me;'—'*Sufficit tibi gratia mea.*' When we have Him, then have we also the purse (Matt. vi. 33.); and if we had the purse, and had not God, what, then, would our gain be? therefore God saith, 'When thou hast me, so hast thou enough.' What saith God in the prophet Ezekiel?—'*Thou son of man, Nebuchadnezzar caused his army to serve a great service against Tyre; yet he had no wages. What shall I give him? I will give the land of Egypt to Nebuchadnezzar, that shall be his wages.*' (Ezekiel, xxix. 18.) Even so," said Luther, "playeth God with great kingdoms: He taketh them from one, and giveth them to another."

"If I had not been a Doctor," said Luther, "Satan had made me work enough. It was no slight and easy matter for one to alter the whole religion of Popedom, which was so deeply rooted in men's minds. But I promised and sware in baptism, that I would hold by Christ and His word, that I would steadfastly believe in Him, and utterly renounce the devil and all his lies. And, indeed, the oath which I took in baptism is renewed in all my tribulations; without this, I could not have resisted them, nor, indeed, have lived;—they would have overwhelmed and made an end of me. I would willingly have shown obedience to the Pope and bishops in any reasonable particulars; but nothing would please them but I must deny Christ, make God a liar, and say the Gospel is a heresy.

"The multitude of books," said Luther, "is much to be lamented; no measure nor end is observed in writing. Every one will write books: some, out of ambition, to purchase praise thereby, and to raise them names; others, for the sake of gain. I fear the Bible by so many books and comments will be buried and obscured, so that the text will be nothing regarded. I could wish," said Luther, "that all my books were buried nine ells deep in the ground, for evil example's sake, in that every one will imitate me in writing many books; and what for?—to purchase praise. But Christ died, not for the sake of our ambition and vainglory, but He died only to the end that His name might be sanctified."

Luther's unfeigned Love to Jesus Christ our Saviour.

"The chiefest study in divinity," said Luther, "is that we learn to know Christ aright; therefore saith St. Peter, '*Grow in the knowledge of Jesus Christ;*' viz. that he is the most merciful, the best, the most just and wise; and," said he, "if I might leave behind me but only this lesson, which with great diligence I have urged and taught, namely, that people would beware and take heed of speculations, and, instead thereof, would take hold on Christ only, in the most plain and simple manner possible, then would I think myself happy, and that I had accomplished much."

"We and the world," said Luther, "are easily parted. Care they nothing for us? so care we much less for them. Yea, through Christ, ' *the world is crucified unto us, and we unto the world.*' Let them go with their wealth, and leave to us our minds and manners. When we have our sweet and loving Saviour, Christ, then are we rich and happy more than enough; we care nothing for their state, honour, and wealth. But oftentimes we lose sight of our Saviour, Christ, and little think that He is in us, and we in Him; that He is ours, and we are His. Yet, although He hideth himself from us (as we think) in the time of need, for a little moment, as He saith, (Isaiah, liv.) still we are comforted in his promise, where he saith, '*I am with you always, even to the world's end.*'"

" Christ, my loving friends, desireth nothing more of us than that we speak of Him. But thou wilt say, — ' If I speak or preach of Him, then I am struck upon my lips.' O!" said Luther, " do not regard that, but hear what Christ saith: — ' *Ask, and it shall be given you,*' &c. Also ' *Call upon me in the time of trouble, so will I hear thee, and thou shalt praise me,*' &c. (Psalm l.) How could we," said Luther, " perform a more easy service to God, and one without all labour or charges? There is no work on earth easier to be accomplished than the true service of God: He loadeth no heavy burdens upon us, neither to cleave wood, nor to carry stones, but will only have that we believe in Him, and preach of Him.[*] True it is," said Luther, " thou mayest count upon being plagued and persecuted for the same; but then cometh our sweet and blessed Saviour to us with His most

[*] Let the reader compare such texts as these, (John, vi. 28, 29. Psalm lxxi. 17, 18. cxix. 32. Matt. xi. 29, 30.) and he will probably understand Luther's meaning,

comfortable promise, where He saith, '*I will be with you in trouble, I will deliver you and honour you.*' &c. (Ps. xci.) I" said Luther, " make no such promise to my servant, when I set him to work, either at the plough or at the cart; but Christ will help me in my need. To conclude, we only fail in believing. We ought to joy in Christ without ceasing, as St. Paul admonisheth us (Phil. iv. 4.); we should leap and sing," said Luther, " for very joy and gladness; yea, in such sort as if we never could be sad and troubled again. But the envious devil doth debar and hinder such our joy, where and how he can; he plagueth and perplexeth us, either without means, through his fiery darts, or through wicked poisoned mouths of men, as oftentimes happeneth to me."

" I have, and know, nothing of Christ," said Luther, " but only His name, seeing I neither have heard or seen Him in the body; yet, notwithstanding, I have (God be praised) learnt so much of Him out of the Scriptures, that I am well and thoroughly satisfied; therefore I have no desire to hear or to see Him corporeally. Over and besides which, when I was forsaken by all men, in my greatest weakness, in trembling, and in fear of death; when I was so persecuted by the false, wicked, world, then I oftentimes found and felt, most evidently, the divine power which this name, Christ Jesus, shewed and witnessed unto me. This name oftentimes pulled me out of the midst of death, and made me live again. It comforted me in the greatest despair, and particularly at the Imperial Assembly at Augsburg, anno 1530, where I was forsaken of every man; insomuch that, by God's grace, I will remain, live, and die, for that name.

"And rather than I will yield," said Luther, " or, through silence, so long as I live, endure that Erasmus of Rotterdam (or any other, whomsoever he be,) should too nearly touch my Lord and Saviour, Jesus Christ, with his ungodly false doctrine, (let him colour, trim, and garnish it as he may,) I say I will rather die; yea, it would be more tolerable for me, with wife and children, to undergo all plagues and torments, and at last to die the most shameful death, than that I should give way thereto."

"I assure myself," said Luther, "that Christ, at the last day, will speak friendly to me also; for here he speaketh (one might say) very unkindly to me. I bear upon me the hate and envy of the whole world; the hate of the Emperor, of the Pope, and of all their retinue. Well,— on! in God's name; seeing I am come into the lists, so will I fight it out: my cause, I know, is just. The greatest adversary I have in it, is the devil, and, indeed, he setteth upon me so fiercely, oftentimes, with this argument, ' Thou art not rightly called,' that he had long since slain me therewith, if I had not been a Doctor of Divinity."

Luther's Firmness and Decision.

"Above all things," said Luther, " let us be sure that this doctrine which we teach is God's word; for when we are sure of that, then we may build thereupon, that this cause shall and must remain, how fiercely soever the devil and the world do rage against the same. I (God be praised!) do know for a certainty that the doctrine which I teach is God's word; and have now hunted from my heart all other doctrines and faiths, which I see do not agree with God's word. And now I have overcome those heavy cogitations and temptations which sometimes tormented me in this manner: — ' Art thou (thought I) the only man that hath God's word pure and clean, while all others fail therein?' In such sort doth Satan vex and assault us, under the name and title of God's church. ' Yea,' saith he, ' that doctrine, which the church so many years hitherto hath held and established for right, wilt thou presume to reject and overthrow the same with thy new doctrine, as if it were false and erroneous, and thereby producest troubles, alteration, and confusion, both in spiritual and temporal government?'

"This argument of the devil," said Luther, " do I find in all the prophets, where the chief heads and members both in church and commonwealth always have upbraided them, and said, ' We are God's people; we are placed, and by God ordained, in an established government; what we do conclude and acknowledge for right, the same must and shall be observed and kept. What fools are ye that will presume to teach us, who are the best and greatest part, there being of you but a handful?' Truly," said Luther, " in this case, we must not only be well armed with God's word, and footed therein, but we must have also the certainty of the doctrine, otherwise we shall not be able to stand in the combat. A man must be able boldly to affirm and say, I know, for certain, that the same which I teach, is, indeed, the word of the High Majesty of God in heaven, His final conclusion, and everlasting unchangeable truth; and whatsoever concurreth and agreeth not with this doctrine, the same is altogether false and spun by the devil. I have before me God's word, which cannot fail, nor can the gates of hell prevail against it; thereby will I remain, although the whole world were opposed to me; and, withal, I have this comfort, that God saith, 'I will give thee people and hearers that shall receive it; cast thy care upon me, I will defend thee; only remain thou stout and steadfast by my word!'"*

"When the devil findeth me idle," said Luther, "and that I do not think on God's word, then he scrupleth my conscience, as if I did not teach aright, but had occasioned a confusion in the government, and, with my doctrine, had raised much offence and rebellion. But when I get hold of God's word, then I have won the game, then I resist the devil, and say thus:—'I know, and, out of God's word, am sure, that this doctrine is not mine, but the doctrine of the Son of God;' then I think thus with myself:—What careth God for the world, though it were ten times as big again. He hath set His Son to be King, and hath set him so fast in his kingdom, that he neither can nor will be removed; for God himself saith, '*This my Son shall ye hear;*' and in Psalm ii. he saith, '*Be wise now, therefore, O ye kings; be instructed, ye judges of the earth; serve the Lord with fear, and rejoice with trembling. Kiss the Son, lest He be angry, and ye perish from the way, &c. If His wrath be kindled even but a little; blessed are all they that put their trust in Him.*' That is, will ye com-

* "I cannot endure the positiveness of you Protestants" (said Sir E. Baynton, a Roman Catholic knight, to Bishop Latimer); "you preach as if you were sure that what you say is God's word, and you could not possibly be in a mistake."—"And what must we say of those," replied Latimer, "who preach what they do not know to be God's word?"

c

bine yourselves against the Son? so shall ye (with all your kingdoms, principalities, governments, rights, orders, law, powers, treasure, and wealth,) be utterly consumed and brought to nothing, like as hath happened to the kingdoms of the Jews and others. Let us," said Luther, " by all means, be sure and certain of our cause. St. Paul boasteth of himself thus:— '*I am an Apostle and servant of Jesus Christ, and a teacher of the Gentiles.*' No carnal-minded person is able to understand this kind of boasting, which at that time was so needful and necessary for St. Paul, as an article of faith.

Dr. Eisleben, at Wittemburg, had stained the university with the Antinomian heresy; and afterward, being sorry for it, would willingly have been reconciled with Luther; and for that end both himself and his wife (weeping bitterly) instantly craved of Luther, that he would receive him again into his accustomed favour. The Prince Elector of Brandenburgh also wrote, earnestly making intercession for him. Notwithstanding which, Luther answered and said, " It is a public cause; if he will make his public confession, in manner following, viz. 'I, Dr. George Eisleben, do confess, that I have played the fool, and done wrong to those of Wittemburg, who teach rightly, and by me were unjustly reproved. I am heartily sorry for the same, and do pray them, for God's sake, to forgive me;' he may then be received again, otherwise, we will accept of no revocation, which he may construe hereafter as he pleaseth,— it must be spoken plainly." Whereupon he made confession, word for word, in this manner, and thereupon he was of Luther embraced and received again.

Luther's Confidence in dangerous Times.

Luther received a letter, written by Philip Melancthon, from the Imperial Assembly. After the reading of it, he said, "What Philip Melancthon writeth hath hands and feet, hath authority and gravity; full of weight, but contained in few words, as I have always found his letters. But I perceive we must have wars; for the Papists would willingly go on, only they want a good stomach; neither may we endure the case to stand as it does at present. Let it therefore proceed, *in nomine Domini*, I will commit all things to God, and will be Crito in the play. I will pray that God would convert our adversaries. We have a good cause, and who would not venture body and blood for God's holy word? Besides, the temporal laws and statutes of policy do also agree with our proceedings, for we always have desired and called for peace; but our princes are provoked, and driven to defend themselves and their subjects, and, of necessity, must resist wrongful power. Our adversaries will not suffer us to live in peace. This letter," said Luther, "was written ten days since;—by this time it is concluded what shall be done. The everlasting merciful God give his grace thereunto. Let us watch and pray, for Satan sleepeth not."

"Let the adversaries rage and swell their fills," said Luther, "and as long as they can. God hath set the sea her bounds. He suffers the same to beat and rage with her waves, as if they would overwhelm every thing; yet they must not pass the shore, although God keeps the waters in their compass, not with iron, but with weak walls of sand." This discourse Luther held at that time when letters were written to him from the Assembly at Frankfort, concerning the intention of the Papists to fall upon the Protestants in all parts.

"The second psalm," said Luther, "is one of the best psalms. I love that psalm with all my heart. It strikes and slashes valiantly among the kings, princes, and high counsellors. If it be true, which this psalm says, then are the purposes of the Papists stark follies. If I were as our Lord God, and had committed the government to my son, as He has to his Son, and these angry gentlemen were as disobedient as they are now, I," said Luther, "should be throwing the world into a lump.

"Mary, the poor maiden of Nazareth, also, scuffleth and ruffleth with these great kings, princes, &c. as she sings, '*He hath put down the mighty from their seat,*' &c. No doubt," said Luther, "she had an excellent undaunted voice. I, for my part, dare not sing so. The tyrants say, '*Let us break their bonds asunder.*' What that is," said he, "present experience teacheth us; for we see how they drown, how they hang, burn, behead, strangle, banish, and torture. And all this they do in despite of God. But he sits above in heaven, and laughs them to scorn. If," said Luther, "God would be pleased to give me a little time that I might expound a couple of small psalms, I would bestir myself so boldly, that (Samson-like) I would take all the Papists away with me." *

---

* Luther's exposition of some of the first psalms has been recently translated, and published, by the Rev. —— Cole.

In the year 1546, Luther was advertised by letters, that Charles the Emperor, and the Pope, swiftly proceeded against that good and godly bishop, Herman of Cologne, intending to hunt and drive him from country and people; whereupon Luther discoursed and said, "The Papists have lost the cause; with God's word they are not able to withstand us, *Ergo volunt sapientiâ, violentiâ, astutiâ practicâ, dolo, vi et armis, pugnare. Ipsi nobis testimonium perhibent quod sapientia Dei, veritas Dei, et verbum Dei, sit.* Here, again," said Luther, "cometh in the second psalm,— '*The kings of the earth stand up, and the rulers take counsel together*'—what to do?—'*against the Lord, and against His Anointed.*' But what followeth? '*He that sitteth in the heavens shall laugh them to scorn; the Lord shall have them in derision.*' God will deal well enough with these angry gentlemen," said Luther, "and will give them small thanks for their labour, in going about to suppress His word and servants. He hath sat in counsel these 5500 years, hath ruled and made laws. Good sirs! be not so choleric; go farther from the wall, lest you knock your pates against it. '*Be wise now, therefore, O ye kings, be instructed ye judges of the earth: serve the Lord in fear,* &c. *Kiss the Son, lest He be angry, and so ye perish.*' That is, Take hold of Christ, or the devil will take hold of you. The second psalm," said Luther, "is a proud psalm against these fellows. It begins mild and simply, but ends stately and rattling,—'*Ne pereatis de via justâ.*' Fire will break out, therefore '*Beati omnes qui confidunt in eum.*' It is a most excellent and a brave, stately psalm, and I am much taken with it. We," said Luther, "have no other comfort against these violent proceedings of the wicked, than that our God, *habitator cæli,* is called, *Deus non a longè, sed a prope,* and also, *Deus misericordiæ.* He seeth all these stratagems, and forgetteth them not, for God hath a great memory.

"I," said Luther, "have now angered the Pope about his images and idolatry. Oh, how the sow raiseth her bristles! I have a great advantage against him; for '*The Lord saith unto my lord, Sit Thou on my right hand, until I make thine enemies thy footstool.*' He saith also, '*I will raise you up at the last day;*' and then He will call, and say, 'Ho! Martin Luther, Philip Melancthon, John Calvin,' &c., arise, come up; and God will call us by our names, as our Saviour Christ, in St. John's Gospel,—'*Et vocat eos nominatim.*' Well, on!" said Luther, "let us be of good comfort."

Luther's Domestic Character.

"We must make a great difference," said Luther, speaking of the Holy Scriptures, "between the word of God, and the word of a man. A man's word is a little sound, which flieth into the air, and soon vanisheth; but the word of God is greater than heaven and earth;—yea, greater than death and hell; for it is the power of God, and remaineth everlastingly; therefore we ought diligently to learn God's word, and we must certainly know and believe, that God himself speaketh with us.

"David saw the same and believed; for he saith, '*God hath spoken in his holiness, therefore I am glad,*' &c. We," said Luther, "should also be glad thereof; but such joy and gladness is, oftentimes, thoroughly powdered and peppered unto us, which

David well found, and endured many trials and temptations about the murder and adultery which he committed. ".I ween," said Luther, " it was thoroughly well-powdered and peppered for his tooth, when he was coursed and hunted from one place to another, to the end he might walk and remain in God's fear; therefore, in the second psalm, he saith, ' *Serve the Lord with fear, and rejoice with trembling.*'

" I," said Luther, " would fain see one that could make these two agree together, *to be joyful,* and *to be afraid.* I cannot behave myself in that manner towards God; but my little son, John, can show himself so towards me; for when I sit in my study, and write or do something else, then my boy sings me a song, and when he will be too loud, then I check him a little; yet, nevertheless, he singeth on, but with a more mild and a softer tone, and somewhat with fear and reverence. Even so will God likewise have us to do; that we should always rejoice in Him, yet with fear and reverence.

Epitaph of Magdalena, Martin Luther's daughter, who died anno 1542, aged 14 years, written by the father himself.

" *Dormio cum sanctis hic Magdalena, Lutheri*
Filia, et hoc strato tecta quiesco meo.
Filia mortis eram, peccati semine nata,
Sanguine sed vivo, Christe, redempta tuo."

" When I hear that a good and godly man is dead," said Luther, " then am I affrighted, and fear that God hateth the world, who taketh away the upright and good, to the end He may fall upon and punish the evil and wicked. Although I die, it maketh no great matter, for I am in the Pope's curse and excommunication; I am his devil,—therefore he hateth and persecuteth me. At Coburg I went about, and sought me out a place for my burial. I thought to have been laid in the channel under the cross; but now I am of another mind. I know I have not long to live; for my head is like a knife from which the steel is wholly whetted away, and is become merely iron: the iron will cut no more, even so it is with my head. Now, loving Lord God, I hope my hour is not far; God help, and give me a happy hour; I desire to live no longer."

———

As on a time, Luther's wife anointed his feet, by reason of some pain which he felt, he said unto her, "In former times, Kate, the wives were anointed by their husbands, but now thou anointest me: for this Latin word uxor, a wife, is derived from anointing, ob ungendo; for, as the Heathen saw that many rubs, lets, and hinderances, were in the state of matrimony, they marked it thus; and, as if to prevent such mishaps, they used to anoint both the legs of the new married woman."

———

"I have oftentimes noted," said Luther, "when women do receive the doctrine of the Gospel, they are far more fervent in faith, they hold on it more fast and steady than men do, as we see in the loving Magdalene, who was more hearty and bold than Peter."

———

A certain English gentleman, very learned, at Wittemburg, was much conversant with Luther at his table: this gentleman had not his Dutch language well, therefore Luther said, " I will give unto you my wife there for a schoolmistress, she shall teach you purely and readily to speak Dutch; for she is very eloquent, and so perfect therein, that she far surpasseth me. Howsoever," said Luther, " when women are ready at speaking, it is not to be commended; it becomes them much better, when they say nothing, or speak little."

" There is no gown or garment becomes a woman worse," said Luther, " than when she will be wise."

Luther's wife said unto him, " Sir, I heard your cousin, John Palner," (who attended on Luther) " preach this afternoon in the parish church, and I understood him better than Dr. Pommer" (Pomeranus), " who is held to be a very excellent preacher." Whereupon Luther made her this answer: — " John Palner preacheth as ye women use to talk, for, what cometh in your mind, the same ye also speak. A preacher ought to remain by the propounded text, and should deliver that which he hath before him, that the people may well understand the same. But such a preacher as will speak every thing that cometh into his mind, I liken to a maid that goeth to market, when another maid meeteth her; then they make a stand, and hold a goose-market, &c. Even so, likewise, do those preachers *qui nimis procul discedunt a proposito*, and think to speak all things at once."

" A woman is, or at least should be," said Luther, " a friendly, courteous, and cheerful companion of the life, from whence they are named of the Holy Ghost willingly gave to the poor; but when it ceased giving, it became poor, as it is still to this day. It fell out that, not long since, a poor man came thither, and desired alms, which was denied; the poor man asked the reason why they refused to give for God's sake? The porter belonging to the monastery answered and said, 'We are become poor;' whereupon the poor man said, 'The cause of your poverty is this;—ye have had in this monastery two brethren, *Date* (Give ye), and *Dabitur* (It shall be given); the one ye have thrust out, and the other is gone away secretly of himself. For after the one brother, *Date*, was put out and cashiered, so hath the other brother, *Dabitur*, lost himself.' Beloved," said Luther, " he that intendeth to have any thing, the same must also give; a liberal hand was never in want nor empty."

In an evening, Luther (walking out to take the air with Dr. Jonas) gave alms to some poor people; the Doctor also gave something, and said, " Who knoweth whether God will give it me again?" Whereat Luther, smiling, answered him, and said, " You speak as if God had not given you this which now you have given to the poor;—we must give freely and willingly," said Luther.

Anno 1538, December 17., Luther invited the singers and musicians to a supper, where they sang fair and sweet anthems; then he said with admiration, " Seeing our Lord God, in this life, (which is a mere *cloaca*) dispenseth unto us such precious gifts, what, then, will be done in the life everlasting, when every thing shall be made in the completest and most delightful manner! here is only *materia prima*—the beginning.

I always loved music," said Luther: "whoso hath skill in this art, the same is of a good kind, fitted for all things; we must, by all means, maintain music in schools; a schoolmaster ought to have skill in music, otherwise, I would not regard him, neither should we ordain young fellows to the office of preaching, except they have been well exercised beforehand, and practised, in the school of music. Music is a fair gift of God, and near allied to divinity. I would not, for a great matter," said Luther, " be destitute of the small skill in music which I have.* The youth ought to be brought up and accustomed to this art, for it maketh fine and expert people."

Luther's Vehemence and Asperity.

" God," said Luther, " is patient, long-suffering, and merciful, in that He can keep silence, and can suffer so long the most wicked wretches to go unpunished; *I* could not do so," said Luther.

" I have no better work," said Luther, " than anger and jealousy †; for when I am angry, I can indite well; I can pray and preach; then my whole dispo-

---

* Luther put the Psalms into verse, and composed many appropriate tunes:—the Old Hundredth Psalm tune is said to be one of them.

† Luther does not speak here of those feelings which arise from impatience of personal injuries or insults, but of an anger and a jealousy similar to that which the Lord Jesus felt (Mark, iii. 5.) at the hardness of some people's hearts, and when he rebuked the Scribes and Pharisees (Matt. xxiii.), and when he turned the buyers and sellers out of the temple (John, ii. 14.); and such anger as Isaiah's (chap. i.), and Elijah's (1 Kings, xix.).

sition is quickened, my understanding sharpened, and all unpleasant cogitations and vexations do depart."

"Dr. Justus Jonas asked me," said Luther, "if the cogitations and words of the prophet Jeremiah were Christian-like, where he curseth the day of his birth? (ch. xx.) I answered thus:—'We must now and then,' said I, 'wake up our Lord God (see Ps. xliv. 23.) with such words. It was, indeed, a right* mur-

---

* It is evident that persons of an ardent and excitable temperament should be peculiarly watchful over their own hearts; lest they miscall that godly zeal, which is the effect of a temper naturally hasty, and impatient of contradiction. Those two "sons of thunder," the apostles James and John, fell into this error (Luke, ix.), and were rebuked for it by the Lord Jesus, who told them, they "*knew not what manner of spirit they were of.*" It would seem that Elijah's jealousy for his Maker's honour was mixed up with much that was selfish: indeed, we perceive, in some of his expressions, the pride and perverseness which so unhappily mark the character of Jonah. Jeremiah was betrayed, through his constitutional vehemence, into very unwarrantable language. He lived in evil days, 'tis true, and was exposed to great provocation; and was, in the main, actuated by a godly zeal; but it is manifest that feelings, which produced such language as we meet with in the twentieth chapter of his prophecies, were sinful and indefensible,— like some of Job's speeches, wrung from him by the force of extreme suffering. St. Paul, also, had his infirmities of natural temper to contend with (as he acknowledges in 2 Cor. xi. 29, 30.): "*Who is offended, and I burn not,*" &c. Every one at all acquainted with Luther's character knows, that he was, as a private person, very friendly and placable; but when he witnessed any dishonour put upon Christ and his doctrines, his spirit was becomingly stirred within him: I say, becomingly, for every one ought to resent a dishonour put upon God, more than one offered to himself. On such occasions Luther would give vent to his feelings, both in

muring in Jeremiah. Our Saviour Christ spake also in that sort,—' *O faithless and perverse generation, how long shall I be with you and suffer you?*' Moses also in such manner set God the stool before the door (as the saying is), where he says, (Numb. xi. 11, &c.) ' *Have I conceived all this people? Have I begotten them, that thou shouldest say unto me, Carry them in thy bosom,*' &c.

"It is impossible but that a man must grieve very much, when from his heart he meaneth good, and is not regarded. I," said Luther, " can never be rid of these cogitations, in wishing I had never begun this business with the Pope. Likewise, I wish myself rather dead, than to hear God's word or his servants contemned: this is our nature's frailty.

"Those that condemn such passions are *theologi in arte speculativâ*, who play with thoughts, and deal with speculations, but when they themselves begin to be truly alive and earnest in the matter, then they will find it, and be sensible thereof. Such histories are very great, and have a high and a deep meaning; we ought not to dispute of them with speculations."

" A short time since," said Luther, " I was very sharply taxed and reprehended by a popish, flattering, courtier, a priest, because I had written with such passion, and so vehemently reproved the people. But I answered him and said, ' Our Lord God must first send a sharp pouring shower with thunder and light-

---

words and writing; and, being not infallible in his judgment, nor always watchful enough over his remarkably ardent temper, was sometimes betrayed into an excess of impatience and of anger.

ning, and afterwards cause it to rain mildly, then it wetteth fairly through. In like manner, a willow, or a hazle twig, I can easily cut with my trencher-knife, but for a hard oak, a man must have and use axes, bills, and such like, and all little enough to fell and cleave it."

———

"There are many," said Luther, "who complain of me, thinking that I am too fierce and violent against popery. I, on the contrary, complain that I am, alas! much too mild; I could wish that I could breathe out thunderclaps against Pope and popedom, and that every word were a thunderbolt."

———

In answer to the question, why Christ cursed so sorely in the 109th Psalm, whereas he forbiddeth to curse (Matt. v.), Luther said, "A Christian, for his own person, neither curseth nor revengeth himself; but faith curseth and revengeth itself. To understand the matter rightly, we must make a distinction between God and man, between the person and the cause. What concerneth God and His cause, we must therein have no patience, neither must we bless; as, for example, when the ungodly do persecute the Gospel, the same toucheth God and his cause; then we are not to bless, nor to wish thereunto good success; but rather we ought to curse and maledict the persecutors and their proceedings.* These," said Luther, "are called the cursings of faith, which (rather than it would suffer God's word to be suppressed and heresy maintained) wisheth that all creatures went to rack, for through heresy we lose God himself. But the

* See Gal. v. 12., and 2 Tim. iv. 14, 15., and Ps. cxxxix. 19—22.

persons ought not to revenge * themselves, but to suffer all things, and (according to Christ's doctrine and the nature of love) to do good to our enemies."

Speaking of the Cardinal of Saltzburg, Luther said,. "This cardinal is not *frater ignorantiæ*†, but *frater malitiæ;* not a brother of ignorance, but a brother of malice; he maketh a show of meekness and good will, but he is not in earnest; he can artificially prepare and accommodate himself to people's humours, like the Italians, who give good words out of false hearts." Luther, deeply sighing over him, said, " Loving Lord and Saviour, Jesus Christ, give me life and strength that I may shave the crown of this prelate, for he is a

* Luther exhibited a striking example of his own doctrine in his dealings with Tetzel, the indulgence dealer, who had sought his destruction. While that wretched man, upheld by his principals, was selling the vile wares of the pretended lord of the Christian church, Luther opposed and denounced him, as the enemy of Christ and His truth; but when deserted, like Judas, by his employers, he was sinking into infamy and despair, Luther wrote to him the letter of a friend, encouraging him to repent and turn to God, that he might be saved.

† Luther remarks thus on this strange fraternity: — " In Italy was a particular order of friars, called *Fratres Ignorantiæ;* that is, Brethren of Ignorance. These were forced to take solemn oaths, that they would neither know, learn, nor understand, any thing at all, but should answer all questions with, *Nescio.* " Truly," said Luther, " all friars are well worthy of that title, for they only read and babble out the words, but care not to understand them. They say, Although we understand not the words, yet the Holy Ghost understandeth them, and the devil flieth away. This was the highest argument of the friars, who are enemies to all good arts and learning; for the Pope and cardinals conclude thus: — Should these brethren study and be learned, so would they master us, &c.; therefore, *saccum per neckum,* hang a bag about their necks, and send them begging, through towns, cities, and countries."

crafty derider of Thy name; he is an offscummed knave; he sticketh not to boast that few of his stratagems have failed him. When lately," said Luther, "I wrote, exceeding harsh and fiercely, to this cardinal, and with grievous words touched him with scoffing and scorning, then he confessed, that in causes of religion he was wrong, and, in them, would give place to Luther, and suffer himself to be reprehended; but, in other temporal and state cases, he would yield nothing unto him. I see," said Luther, "I must rouse him better up. Ah, Lord God!" said he, "we ought not to dally with Thee, nor to abuse thy holy name; sufficient it is that we have sinned against Thee; we ought, therefore, to repent and to be sorry for our sins. Surely this cardinal is like unto that soldier, who lately came to me, and when I admonished him to desist from his wicked kind of life, he answered me and said, 'If I should think of this, then should I never go to the wars again;' even so it is with this cardinal.

"The good and godly Princess Electress of Saxony lately asked me," said Luther, "if there were yet any hope of this cardinal's conversion? I answered, 'I believe not; however, it would be a great joy to me, if in time he recalled himself, were won, and repented; but there is little hope thereof; I would rather hope the same in Pilate, Herod, and Dioclesian, who sinned openly.' The Princess replied and said, 'God is almighty and merciful, who would have received Judas again, if he had repented.' Luther answered — 'True, gracious madam, God would also receive Satan to mercy, if from his heart he could say — " God be merciful to me a sinner!"' But, alas! of this cardinal there is no hope, for he opposeth himself to the acknowledged truth. A few days since he caused thirteen Christians lamentably to be slain, for receiving of the communion in both kinds. True it is, God is almighty and merciful; He can do more than we are able to think; but He will do no more than He hath concluded to do, as St. Paul, — ' *Whom He did predestinate them He also called,*' &c. When our Lord God saith, I will not do this or that, then it is time for us to be gone, and to set our hearts at rest, as God said to Samuel, — ' *Why mournest thou for Saul, seeing I have rejected him?*' Therefore," said Luther, " all my hope is gone touching this cardinal; I commit the case to God, He will order the same.

"This cardinal," said Luther, "wrote oftentimes very friendly unto me, thinking to oil my lips, insomuch that I actually advised him to take a wife; but, in the mean time, he intended with smooth words to deceive me. At the Imperial Diet at Augsburg I became acquainted with his real character; yet he still pretended great friendship towards me, and in causes of weight would make choice of me to be an umpire.[*] After my departure from the Diet he assembled the citizens together, and uttered unto them these words: — ' Loving people, be obedient unto me, and receive the sacrament in one kind, so will I not only be a gracious lord unto you, but also a father, a brother, and a friend; and I will procure from the Emperor great privileges for you. But in case you refuse to be

[*] Luther's character for sound judgment and honest principle were so generally acknowledged by those who knew him, that he appears to have been, not unfrequently, chosen arbitrator in important civil causes. It is well known that his death took place while he was engaged in business of this nature, settling some disputed claims between the Counts of Mansfeldt.

obedient herein, so will I be altogether your enemy. I will bring you and your city into the utmost confusion.' Were not these," said Luther, "rather the words of Rabshakeh, or of the Turkish emperor, than of a Christian prelate?

"I will leave this testimony behind me," said Luther, " touching this cardinal; namely, excepting Nero and Caligula, he is the greatest knave that ever came on earth. He sought wonderfully to ensnare me; insomuch that if our Lord God had not, in special manner, preserved me, he had taken me captive. And in 1525 he sent one of his doctors unto me with a present of 200 Hungarian ducats, which he caused to be given to Kate my wife; but I refused to receive them, and charged my wife not to meddle therewith; for (God be praised) I never had the name to be a money-seeker."*

"I hate Erasmus† from my heart," said Luther:

---

* The same may be said of all the leading Reformers: Luther, Melancthon, Calvin, Zuingle, Bucer, &c. &c., all lived and died in very moderate circumstances; and our own Cranmer and Ridley, whose incomes were considerable, appear to have left very little wealth behind them.

† This remarkable man, whose extensive knowledge, ready wit, and classical style of writing, gained him the admiration of all the learned in Europe, while his exposure of the folly and ungodliness of the Romish clergy, and his endeavours to promote the study of the Holy Scriptures, conciliated, in the beginning of the Reformation, the respect of the religious, was, above most others, the character which Luther's honest mind could least endure. He appears, by all accounts, to have been of a cowardly, trimming, time-serving, spirit. His reputation was his idol; and to enjoy literary pre-eminence, and the favours of the rich and the great, were the objects for which he lived.

"he makes use of the very same argument that Caiaphas advised, when he said, — '*It is expedient that one man should die for the people.*' Even so saith Erasmus, and all Epicures. It is expedient and better that the Gospel go down, or be not preached, than that the whole of Germany, with all the princes, should go together by the ears, and that all Christendom should be moved. St. John, the evangelist, by reason of this advice, became an utter enemy to Caiaphas. In like manner, Christ gave Caiaphas such a blow, as (I fear) everlastingly he will feel, when He said to Pilate, — '*He that delivered me unto thee hath the greater sin.*'" Luther then (with great and earnest zeal of heart) said to Dr. Jonas, and to Pomeranus, "I charge you, in my will and testament, that you hate and lothe Erasmus, that viper. I regard not his words; indeed they are well adorned, but they are merely Democritical and Epicurean things; for, of set purpose, he speaketh of every matter doubtfully: his words are

---

To Erasmus may be truly applied those remarkable words in St. John, ch. xii. 42, 43. : — " Nevertheless, among the chief rulers also many believed on Him; but because of the Pharisees *they did not confess Him: for they loved the praise of men more than the praise of God;*" the severest censure which the Evangelists have passed upon any of their adversaries! Nothing can more clearly mark the sense of the Holy Ghost upon the subject; nor can there be a doubt, but that "the elect angels," and "the spirits of the just," take the same view of such dissemblers as Luther did of Erasmus. So that, whatever we may think of Luther's language towards this equivocating, double-minded man, *this* every Christian will acknowledge, that it is no honour to any man to be indifferent to the treatment which our Maker receives from his creatures; and, that there is less danger, in ordinary minds, of being too angry with the enemies of God, than of being too complaisant towards them.

wavering, and (as we say) screwed[*] words, which he may construe as he pleaseth. Such words beseem not any honest human creature, much less a Christian. For, behold, what poison he spitteth out in his Colloquies, under feigned characters, and finely applieth himself, according to the humour of youth, thereby to infect them. So soon," said Luther, " as it shall please God to help me on my legs again, I will use against him the sentence of Isaiah[†] concerning the eggs of the cockatrice: they are finely dressed for Erasmus's tooth." Afterwards, Luther, lying in his bed, made these two verses on the same Erasmus of Rotterdam:—

" Qui Satanam non odit, amet tua carmina, Erasme,
Atque idem jungat farras et unguat urnam."

The first day of April, 1526, Luther, lying sick in bed, spent almost the whole day in reading Erasmus's prefaces to the New Testament; and being much therewith moved, he said, " Although this snake be slippery, so that we cannot well fasten it, yet, nevertheless, we and our church will condemn him with his books; and although many worldly people will be displeased with us, and offended at our doing so, yet it is better for us to leave them, than to deny Christ our Saviour.

" Erasmus," said Luther, " makes very base and heavy prefaces (howsoever he soften them); for he makes no difference, in a manner, between Christ our Saviour, and the wise heathen lawyer Solon. He also

[*] Not like a nail, fixed and fast, but like a screw, which will bear turning either way.
[†] Isaiah, lix. 5.

contemneth St. Paul and St. John, as his preface to the Epistle to the Romans and to St. John witnesseth. He writes as though the same were stark naught, where he says, 'The Epistle to the Romans is neither qualified nor pertinent to these times, and that it is more troublesome and heavy than profitable,' &c. Is not this fair praise and credit for the master of that book? Fie on thee, thou maledicted wretch!

"Erasmus," said Luther, "is a right Momus: he derideth every thing, insomuch that his equivocating books may be read by the Turks. For when one thinketh he hath said much, he hath, in fact, said nothing at all. He can be caught neither by us nor by the Papists, unless his wavering and screwed words were abolished, which, both in the Holy Scriptures and in the imperial laws, are forbidden; for they write thus:—'Whoso useth doubtful, dark, and uncertain words, the same shall be construed and understood against him that speaketh them.'

"This," said Luther, "I do leave behind me in my will and testament, whereunto I call you for witnesses; I hold Erasmus of Rotterdam for Christ's most bitter enemy. In his Catechism, which of all his writings I can endure the least, he teacheth nothing certain; there is not one word which saith, 'Do this,' or 'Do not this.' He only maketh the young people's consciences to err and despair. He wrote a book against me (called *Hyperaspistes*), wherein he intended to defend his book on Free Will, against which I wrote my book touching the Bondage of the Will: that same book of mine hath not yet been confuted, neither shall he ever be able to confute it; for I am sure and certain that what I wrote therein, touching that particular, is the unchangeable truth of God. But if God liveth in heaven, then Erasmus shall feel and know what he hath done.

"Erasmus is an enemy to true religion, a particular adversary to Christ, a complete picture and image of an Epicure, and of Lucian.

"This have I, Martin Luther, written with mine own hand, to thee my beloved son John, and through thee, to all my children, and to the holy Christian church.

"*Sensibus hæc imis (res est non parva) reponas.*"

Anno 1543, November 8. Gaspar Schwenckfield sent one of his books to Luther, entitled, "Of the Glory;" whereupon Luther brake out with fervent zeal and said, "Schwenckfield is a silly creature, *qui non habet ingenium, nec spiritum, sed est attonitus,* as all seducers are: he knoweth not what he babbleth, but this is his meaning and his principle:—*creatura non est adoranda, quia scriptum est,* '*Dominum Deum tuum adorabis, et ei soli servies.*' The creature is not to be worshipped, because it is written, ' Thou shalt worship the Lord thy God, and Him only shalt thou serve;' so that he thinketh *Christus est creatura,* Christ is a creature, therefore Christ ought not to be worshipped as a human creature: he feigneth two Christs, and saith, that, after the resurrection and glorification, the creature is transformed into the Deity, and is therefore to be worshipped. He deceiveth in such sort the people with the glorious name of Christ, as he writeth " To the praise of Christ."

"A little child goeth plainly to work, and saith, '*I believe in Jesus Christ our Lord, who was conceived of the Holy Ghost, born of the Virgin Mary,*' &c.; but this idiot will make two Christs," said Luther, "one that hanged on the cross, and another that ascended into heaven, and sitteth at the right hand of God, His heavenly Father. 'We ought not,' saith Schwenckfield, 'to worship that Christ which hung on the cross, and lived on earth.' But," said Luther, "Christ suffered himself to be worshipped when the man fell down before him, and Christ himself said, ' *Whoso believeth in me, believeth also in him that sent me;*' also, '*All men should honour the Son even as they honour the Father*.' This fantastical gentleman hath filched certain words out of my book, on the last words of David; therewith the fellow will trim himself, as *communicationem idiomatum*, communication of properties, and *identitatem personæ*, the identity of person, he mingleth my phrases with his own, and sets it forth as if it were all my meaning. He will teach me what Christ is, and how I shall worship Him. I have (God be praised!) better learned it than he; I know my Christ well, therefore let him trouble me no more." Then spake Dr. Rorer to Luther, and said, " O, sir, that is somewhat too harsh." Luther answered him, " Such fellows teach me to be harsh, we must talk so with the devil.* Let Schwenckfield, by public writing, revoke that heresy about the sacrament, and bring me testimony from Dr. John Hessen and from Dr. John Moibane of Breslaw, otherwise," said Luther, "I will not believe him, though he sware unto me that he had laid his fingers in the wounds."

Luther, afterwards, gave to the messenger that

---

* Agreeably to our Lord's reply to Peter, — " Get thee behind me, Satan," &c.

brought him the book, an open letter with this superscription:—"Luther's Answer to Schwenckfield's messenger;" and spake these words unto him:—"My loving messenger, thou shalt return this answer from me to thy master, Gaspar Schwençkfield, and say that I have received from thee the book; I would that he abstained from these proceedings, for he hath heretofore kindled a fire in Silesia which is not yet quenched, and I fear will burn him eternally; besides this, he goes on with his Eutychianism and creaturality, and maketh the church to err, he having from God no command, neither hath God sent him. Give thou unto him this note also" (wherein were these Latin lines):—"*Increpet Dominus te, Satan. Et sit spiritus tuus qui vocavit te, et cursus tuus quo curris, et omnes qui participant tibi, sacramentarii et Eutychiani, tecum et vestris blasphemiis, in perditionem, sicut scriptum est; currebant, et non mittebam eos, loquebantur et nihil mandavi eis.*"

Luther's Constitutional Melancholy, and Attendant Tribulations.

"Heavy thoughts," said Luther, "do enforce rheums: when the soul is busied with grievous cogitations, and the heart troubled therewith, then the body must partake of the same. Austin said well, '*Anima plus est ubi amat, quàm ubi animat.*' When cares, heavy cogitations, sorrows, and passions, do exceed, then they weaken the body, which, without the soul, is dead, or like a horse without one to rule it. But when the heart is at rest and quiet, then it taketh care of the body, and giveth what thereunto pertaineth. Therefore we ought to abandon and resist heavy cogitations by all possible means. My greatest strife is when I fight with the devil with my cogitations.*

---

* The Almighty had, of course, wise and good reasons for exercising the spirit of this extraordinary man with this most afflictive of all maladies. We may believe that they were such as these: —

1. To give him a more affecting sense of his wretchedness as a sinner.

2. Thus to fix more firmly upon his mind the supreme importance of those doctrines, the knowledge of which he was to be a principal means of restoring to the Church.

3. To restrain and subdue his pride, which the great success and distinguished honour that attended his labours were calculated to inflame.

4. To enable him to sympathise freely with afflicted consciences, and apply the doctrines of the Gospel, more judiciously and tenderly, to their relief.

Independent of any direct temptation of the devil and his angels, a sincere Christian is *likely* to suffer more severely than others under the influence of this malady. It is the nature of it to fill the mind with the most gloomy imaginations respecting every subject with which it may be occupied; and the Christian's mind being habitually engaged with the most solemn subjects, it follows of course, that when the gloomy doubts and apprehensions, incident to melancholy, are exercised upon them, his sufferings will be proportionably greater than those of the man whose thoughts are, for the most part, limited to the affairs of this world. Yet how many, even of this latter description of persons, are driven to the perpetration of self-murder, in the hope of escaping from reflections which seem intolerably oppressive!

It is impossible to determine, in any case, how far the agency of evil spirits may aggravate the symptoms of the disorder; but it is reasonable to suppose, that spirits, so subtle and malicious as the evil angels, will not fail to take advantage of a season of weakness to assault and harass the mind of the unhappy patient, in the

"I have found by myself," said Luther, "that in my highest tribulations (which tormented and exhausted my body so much that I could scarcely pant and take my breath), I went dried up and pressed out like a sponge. No creature was able to comfort me, insomuch that I said, 'Am I alone the man that must feel such tribulations in the spirit?' But ten years past, when I was solitary and alone, God comforted me again through his angels, and enabled me to strive and fight against the Pope."

Dr. Jeronymus Weller being deeply plunged into melancholy fits and humours, Luther said unto him, "Be of good courage; you are not alone that suffereth tribulation; I also am one; and as for sins, I have greater upon me than you and your father have; for I blasphemed my God fifteen years together, with celebrating that abominable idol, the Mass, insomuch that I wish from my heart that I had been at that time rather a pander or a thief.*

---

hope either of driving him to despair, or of urging him (as they did Job) to some dangerous and sinful expedient for obtaining relief.

The reader who has the candour to consider, and the judgment to combine, what follows in Luther's conversations on this subject, will perceive, that while he attributed much of his inward trials and distresses to the agency of evil spirits, he was fully aware of the influence of those natural and sensible causes of his sufferings, by which alone a *Saducee* would account for them all, — for Luther was a man of remarkable good-sense. The following portions of Scripture may be referred to, — Psalms lxxvii. and cii., Lam. ch. iii., the Book of Job. Mr. Rogers's work on Trouble of Mind may also be consulted with advantage.

* This language of Luther, so characteristically strong, is

"When I," said Luther, " am troubled with melancholy thoughts concerning temporal or domestic affairs, then I take a psalm, or a sentence out of St. Paul, and so I lay me down to rest and sleep. But the cogitations that come of the devil are somewhat more chargeable unto me; then I must look strongly about me, and valiantly must strive to work myself thereout."

"When heavy plaguesome cogitations come upon thee," said Luther, "expel them by whatever means thou best mayest; talk and discourse with good friends of such things as thou takest delight in. But here a man may say, 'Without due cogitations, nothing that is good can be effected.' Hereunto," said Luther, "I make this answer:—'We must make a difference of cogitations. Cogitations of the understanding produce no melancholy; it is the cogitations of the will which cause sadness; as, when one is grieved at a thing, or when one doth sigh and complain, those are melancholy and sad cogitations; but the understanding is not melancholy.'"

"When I," said Luther, "write against the Pope, I am not melancholy; for then I labour with the brains and understanding; then I write with joy of heart: insomuch that not long since Dr. Reisinpusch said to me—'I much marvel that you can be so merry; if the case were mine, it would go near to

readily accounted for. It was his opinion, that he should have dishonoured God less, and, certainly, been less injurious to his neighbour, by a life of gross sensuality and dishonesty, than by carrying on and countenancing the system of deception and idolatry which is practised by the massing priest.

kill me.' Whereupon I answered him and said,— 'Neither the Pope nor all his shaven retinue can make me sad; for I know that they are Christ's enemies, therefore I fight against them with joyful courage.'

"Since the time that Silvester Prierias wrote against me," said Luther, "and in the beginning of his book calleth himself by this title,—'The Master of the Holy Palace,' and that I saw the bacchant wrote such stuff as forced me thereat to laugh and jest, since that time, I say, I scorned him, his master the Pope, and all his popish crew."

"Now, in this my age, I am vexed and tormented with nothing except the tribulations of the devil, who walketh with me in my bedchamber; he strongly scowleth upon me. When he can gain nothing of me in my heart, he falleth on my head, and soundly plagueth me.

"He often troubles me on the subject of prayer. He striketh cogitations into my heart, as though I neglected to pray diligently; although I know, that in one day I pray more than all the popish priests and friars, only I babble not so much. My earnest advice is," said Luther, "that no man despise written or described prayers; for whoso prayeth a psalm, the same shall be made thoroughly warm."

"The devil oftentimes objecteth against me the whole cause which (through God's grace) I lead. He objecteth also against Christ; but better were it that the temple brake in pieces than that Christ should therein remain obscure and hid.

"What I teach, write, preach, and intend, the

same," said Luther, " I bring forth openly to the clear daylight; it is not hidden in a corner. I direct and square it all by the Gospel, by baptism, and by the Lord's Prayer. Christ standeth here; Him I cannot deny : upon the Gospel do I ground my cause. Yet, notwithstanding all this, the devil bringeth it so near to me with his crafty disputing, that the sweat of anguish droppeth from me, so that many times I can feel and understand that he sleepeth nearer to me than my wife Kate doth *; that is to say, he disquieteth more than she comforteth or pleaseth me."

" It is a fearful thing," said Luther, " when Satan intendeth to torment the sorrowful consciences with intolerable melancholy; then the wicked villain, master-like, can mask and disguise himself into the person

* Luther here explains his meaning, which is not always the case; otherwise, how readily might a careless reader, fond of a jest, run away with the impression, that Luther's ideas of Satan's temptations were exceedingly gross and absurd. Luther believed that evil spirits have, more or less, to do with every thing that disquiets the Christian's mind, or tends to draw away his heart from a comfortable confidence in his Saviour's love. He was not only a very conscientious man, but his feelings were tender and sensitive; he was what we call a warm-hearted man; hence Satan took occasion of suggesting doubts (notwithstanding Luther's well-grounded conviction of the justice of his cause) whether he were, or could be, justified in making such opposition to the Romish errors as he had done. " Behold," said he (within the heart of Luther), " what contention, and misery, and bloodshed, hast thou occasioned with thy gospel! Why could you not be quiet? If thou shouldest be wrong in this matter, what awful guilt is upon thee!" &c. &c. Doubts on this point must have been intensely distressing to one of Luther's spirit. To Melancthon's mind they appear to have been, at times, and especially at the Diet of Augsburg, almost overpowering.

of Christ, so that it is impossible for a poor human creature (whose conscience is troubled with such great and heavy tribulations) to mark and discover the villany of the devil. Hence it happens, that many of those who are not aware of this do run headlong to despair, do kill and make away with themselves: for they are blinded and deceived so powerfully by the devil, as to be fully persuaded it is not the devil, but Christ himself, that vexeth and tormenteth them in such sort.

"I," said Luther, "am a Doctor in Holy Scripture, and for some years have preached Christ; yet, to this day, I am not able to put Satan off, nor to drive him away from me, as willingly I would; neither am I able so to comprehend Christ, and to take hold of Him, as in Holy Scripture he is placed before me; but the devil continually seeketh how to put another Christ into my mind. Nevertheless, we ought to render thanks to Almighty God, who hath hitherto held and preserved us, by His holy word, by faith, and prayer; so that we know how to walk before Him in humility and fear; and we ought nothing at all to depend or presume upon our own wisdom, understanding, righteousness, art, strength, and power, but should comfort and cheer up ourselves in the strength of Christ alone, who always, above sufficiency, is strong and powerful; and although we be weak and faint, yet He continually vanquisheth in us poor feeble creatures: His holy name be blessed and magnified for evermore. Amen."

"It is written of St. Paul, that when he had suffered shipwreck and great hunger, fourteen days together, he went afterwards to his brethren, of whom being courteously received, he recovered himself again, was refreshed, and comforted. Even so," said Luther, " when I am in heavy tribulations, then I go rather to my swineherd and swine, than to be and remain alone. The heart of a human creature is like a millstone in a mill: when corn is shaken thereon, it runneth about, rubbeth and grindeth it to meal; but if no corn be present, (the stone, nevertheless, running still about,) then it rubbeth and grindeth away itself: so it is with the heart of a human creature; it will be occupied; if it have not the works of its vocation in hand to be busied with, then cometh the devil and shooteth thereinto tribulations, heavy, painful thoughts, and vexation; then the heart consumeth itself with' melancholy, insomuch that it must starve and famish. Many a one therewith grieveth and perplexeth himself to death, as Syrach saith, — ' Sorrow killeth many people, and melancholy consumeth marrow and bone;' it produceth no profit at all. Truly," said Luther, " such evil cogitations have plagued me more than all my labours, which have been innumerable."

"Whoso," said Luther, " is possessed with these and the like spiritual trials, the same should frequent the company of people, and, in any case, not be alone, nor hide himself, and so bite and torment himself with his and the devil's cogitations and possessings, for the Holy Ghost saith, — ' *Woe to him that is alone.*' * When I," said Luther, " am in melancholy, unpleasant, and heavy-minded, then I abandon solitariness, and repair to people and talk with them."

* Eccles. iv. 10.

"I have need often, in my tribulations," said Luther, "to talk even with a child, thereby to expel such cogitations as the devil possesseth me with. The same is done to the end we may not boast, as if we were of ourselves able sufficiently to help ourselves, and to subsist, but should know, that the strength of Christ in us ought to be extolled and praised. Therefore, sometimes, such a one must help me, who in his whole body hath not so much divinity as I have in one finger, for the purpose of teaching me, that without Christ I can do nothing. It was said to St. Paul,— '*My strength is made perfect in weakness.*' This is not such a strength as striveth with raging and power; but it striveth and fighteth in weakness, in silence, and in patience; so that an afflicted heart saith,—'I, poor sinner, do believe in thee, O Christ, let it go with me as it will. Hast thou forsaken me? or art thou angry with me? yet will I be a Christian; I will still remain in that faith, that thou, O Christ, diedst for me,' &c. Now, when this remains steadfast and unremoved, which is the substance, then," said Luther, "all the rest, being accidental, must go and depart. Therefore, thou that art in tribulation, fear God, and doubt not thou art a member washed with Christ's blood, and delivered from Satan's bands and chains; ease thy corporeal smart with spiritual joy," said Luther; "have patience, and thou shalt see and find, that Christ will keep and preserve thee in thy faith, and will deal with thee according to His good and gracious fatherly will."

———

"My tribulations," said Luther, "are more necessary for me than meat and drink; therefore those that feel them ought to accustom themselves thereunto, and learn to bear them. If Satan, in such manner, had not plagued and vexed me, then I should not have been so great an enemy to him, neither should I have been able to do him so much hurt. Tribulations do keep us from pride, and therewithal they increase the acknowledgment of Christ, and of God's gifts and benefits. For from the time that I began to be in tribulation, God gave me the glorious victory in overcoming that confounded and blasphemous kind of life wherein I lived in cursed Popedom. And truly," said Luther, "seeing God frameth the business in such sort, that neither the Emperor nor the Pope are able to suppress me, therefore the devil must come and set upon me, to the end that, in my weakness, God's strength may be known. We that feel our sins have no cause to fear; they that are not sensible of their sins may, indeed, justly be afraid."

"Our tribulations and heavy cogitations," said Luther, "wherewith the devil plagueth and tormenteth, can by no means be driven away better than by spiteful contemning of the devil; for like as when one contemneth a fierce currish dog, by passing quietly by him, the dog then not only desisteth from biting, but also from barking; but when one eggeth him on by throwing or striking at him, then it is to be feared that he will fall upon and bite one. Even so, when the devil seeth that we do not contemn, but fear him, then he ceaseth not to torment and plague us with such tribulations and temptations."

"Ah!" said Luther, one day in his sickness, "how willingly would I now die, for I am faint and overwrought; and at this time I have a joyful and peaceable heart and conscience. I know full well, so soon as I shall be well again, no peace nor rest, but sorrow, weariness, and tribulations, do await me. For could that great man, St. Paul, not be freed or exempted from tribulation, (who made complaint of Satan's angel buffeting him, 2 Cor. xii. 7.) how then should I, poor man, have peace, and be without vexations and troubles of heart? ' *Through much tribulation we must enter into the kingdom of God.*' How willingly would I be instructed of St. Paul, if he were now living, what manner of tribulations his were."

Luther's warm and humble Piety.

" I," said Luther, " out of my own experience, am able to bear witness, that Jesus Christ is true God; I will be no Epicure; I know full well, and have found, what the name of Jesus hath done for me. It is, indeed, well spoken and the plain truth, where we sing in the psalm, — ' God layeth a burden upon us, but He helpeth also;' ' We have a God that helpeth,' and a ' Lord of lords, that delivereth from death.' (Ps. lxviii.) Therefore (by God's grace) no troubles, no tribulations, or other creatures whatsoever, shall separate me from Christ. I," said he, " have oftentimes been so near death, that I thought, verily now I must die, because I teach His word to the wicked world, and acknowledge Him; but He always put life into me, refreshed and comforted me. Therefore let us use diligence only to keep Him, and then all is safe, though the devil were never so wicked and crafty, and the world never so evil and false. Let whatsoever will or can befall me," said Luther, " I will surely cleave by my sweet Saviour, Jesus Christ; for in him I am baptized. I neither can do nor know any thing but what He has taught me. But truly it is a very difficult art, whereunto appertain much and manifold trials and experiences, when one from his heart can name Christ, a Lord and a God that delivereth from death."

"Let us," said Luther, "fix and impose all our trust and confidence in Christ Jesus. Let it please the Lord to take me out of this world this hour, or on the morrow, or whensoever, so will I leave this behind me, that I do and will acknowledge Christ Jesus for my Lord and my God. I have not this out of Scripture only, but also by great and manifold experience; for the name Jesus hath oftentimes holpen me, when no creature besides could help or comfort me.

"In this manner I have before me the word and the deed, Scripture and experience; the loving Lord hath given them both richly unto me; and thereupon I have endured many heavy trials and temptations; but they were all necessary and good for me."

"Oh!" said Luther, "His grace and goodness towards us is so unmeasurably great, that without great assaults and trials it cannot rightly be understood. If the tyrants and false brethren had not set themselves so fiercely against me, against my writings and proceedings, then should I," said Luther, "have vaunted myself too much of my poor gifts and qualities; nor should I, with such fervency of heart, have directed my prayers to God for His divine assistance; I should not then have adscribed all to

God's grace, but to my own dexterity and power; and so I should have flown to the devil, with all my art and doings, &c. &c.

"But," said Luther, "to prevent this, my gracious Lord and Saviour Christ caused me to be chastised and whipped. He ordained that the devil should plague and torment me, inwardly, with his fiery darts; outwardly, through tyrants, as through the Pope and other heretics; and all this Christ suffered to be done for my best good, as in Psalm cxix. is written,—'*It is good for me that I have been in trouble, that I may learn thy statutes.*'"

Luther, speaking of those words of St. Paul to the Corinthians, (1 Cor. ii. 2.)— "*I was with you in weakness, and in fear, and in much trembling;*" and 2 Cor. vii. 5., "*Without were fightings, within were fears,*" &c. "Hereby," said he, "it is evident that he was not always strong in faith; and, moreover, the Lord was fain to comfort him, saying,—'*My grace is sufficient for thee, for my strength is made perfect in weakness.*'

"This is to me," said Luther, "and to all Christians, a comfortable doctrine to hear; for I persuade myself, also, that I have faith, but it is so so, and might well be better; and yet I teach the faith to others; and this I know, that my teaching and preaching is right; but, I confess it, I come very short of faith. Sometimes I commune thus with myself:— 'Thou preachest God's word; this office is committed to thee, and thou art called thereto without thy will or seeking; thou confessest Christ, and preachest Him, which is not fruitless, for many thereby are amended;' but when I consider and behold my own weakness, (I eat, I drink, sometimes I am merry, yea, also, now and then, I play the good-fellow *,) then I begin to doubt and say, ' Ah! that we could but only believe!' Therefore," said Luther, " the secure and presumptuous spirits (heretics and all false Christians) are irksome and dangerous people, who, when they have only looked on the Bible, or have heard a few sermons, do presently think that they have the Holy Ghost, that they understand and know all. But good and godly souls are otherwise minded, and do daily pray, ' *Lord, increase our faith.*' "

" Is it not," said Luther, " a perverse thing in the heretics, hypocrites, and in all false Christians, who do think they know all this well enough, and that they cannot be deceived? but I fail herein, and such as I am," said Luther, " that daily take in hand the Scriptures; so that it maketh me sad, and full of sorrow: for it is a spiteful thing, and the devil's witchcraft in us, that we put more trust in human creatures than in God.

" I, for example," said Luther, " do expect more from Kate, my wife, from Philip Melancthon, and other of my friends, than from my sweet and blessed Saviour Christ; and yet I know for certainty, that

---

* Luther was an edifying and interesting companion, and *could be* a very amusing one. Possessed of rare talents, a great fund of various information, and of a remarkably social temper of mind, he would, it seems, now and then, play the good-fellow; that is, he indulged, too freely, his natural turn for pleasantry, especially when young people were of the party, and made his company more merry than wise. His conscience reproved him for it afterwards, and he was humbled; feeling, no doubt, that he dishonoured his Master by such ebullitions of folly, and lowered the dignity of his office. (See Ephes. v. 4., Col. iv. 5, 6., 1 Tim. iv. 12.; also Eccles. x. 1.)

neither she, nor any other person on earth, hath suffered, or will, or can suffer for me that which He hath suffered. Why, then, should I be afraid of Him?

"This, my foolish weakness," said Luther, "grieveth me much. We plainly see in the Gospel how mild and gentle He showeth himself towards His disciples; how familiarly and friendly He passeth over their weakness, their presumption, yea, their foolishness, &c. He checketh their unbelief, and, in all gentleness, admonisheth them to amendment. Moreover, the Scripture (which is most sure) saith, '*Blessed are all they that put their trust in Him.*' Fie on our unbelieving hearts, that we should be afraid of this Man, who, notwithstanding, is more loving, more friendly, more gentle-minded, and more compassionate towards us, than are our natural kindred, our brethren, and sisters, yea, than parents themselves are towards their own children."

"The devil oftentimes," said Luther, "hath cast these cogitations into my breast, namely, 'How, if thy doctrine be false and erroneous, wherewith the Pope, the mass, friars, and nuns are thus dejected and startled?' And, indeed, the devil hath oftentimes in such manner assaulted me, that the sour sweat hath drizzled from me. But at last, when I saw he would not leave me, I gave him this answer, — 'Avaunt, Satan; address thyself to my God, and talk with Him about it, for the doctrine is not mine, but His; He hath commanded me to hear this Christ; yea, this Christ must only do the deed.' We Christians," said Luther, "ought, in such temptations of the devil, to leave and commit our cause to Christ, He will answer for us."

"If," said Luther, "I were addicted to God's word at all times alike, and had always such love and desire thereto as sometimes I have, then should I account myself the most blessed man on earth. But the loving apostle, St. Paul, failed also thereof, as he complaineth with sighs of heart, saying,—'*I see another law in my members, warring against the law of my mind,*' &c." Rom. vii.

LUTHER'S REMARKS ON SOME OF THE ERRORS AND ABOMINATIONS IN POPEDOM.

The Book of the Birth and Generation of Antichrist, the Son of Hypocrisy, the Son of the Devil.

"The Devil begat Darkness, Darkness begat Ignorance, Ignorance begat Error and his brethren, Error begat Free Will and Presumption out of Self-Conceit, Free Will begat Merit, Merit begat Forgetfulness of God, Forgetfulness begat Transgression, Transgression begat Superstition, Superstition begat Satisfaction, Satisfaction begat the Mass Offering, the Mass Offering begat, of Unction, the Priest, the Priest of Unction begat Misbelief, Misbelief begat King Hypocrisy, Hypocrisy begat Trading with Offerings for Gain, Trading for Gain begat Purgatory, Purgatory begat the yearly solemn Vigils, yearly Vigils begat Church Livings, Church Livings begat Mammon, Mammon begat Swelling Superfluity, Swelling Superfluity begat Fulness, Fulness begat Rage, Rage begat Licentiousness, Licentiousness begat Rule and Dominion, Dominion begat Pomp, Pomp begat Ambition, Ambition begat Simony,

Simony begat the Pope and his brethren about the time of the Babylonian captivity.—After the Babylonian captivity the Pope begat the Mystery of Iniquity, the Mystery of Iniquity begat Sophistical Divinity, Sophistical Divinity begat Rejection of Holy Scripture, Rejection of the Holy Scripture begat Tyranny, Tyranny begat Slaughtering of the Saints, Slaughtering of the Saints begat Contempt of God, Contempt of God begat Dispensation, Dispensation begat Wilful Sin, Wilful Sin begat Abomination, Abomination begat Desolation, Desolation begat Questioning, Questioning begat Searching out the Grounds of Truth, out of which the Desolator, the Pope (called Antichrist), is revealed."

"St. Paul," said Luther, "complaineth and saith, '*The time will come when they will not endure sound doctrine, but after their own lusts shall heap to themselves teachers, having itching ears; and they shall turn away their ears from the truth, and they shall be turned unto fables,*' &c. In like manner St. Paul saith, '*This know also, that in the last days perilous times shall come, for men shall be lovers of their own selves,*' &c. When first I read these sentences," said Luther, "I never looked toward Rome, but thought they had been spoken of the Jews and Turks."

Luther's Opposition to the Popish Doctrine.

"The manner of life," said Luther, "is as evil among us as among the Papists; wherefore we strive not with them by reason of the manner of life, but for and about the doctrine. Wickliffe and Huss opposed and assaulted the manner of life and conversation in

Popedom. But I (chiefly) do oppose and resist their doctrine: I affirm, soundly and plainly, that they teach not aright;—thereunto am I called. I take the goose by the neck," said Luther, "and set the knife to the throat. When I can maintain that the Pope's doctrine is false (which I have proved and maintained), then will I easily prove that their manner of life is evil. The Pope hath taken away the pure word and doctrine, and hath brought another word and doctrine, and hanged the same upon the church. I startled whole Popedom only with this one point, in that I teach uprightly, and meddle with nothing else. We must press upon the doctrine, for that breaketh the neck of the Pope. Therefore the prophet Daniel rightly pictured out the Pope, that he will be such a king as shall do according to his will; that is, he will regard neither spirituality nor temporality, but will, short and roundly, say, 'Thus and thus will I have it.' For the Pope is instituted and ordained neither by divine or human right; but is a self-chosen human creature, who hath intruded himself. St. Paul read Daniel thoroughly, and useth nearly his words, where he saith, '*And he will exalt himself above all that is called God, or that is worshipped.*' " 2 Thess. ii.

" In my time, when I was at Rome," said Luther, " a disputation was openly held (in which, beside myself, were thirty learned masters,) against the power of the Pope, who boasted that with his right hand he commanded the angels in heaven, but with the left he drew souls out of purgatory, and that his person was mixed or mingled with the Godhead.* But Calixtus

* Popery, in its external appearances, the extent of its pre-

disputed against the same, and showed that power was given to the Pope to bind and loose only upon earth. But when the others outrageously opposed him with exceeding great vehemency, then Calixtus concluded by saying, ' That he spake it only by way of dispute, and did not believe as he said.' "

"For the space of many hundred years," said Luther, " there hath not been one bishop who undertook any earnest care about schools, baptism, and preaching; the same would have been too great labour and trouble to them, such enemies were they to God. I have heard divers learned fathers affirm," said Luther, " that the church long since stood in need of a reformation; but no man hath been so bold as to fall upon Popedom, for the Pope carrieth this style, ' *Noli me tangere*—touch me not,' therefore every man was silent. Dr. Staupitz said once to me, ' If you meddle with Popedom, you will have the whole world against you;' and he said, further, ' Nevertheless the church is grounded upon blood, and in and with blood must be dewed, sprinkled, cut, clipped, and planted.'

"Therefore," said Luther, "I could wish that all

---

tensions, and its methods of defence, varies greatly in different times and countries. Arguments and assertions common among English Roman Catholics would not be tolerated in the metropolis of their religion, though (for reasons of policy it is to be presumed) the use of them is not prohibited *in England*. While intelligent Roman Catholics from England,—till being at Rome they have learned to do as they do at Rome,—would be startled to hear the Roman Catholic sentiment of Italy, Spain, or Portugal; that is to say, if they were *at all serious* in their religious views.

those who intend to preach the Gospel would diligently read the popish abominations, their decrees and books, and, above all things, well and thoroughly consider the horrors of the mass, (for the sake of which idol, God, in justice, might have drowned and destroyed the whole world,) to the end their consciences may be armed and confirmed against the adversaries, and the present offences."

———

" The Pope and his crew," said Luther, " can in no wise endure a reformation; the very word Reformation is more hated at Rome than thunderbolts from heaven, or the last day of judgment: as a cardinal said lately, ' Let them eat and drink, and do what they please; but in that they think to reform us, the same is in vain, and we will not endure it.' Neither will we that are Protestants," said Luther, "be satisfied with them, although they administered the sacrament in both kinds, and permitted priests to marry; but we will have also the doctrine of faith pure and unfalsified; and we will have the righteousness that justifieth and saveth before God, which driveth away all idolatry and false worship, which being gone and banished, the foundation upon which Popedom is built falleth also."

———

" The Pope," said Luther, " hath two pillars or bases, on which he standeth: the one is called, ' *Whatsoever ye shall bind on earth shall be bound in heaven,*' &c.; the other is that which our Saviour Christ said to Peter, ' *Feed my sheep,*' &c. These two sentences the Pope hath wrested so far, that thereby he assumeth power and authority to do and deal in the church, and in temporal government, according to his own will and pleasure. Therefore he hath taught such things as he dreamed of; hath altered the true doctrine, hath damned and saved whom he would. Afterwards, also, he deposed emperors, kings, and princes according to his pleasure, as if our Saviour Christ had given that binding and loosing to such external and temporal power, which belongeth to sorrowful and broken consciences alone, and to the doctrine of faith. It became at length one of his canons, *Quod auctoritas sacræ Scripturæ pendeat a sede Romana.* Now when the Pope had made the people believe this, then he might teach what he pleased. He brought it, in fact, so far, that a Christian denied the bloodshed of our Saviour Christ, and put on a friar's hood*, therein seeking his salvation. This was such an abominable fall, that if the same had been done among heathens, it had been too much. Oh!" said Luther, "how do I, oftentimes, wonder that such darkness hath been in Popedom! I know no other way of judging of it, but according to St. Paul's speech, where he saith, '*Because they received not the love of the truth that they might be saved, God shall send them strong delusion that they should believe a lie,*' &c." 2 Thess. ii.†

"When I was at Worms," said Luther, "the Bishop of Magdeburgh came to me, and said, 'I know we have an evil cause in hand, and that your doctrine is right, yet, for some reasons best known to ourselves, we

---

* He alludes, probably, to the custom of burying the dead in a friar's cloak, as well as to the practice of becoming friars in order to please God better than by remaining in an ordinary state of life.

† This plain solution of the strange phenomena of Popery is too little considered by Protestants.

neither can nor will receive it.' In like manner, the Cardinal of Saltzburg said to me, ' We know, and it is written in our consciences, that priests justly might marry, and that matrimony is far better than the shameless wicked way of life which priests drive and use; yet,' said he, ' we must neither alter nor reform it, for the Emperor will not suffer Germany to be disturbed for the conscience sake.'

"What is this," said Luther, "but a flat contemning of God! These are devilish words, and God also contemneth and derideth them again; as we see that emperors, kings, and princes, and all the Imperial cities, do leave and forsake them.

" They can only defend themselves," said Luther, " under the name of the church *; their raging and tyranny are against their own consciences; for they know full well that the church is made subject to God's word, and can only be where Christ is taught and preached; therefore (no thanks to them) they must confess that our doctrine is the doctrine of Christ. The wretches know that Popedom is not God's church; yet they will not hear us, nor will they yield nor allow that God is above the church, but that the church is over and above God; therefore Popedom is not the church of God."

In the year 1530, the 9th of May, Luther held a

* Grant the Roman Catholic that his church is the Holy Catholic Church, — the Holy Church throughout all the world, — and he will manage to prove whatever his church has enjoined in faith or practice. Deny this claim, and bring both church and doctrine to the test of Scripture, they have nothing on which to base an argument.

very sharp disputation, at Wittemberg (which continued three hours), against " that abominable monster, the Pope, that bear-wolf, who exceedeth all tyranny and oppression," said Luther, " as he that will, alone, be *exlex* (lawless), will live secure and free, and do according to his will, — yea, and will even be adored and worshipped, under pain of damnation and loss of many poor souls.

" Therefore, whoso," said he, " regardeth and tendereth God's honour, and endeavoureth the saving health of his soul, the same ought to withstand the Pope with all his might.

" I hope," said Luther, " he hath done his worst; and though he fall not altogether, yet he shall increase no more, but rather decrease. The ancient popes were more upright and honest; but when they began to look after government and domination (fearing they might become servants again), then Cain could no longer endure his brother. The Papists never ought to be trusted [*], though they promise peace by articles, covenants, and under hand and seal, or by what confirmation soever may be thought sure and sufficient. At the Imperial and princely Diet at Nuremberg, they detained us with deceitful disputations, to the end they might, in the mean time, over-run and suppress us. Let us watch," said he, " and pray, in this time

[*] This, of course, refers to political transactions, when the honour and interests of their church are concerned: otherwise a Papist may be a very respectable moral character; a praise which cannot be denied even to many heathens. There may be a high degree of morality completely independent of religion; as there may be a very great refinement and elegance of manners without morality.

of cessation of arms, that, through the light of the Gospel, God's name may be hallowed."

"I am persuaded," said Luther, "that if at this time St. Peter, in person, should preach all the articles of Holy Scripture, and should only deny the Pope's authority, power, and primacy, saying that the Pope was not the chief head of all Christendom, then, surely, they would cause him to be hanged. Yea, if Christ himself were yet on earth, and should preach, then, without all doubt, the Pope would crucify Him again. Therefore," said Luther, "let us expect the same entertainment; better it is to build upon Christ than upon the Pope. If," said Luther, "I did not from my heart believe that after this life there is another, then I would sing another song, and lay the burden on another's neck."

"The Papists," said Luther, "are proud people, unlearned in the Holy Scriptures; they understand nothing they read, and write nothing sincerely: but stiffly do they sit in the seat of government; they exclaim, — ' The decrees and conclusions of the fathers must not be put in any doubt, nor disputed.' Therefore, the Pope (as he that is full of devils) defendeth his tyranny, and very strongly doth maintain it, as we see in his Decrees *, *Si Papa, &c.* 40. *Dist.* There it is

---

* The Decretals contain the laws and ordinances of the Romish Church. The particular decree to which Luther here refers is as follows: —

" If the Pope is found careless of his own, and of his brethren's salvation; useless and inattentive in the employment of his means; and, moreover (which is more prejudicial to himself and to all

clearly written, although the Pope did lead the whole world into hell, yet no human creature must presume to question him for the same, nor once must dare to ask, 'Why and wherefore he did so?'

"This," said Luther, "is most fearful and abominable, that, for the sake of his usurped authority, we should lose our souls, which Christ, with His precious blood, so dearly earned and delivered. Christ saith, '*Whoso cometh unto me, him will I in no wise cast out*,' &c. Against this, the Pope saith[*], 'Thus do I command, thus will I have it, shortly and roundly. Rather than my command shall be neglected, ye shall all be made away and lost.' Yet, notwithstanding all this and more, our princes do fall down before him,

---

men), shall neglect to speak what is good: notwithstanding his leading innumerable people in crowds, with himself, to that chief slave of hell, with whom he shall be beaten with many stripes for eternity, yet no mortal man must presume to reprove this person's faults herein. He, who is himself to be the judge of all, is to be judged of no man; unless he be caught departing from the faith. For whose everlasting state the whole body of the faithful must the more earnestly pray, inasmuch as they perceive that their own salvation depends, after God, more particularly upon his safety."

[*] It is the creed of every intelligent and *honest* Roman Catholic, that the church of Rome is the mother and mistress of all churches, and the Pope the head of the church. It is also his creed, that out of the Romish church there is no salvation; that is to say, that none but Roman Catholics can be saved. (See Pope Pius's Creed, Art. XI., and the Ratification of it.) Hence, naturally enough, the enquiry of every *sincere* Roman Catholic, respecting one for whose salvation he feels interested, is, "Does he belong to our church? Is he a Roman Catholic?" And the labour of the sincere Roman Catholic priest is, to bring men into *his church*. The Protestant is lost simply as a Protestant; *i. e.* as one who protests against the errors of the church of Rome,

worship him, and kiss his feet*; therefore we ought to withstand and resist him, and beat him down with God's word and prayer.

"But," said Luther, "who, thirty years past, durst so much as have had such a thought of the Pope? For, in those days, he would cast whom he pleased headlong into hell, and fetch them out again."

The Pope's Decrees.

"In the Pope's Decrees many foul and devilish canons are contained: the church is in a particular manner plagued and fouled by them. The Pope, void of all shame, presumeth therein to say, 'Whoso believed and observed not his decrees, it were in vain for such a one to believe in Christ, or to give credit to the four Evangelists.' 'Is not this," said Luther, "the devil himself, and the utmost ruin and poison of the church? Likewise, the Pope saith, in one of his decrees, although he led people into hell, yet they ought to follow him; when, on the contrary, his office is to comfort the broken and sorrowful hearts, and to lead them to Christ. Fie upon this maledicted villain! — must he teach the consciences to despair in this sort?

---

and renounces communion with it. Christ says, "Come to *me*, all," &c. "He that believeth in *me* hath everlasting life." The Roman Catholic religion diverts men's minds from the grand object of faith (Jesus Christ), and directs them to the church; that is, in fact, to the church ministers, whose prayers, masses, unctions, &c., are to do what is needful for the saving of the soul.

* "For God hath put in their hearts to fulfil his will, and to agree and to give their kingdom unto the beast, until the words of God shall be fulfilled." — Rev. xvii. 17.

"Whoso readeth his decrees," said Luther, "shall oftentimes find, that an article is proved with fair sentences of Holy Scripture. But when he hath cited every fit part of Scripture, then he argueth against them, and saith, ' The Romish church hath otherwise concluded:' and so, like a hell-hound, dareth presume to make God's word subject to human creatures.

"Even so, likewise, doth Thomas Aquinas, who in his books disputeth *pro et contra;* and when he citeth a place in Scripture, then, by and by, he concludeth thus :— ' Aristotle, *in sexto libro Ethicorum*, holdeth the contrary.' Here," said Luther, " the Holy Scripture must give place to Aristotle, the heathen writer. Such abominable darkness the world will not observe; but despise the truth, and fall into horrible errors. Therefore, let us make good use of the time, for it will not always remain as now it is."

Of the Idolatry in Popedom.

"When people will serve God without his word and commands," said Luther, " all their religion, let it have never so great a name and lustre of holiness, is nothing else but plain idolatry. And the more holy and spiritual such a religion seemeth to be, the more hurtful and venomous it is; for it seduceth people away from the faith of Christ, and maketh them depend upon their own strength, works, and righteousness. Thus all kinds of Orders in Popedom, all their fastings, prayers, hairy shirts, the holiest works of the Capuchins (which in Popedom are held to be the most holy of all), are altogether works of the flesh: and why? because they hold that they are holy, and shall be saved — not through Christ (whom they hold and fear as a severe and angry judge*) — but through the rules of their order," &c.

"Hypocrites and idolaters," said Luther, "have the same quality and nature in them that those singers have, who will scarcely sing at all when entreated thereto, but being not desired they never leave off singing. Even so are the false workers of holiness; when God bids them obey His commandments, viz., in loving their neighbour, and helping him as they are able, with advice, with lending, giving, reproving, comforting, &c., then no man can bring them to those points; but, on the contrary, what they themselves make choice of, and pretend, out of their own devotion and good meaning, to honour and serve God with (as they dream), thereon do they hold fast and sure.

---

* Should this be denied by any Roman Catholic, let him enquire, why (if Christ be not regarded as an object of fear rather than of comfortable confidence) is there so much use made by the Romish church of the *intercession of the saints,* and especially of the Virgin Mary, whose great prerogative it is (if we may judge by Roman Catholic Prayer-Books) to make her Son propitious to those who court her patronage? The following are *specimens* of the prayers offered to that blessed woman, by the Roman Catholics, according to their Common Prayer-Book: — " Blessed mother, and spotless virgin, glorious queen of the world, pray to the Lord for us." Again, — " We flee to *thee* for succour, O holy mother of God; despise not our prayers in our necessities, but deliver us from all dangers, thou ever glorious and blessed virgin." These are, absolutely! the prayers commanded by the infallible church to be offered up (in Latin) to that blessed woman. Here, also, is part of a hymn to be sung (in Latin) to her praise: —
" Hail, star of the sea, sweet mother of God, and always a virgin, happy gate of Heaven; loose the guilty from their chains, give light to the blind, drive from us all evil things, demand for us all that are good; show that thou art the mother; let Him who sub-

They plague and torment their bodies with fasting, with praying, singing, reading, hard lying, &c.; they pretend great humility and holiness, and do all things with a wonderful zeal, and fervency, and devotion, without ceasing. But, such as the service and work is, such will also the reward be, as Christ himself saith, Matthew, xv., '*In vain do they worship me, teaching for doctrines the commandments of men.*'"

Speaking of the worship of the idol Moloch, Luther said:—" This idolatry, I apprehend, had a glorious show, as though it were a kind of worshipping which was more pleasing to God than the common service commanded by Moses; from whence many people, that in outward show were devout in holiness, when they intended to perform an acceptable service to God, did, out of great love and zeal in honour of God (as they dreamed), offer up and sacrifice their sons and daughters: they thought, no doubt, that, in doing this, they followed the example of Abraham, Gen. xxii., and did that which was highly pleasing to God.

" Against this idolatry," said Luther, " the prophets preached with hot-burning jealousy : they call the same, not offerings to God, but to idols and to devils, as the 106th Psalm showeth, and Jer. xxxii., &c. But they held the prophets, no doubt, to be liars and cursed heretics.

---

mitted to be thy son for us, receive *through thee* our prayers." Reader, what honest man, reading, as he may (in Latin), these prayers, which the Romish church prescribes to be used by all its members, but must be both ashamed and afraid to submit his conscience to the government of such a body of men? " Unto their assembly mine honour be not thou united," (Gen. xlix. 5.); for if this be not idolatry, what is?

"This worshipping of idols was, in Popedom, very frequent in my time, and still is," said Luther, "though in another manner: for those parents, in Popedom, were held and esteemed holy people, that gave one or more of their children into the monasteries, to become either friars or nuns, that so they might 'serve God day and night,' &c. Hence came the common proverb, 'Oh! blessed is the mother that hath borne such a child, as is to be made a spiritual person.' Now, true it is," said Luther, "though those sons and daughters are not burned corporeally, and offered to idols, as were the others spoken of before, yet are they (which is far worse) thrust spiritually into the throat of the devil, who (through his disciples, the Pope and his shaved crew,) lamentably doth murder their souls with false doctrine, in that they rely only upon their own good works, &c.

"The Jews," said Luther, "out of hate and malice to the Gentiles, do write, 'That the service of Baal Peor was such, that they used to lift up their tails, and fouled before that image.' But the meaning thereof was not so; for all idolatry and worshipping of idols have always been performed in such sort, that they have had a colour and show of sanctity. I am persuaded," said he, "it was such a service and concourse of people as by us was in Popedom to St. Valentine, St. Antony, St. Cyriac, St. Roche, &c., to the end Baal Peor should not hurt the people, nor destroy them with pestilence, with cold, or heat, or St. Valentine's disease, or other plagues. I hold also, it was a confused doing in all things, like to our pilgrimages and church marts: that they (as it is written, Exod. xxxii., of worshipping the calf,) rose early in the morning, prayed, and offered, and afterwards did eat and drink, and then dispersed themselves here and there to accomplish their licentious wickedness.

"This manner," said Luther, "was very common in my time, when I was bewitched with that cursed Popedom. Then they went out and performed their pilgrimage in passion week, they visited holy places or churches two or three miles from the towns. And when parties could not consort together as they would at other times, then they went out on such pilgrimages, and fulfilled their wicked purposes; and this they did all under the colour of divine and holy service. Such abominable doings are continually practised in that cursed Popedom; God put an end to it! Amen."

"There must needs be sectaries and seducers," said Luther, "to practise idolatry, so long as the world standeth, who (with seeming high devotion) do give a great inducement to errors. Let us but consider, what a howling and crying parents made in Popedom when they first blessed and gave their children into monasteries, especially the daughters, when they sung that '*Regnum mundi,*'" &c.

Idolatrous Religions encouraged in the World.

"The invocation of saints," said Luther, "is a most abominable blindness and heresy; yet, nevertheless, the Papists will not consider, much less acknowledge, and amend it. The Pope hath had his greatest profit from the dead, much more than from the living; for the calling on the dead saints hath brought unto him infinite sums of money and riches. But thus it goeth in the world; superstition, unbelief, false doctrine and worshipping, obtaineth more than the upright, true, and pure religion. She, in this world, is the maid, but the other is *domina* and empress. Eight hundred prophets of Baal could be fed and maintained from Jezebel's table; but the whole kingdom of Israel could not maintain the one prophet, Elijah: he was fed by the widow of Sarepta among the heathen."

The slavish Praying in Popedom.

" Certain students of Bononia sought of the Pope a dispensation touching the praying of the Canonical Hours. The Pope thereupon wrote to them thus:— ' *Surge mantiùs et ora citiùs;*' i.e., Rise earlier and pray quicker. Which rule was followed by Mercurinus, chancellor to the Emperor Charles V., who, on a time, arose up early and in haste to pray. The devil appeared unto him in the likeness of a poor soul, and said to him, ' *Tu non justd hord oras!*' i.e., ' Thou prayest not at the right hour!' In such sort," said Luther, " could the devil scoff and flout them. In my time there was a brother in the monastery at Erfurt, who, by reason of many engagements, neglected divers hours in his prayers, and whereas he could obtain no dispensation, therefore he was forced to hire one to pray for him, that so he might have time to read twice in the day."

The Value of holy Places, and of Relics.

" I believe," said Luther, " that the Pope, out of special consideration, appointed and ordained the feast of St. Sylvester and Thomas of Canterbury to be celebrated eight days after Christmas-day. The one brought to the Pope the kingdom of England, the other the Romish empire.

" The apostle St. Thomas," said Luther, " was, by the Pope, held in no esteem in comparison with this

Thomas of Canterbury; for the Pope's chief aim is securing the livings. Therefore have I noted and shown all the robberies in the Pope's keys, which will vex and anger him much; for his acts and deeds will plainly appear to agree with my words. It was high time to have this wickedness discovered to the world.

"Although the errors and deceits of the Pope, before the light of the Gospel came, were great, yet we worshipped and adored them; to think whereof we are now ashamed. There were the relics of Joseph's breeches, and St. Francis's under-drawers, which have been shown here at Wittemberg.

"The Bishop of Mentz boasted that he had a flame of the bush which Moses beheld burning. At the Black Star at Compostella, in Spain, they show, for a holy relic, the ensign of the victory which Christ had in hell; they likewise show his crown, the cross, the nails," &c.

A Friar at Compostella.

"In Popedom," said Luther, "they went on pilgrimage to the dead saints; they went to Rome, to Jerusalem, and to St. James at Compostella, to make satisfaction and payment for their sins. A certain prince in Germany, well known to myself," said Luther, "went to Compostella, in Spain, where 'tis thought St. James (the brother of St. John) was buried. Now, as this prince made his confession to a barefoot friar, who was an honest friar, and as the custom hath been in Popedom to fetch from thence great Romish indulgences and pardons for sins, which there they bestowed on those who gave money for them, the friar asked the prince if he were a German. The prince answered, 'Yea;' upon which the friar said, 'O, loving child! why seekest thou so far for that which thou hast so much better in Germany? For I have seen and read the writings of an Austin friar touching indulgences and pardons for sins, wherein he powerfully concludeth that the true pardons and remissions of sins do only consist in the merits and sufferings of our Lord and Saviour, Jesus Christ, wherein is found the forgiveness of all. O, loving child!' said the friar, 'remain thereby, and suffer not thyself to be otherwise persuaded. I purpose shortly (God willing) to leave this unchristian life, to repair to your Germany, and join myself to this same Austin friar.'"

Of Rome and Jerusalem.

"Christ," said Luther, "lived three-and-thirty years on earth, and went up every year thrice to Jerusalem, which maketh ninety and nine times that he went thither. If the Pope could show that Christ had been but once at Rome, what a boasting and bragging would he then make? Yet, notwithstanding, Jerusalem was destroyed to the ground."

Celibacy in Popedom.

"That unmarried life, so cried up in Popedom," said Luther, "is great hypocrisy and wickedness; under colour of it the fathers of the church were deceived. Austin, although he lived in the better time, was deceived through the crowning of monastery nuns and virgins: and although he allowed them to marry if they would, yet he said they sinned in marrying, and did not rightly toward God. Afterwards, when the time of wrath and blindness came, and the truth was hunted away, and lying got the upper hand, then, under colour of great holiness, which, in truth, was mere hypocrisy, the generation of poor womankind was contemned.* But Christ, with only one sentence, confuteth all their arguments,—namely, ' *God created them male and female.*' "

The Social Life is the best.

" To live in an open public state," said Luther, " is the safest; Christ also did live and walk in an open and public state here on earth amongst the people, and did warn those that are his, saying, ' *When they shall say, behold He is in the wilderness, go not forth; or in the secret chambers, believe it not;*' for in such cells and corners," said Luther, " have the wicked wretches (the monks, friars, and nuns) used and led shameful and beastly lives. But openly, and among people, a man must live civilly and honestly, must fear God and man," &c.

" I much admire," said Luther, " the madness and bitterness of Witzell, in undertaking to write much against the Protestants, when, in truth, he had neither cause nor matter, but (as we use to say) brake a cause from the hedge, and sought occasion; as, for example, in blaspheming this saying of ours;—' The

---

* The Scripture, speaking generally, saith,—" *Marriage is honourable among all men.*" Again, referring to a period of distress and persecution, when great personal suffering was likely to be the lot of all, and of the married Christians more particularly, it declared it to be better, under existing circumstances, for Christians to abstain from marriage. The Pope (*i.e.*, the Romish church), in his tyrannical way, took advantage of the recommendation contained in 1 Cor. vii., to bind young women, by a heavy curse, to keep the vows of single life which they had been tempted to make; and to confine them for life to the rules, and, mostly, within the walls, of a nunnery.

works and labours of a farmer, a husbandman, or any other good and godly Christian (if they be done in faith) are far better in the sight of God, than all the works of monks, friars, nuns,' &c. Therefore this poor, simple, and ignorant fellow," said Luther, " maketh himself very angry and busy against us. He looketh not upon the works which God hath commanded and imposed upon every one in his station and calling. These he regardeth not at all; but gapeth only after superstitious, prancing, and shining works, which God neither commandeth nor regardeth.

" St. Paul wrote more richly and naturally of good works and virtues than all the philosophers; for he extolleth with high commendation the works of good and godly Christians, in their common callings in the world. Let Witzell know," said Luther, " that David's wars and battles which he fought, were more pleasing to God than the fastings and prayings of the best, the honestest, and holiest monks and friars, much more than the works of our now ridiculous and superstitious friars."

A Friar's Fast in Popedom.

" In Popedom," said Luther, " every thing is done without trouble*; their fasting is more easy unto them than our eating is to us. To one fasting day belong three days of devouring. Every friar to his evening collation hath two quarts of beer, a quart of wine, spice cakes, or bread prepared with spice and salt, the better to relish their drink. Thus went

---

* *i. e.*, To those who were inclined to take things easily; while, to the conscientious, it was exceedingly burdensome and injurious.

these poor fasting brethren; they grew so pale and wan, that they were like to the fiery angels."*

The People's Fasting.

"The Popish fasting," said Luther, "is a right cave of murder, whereby many young people have been utterly spoiled, in observing all their times without distinction, and in eating generally one sort of food, so that nature's strength is thereby wholly weakened. For this cause Gerson, that ancient teacher at Paris, was constrained to write a book of *Comfort for troubled and perplexed Consciences*, to the end they might not be discouraged nor reduced to despair; for those that fast as some do in Popedom do weaken their strength, and break and spoil their constitutions. Such darkness hath been in Popedom, where they neither taught, nor intended to teach, the Ten Commandments, the Creed, nor the Lord's Prayer."

Auricular Confession.

"The Papists," said Luther, "in private confession do only regard the work itself. There was such a running to confession, that they never could be satisfied with confessing; for in case one had forgotten to confess any thing (be it ever so little) which haply afterwards came to his remembrance, then presently he must return to his confessor, and confess over again; for they must make confession of every particular sin, insomuch that a priest said once to me (being tired with his clients' innumerable confessions), 'God hath

---

* It is a common remark of travellers, that the friars in Popish countries are a plump, corpulent race of men.

charged and commanded that we should hope in his mercy.' I knew a doctor in law," said Luther, " who was so tormented with this confessing, that, before he could receive the sacrament, he was obliged to go three times to confess to his confessor.

" In my time, when in Popedom, we made our confessors weary, and they again much perplexed us with their conditional absolutions; for they absolved in this manner:—' *I absolve and speak thee loose, by reason of the merits of our Lord Jesus Christ, by reason of the sorrow of thy heart, of thy mouth's confession, of the satisfaction of thy works,*' &c. These conditions, and what thereunto pertained, were causes of all mischiefs.

" All this we did out of fear, and hoping thereby to be justified and saved before God. We were so troubled and overburdened with the ' traditions of men,' that Gerson felt himself constrained to slack the bridle of the conscience, and to give it some relief. Gerson was the first to break out of this prison; for he wrote that it was no mortal sin to neglect the ordinances and commandments of the church, or to do contrary to the same, unless it were done out of contempt, wilfully, or out of a stubborn mind. These words, though they were but weak and few, raised up and comforted many consciences. The Pope*," said Luther, " laughed in his fist at these dark errors; he took pleasure and delight in domineering, in vexing and tormenting of the poor consciences.

" Against such bondage and forcements," said Luther, " I wrote a book concerning Christian freedom, showing that such strict laws and ordinances of

* The head, and so, the personification, of the ruling authorities in the Romish church.

human invention ought not to be observed. But there are now certain gross, misunderstanding, and inexperienced fellows (who never felt such captivity), that presumptuously undertake utterly to contemn and reject all laws and ordinances.

"To conclude, the consciences in Popedom were so plagued and tormented that a man could scarcely believe it. If we had not their books and our own experience to witness the same, no man would imagine that the blindness were so great.*

"And although the Pope sinned and did wrong in nothing else, but only with forcing confessions in the days of the passion week; yet, by reason of that wickedness, he deserved to be torn in pieces with hot glimmering fiery pincers.† Our people in these days," said Luther, "know nothing of that tormenting captivity of the consciences, but they live in great freedom; they are now secure, being sensible neither of the law nor of Christ."

The Pope's Perversion of the Bible and Sacraments.

"The Pope," said Luther, "denieth not the Sacrament, but he hath stolen from the laity the one part or

* So it is at present; many well-meaning people, who see Popery only as it is exhibited before Protestants in England, have a most imperfect idea of what the spirit of Popery, and of what its practice, is, to this day, in countries where its power is undisputed.

† This, again, is one of those vehement expressions of Luther, which, when separated from its context, or taken without its appropriate grain of salt, might give a modern reader, ignorant of the great reformer's character, a very unfavourable opinion of him. It should be known, that Luther always discouraged persecution: "Let us fight against the Pope," said he, "*with the word of God and prayer.*"

kind thereof, neither doth he teach the true use of the sacrament. The Pope rejecteth not the Bible, but he persecuteth and killeth upright and godly teachers. So did the Jews: they persecuted and slew the prophets who truly expounded and taught the Holy Scripture. The Pope will permit the substance and essence of the Sacrament and Bible to remain, but he will compel us to use the same according as it is his will and pleasure to describe it; and he will force us to believe the falsely feigned and invented transubstantiation, and the real presence, *corporaliter*.* The Pope doth nothing else but pervert and abuse all that God hath ordained and commanded."†

The True Use and Understanding of the Sacrament.

"The operative cause of this Sacrament," said Luther, " is the word and institution of Christ, who ordained and erected it. The substance is bread and wine; the form is the true body and blood of Christ, which is spiritually received by faith; the final cause of instituting the same, is the benefit and fruit in that we strengthen our faith, and doubt not but that Christ's body and blood was given and shed for us, and that

---

* Luther, who had, in early life, embraced with all his heart, the whole system of Popery, and been used to submit his judgment to the authority of the church till near his thirtieth year, could not divest himself of the idea of the real presence of Christ's body and blood in the bread and wine of the Lord's Supper; but he rejected the Romish opinions as to the nature of the change: and — as to the offering of the wafer in sacrifice, and the adoration of it as God, — these he entirely disallowed and abolished.

† This will be found to be the distinguishing peculiarity of Popery, which has justly been called " Satan's masterpiece." It is a system into which he admits the whole canon of truth, yet makes it speak (in a manner) nothing but error.

depend thereon so fast and sure, and are of opinion that whoso has heard Mass no evil can happen to him that day, but he is free from all danger, neither can he sin in whatsoever he taketh in hand; from hence it came to pass that, after hearing Mass, many sins and murders were committed. When I was at Rome, I remember there was one that had sought after his enemy two whole years to be revenged of him; at last he spied him in that church where he himself had heard Mass, and newly was risen from before the altar: he stepped up to him, and at once stabbed * him to death in the church, and afterwards fled away. My book," said Luther, " on the abolishing of the Mass is very harshly written against the adversaries, the blasphemers. It is not for those that are new beginners, nor for young milk-christians, — such thereat are offended, and no marvel: if, twenty years ago, any one had attempted to take the mass from me, the same should have tugged hard before he had gotten it from me; for my heart did hang thereon, — I did adore it. Now, God be praised! I am of another mind, and am fully assured that the foundation of the Mass, — and of Popedom altogether, — is nothing but a deceitful trade, and an abominable extortion and idolatry."

" The Mass," said Luther, " is a double impiety and

---

* The practice of private assassination, so frequent among modern Italians, at least so generally charged upon them, may be owing to constitutional temperament, and entirely unconnected with their religion. Yet, I think, we do not read that the inhabitants of Italy were addicted to it before the establishment of Popery. The cause of the evil is, probably, of a mixed character.

† 1 Cor. iii. 2.

abomination:—1st, It is a divine blasphemy of God: 2dly, A political sin; namely, a deceit and a theft."*

Of Purgatory.

"Austin, Ambrose, and Jerome," said Luther, "held nothing at all of Purgatory. Gregory (being in the night time deceived by a vision) taught something of it. But as God commands us to enquire, not of visions and spirits, but of Moses and the prophets; therefore the opinion of Gregory on this point must go for nothing with us.

"God," said Luther, "hath set before us two ways in his word: one which, by faith, leadeth to salvation; the other, by unbelief, to damnation. As for Purgatory, no place in Scripture maketh mention of it, neither must we any way allow of it; for it darkeneth and undervalueth the grace, the benefits, and merits of our blessed sweet Saviour, Jesus Christ.

"In this world," said Luther, "we may leave Purgatory in its circle and bounds; for here, in this life, the upright, good, and true godly Christians are well and soundly scoured and purged."

The Pope's Covetousness.

"The covetousness of the Popes has exceeded all others; therefore," said Luther, "the devil made choice of Rome to be their habitation, for the ancients said, 'Rome is a den of covetousness, the root of all wickedness.' Truly," said Luther, "there is at Rome a most abominable trading with covetousness; for all is

---

* Being celebrated for money, under the pretence of its being available for expiating the sins of the living and the dead, and delivering souls out of the Romish purgatory; and this without any warrant from God in the Scripture.

† i. e., By tribulations.

raked to their hands without preaching or church-service, but only with superstition and idolatry, and with selling their good works to the poor ignorant lay-people for money: therefore St. Peter describeth such covetousness with express and clear words, when he saith, '*They have a heart exercised with covetous practices.*' I am persuaded a man knows not what the disease of covetousness is unless he knoweth Rome; for the deceits and jugglings in other parts are nothing in comparison with those at Rome. Therefore, anno 1521, at the Imperial Diet held at Worms, the states of the whole empire made supplication against such covetousness, and desired that his Imperial Majesty would be pleased to suppress the same."

A Lying Wonder.

"In the monastery at Isenach standeth an image, which," said Luther, "I have seen. It is the image of Mary and her child. When a wealthy person came to pray thereunto, then the child turned away his face from the sinner to his mother, as if it refused to give ear to his praying; and he was to seek mediation and help from the Virgin his mother. But if the sinner gave liberally to that monastery, then the child turned to him again; and if he promised to give more, then the child showed itself very friendly and loving towards him, and, with outstretched arms, made over him a cross. The image," said Luther, "was made hollow within, and prepared with locks, lines, and screws, and behind stood a knave to work them. In such sort were the people mocked and deceived, who took it for a miracle, and that it moved by Divine providence."

Self-righteousness of Popedom.

"It is impossible," said Luther, "that a Papist should

understand this article:—'*I believe the forgiveness of sins;*' for the Papists are drowned (as I also was when among them) in their cogitations of inherent righteousness."

"A Capuchin friar saith, 'Wear a grey coat and a hood, wear a halter about thee, and put clogs on thy feet;' a preacher friar saith, 'Put on a black hood;' a Papist saith, 'Do this or that work, hear mass, pray, fast, give alms;' but a true Christian saith, 'I am made good, righteous, and saved, only by faith in Christ, without any of my works or deserts.'* Compare, now, these two together," said Luther, "and judge which may be the true righteousness.

"In Italy," said Luther, "the hospitals are very well provided; they have fair buildings, good meat and drink, diligent attendance, and learned physicians; the bedding and furniture are clean and neat, the dwelling-places are fairly painted. As soon as a sick person is brought in, they take off his clothes in the presence of a public notary, who takes account thereof in writing: these are carefully laid up; and they put upon him a white coat, and lay him in a well-prepared bed. Soon after, they bring two physicians; and the servants bring meat and drink in pure glass vessels and cups, which they touch only with one finger. Then also certain married women (whose faces are covered) come and administer to the poor, as unknown, and afterwards go home again. Now," said Luther, "these works are good and laudable; only the mischief is that they think thereby to merit heaven, and to be jus-

---

* 1 Cor. i. 30.

tified and saved by reason of such their works. This spoileth all."

A Popish Argument.

"The chiefest argument which the Papists do use against us," said Luther, "is this:—'Ye at Wittemberg,' say they, 'are nothing bettered by your preaching:' from which they conclude that our doctrine is not right. They would have us teach according to their humours; that is, we should depend upon our own righteousness. But," said Luther, "they have not the art to know the difference between the seed falling on the stony and on the good ground; nor between the tares and the wheat. Ah! it is a great folly in them to censure the word by the fruits. "For the Gospel is the power of God, which saveth only those that believe therein."*

ANECDOTES RELATIVE TO THE REFORMATION.

Bishop of Mentz and the Bible.

"Anno 1530," said Luther, "at the Imperial Assembly at Augsburg, Albert, Bishop of Mentz†, by

---

* Rom. i. 16. See also 2 Cor. ii. 15—17.

† The Archbishop of Mentz was, after him of Toledo, in Spain, the richest prelate in the Pope's kingdom; being not only a bishop, but a prince elector of the German empire. Albert seems to have considered himself rather as a political than a religious character.

chance had got into his hands the Bible, and for the space of four hours he continued reading in it. At last one of his council came on a sudden into his bedchamber, where he was, and seeing the Bible in the bishop's hand, was much amazed thereat, and said unto him, 'What doth your highness with that book?' The archbishop thereupon answered him, and said, 'I know not what this book is, but sure I am that all which is written therein is quite against us.'

"Dr. Esk confessed openly, and said, 'The Protestants cannot be confuted and opposed out of holy Scripture:' therefore the Bishop of Mentz said unto him, 'O! how finely do our learned divines defend us and our doctrine!' The Bishop of Mentz," said Luther, "holdeth our doctrine to be upright and true: but he courteth the Pope; otherwise, long time before this, he would have played strange pranks with His Holiness."

The World's Judgment of the Bible.

"Dr. Ussinger (an Austin friar with me in the monastery at Erfurt) said once unto me, as he saw that I diligently read and affected the Bible, 'Brother Martin, what is the Bible? Let us,' said he 'read the ancient teachers and fathers, for[*] they have sucked the juice and truth out of the Bible; the Bible is the cause of all dissension and rebellion.' This," said Luther, "is the censure of the world concerning

[*] The very same argument is in use with the Roman Catholic priesthood of the present day. "What is the use of your reading the Bible for yourselves, when in *our books* you may find all that may be gotten from the Bible? The reading of the Bible will only unsettle your minds, and produce discord."

God's Word; therefore we must let them run on their course towards that place which is appointed for them."

Elector Frederick's Judgment.

"Frederick, Prince Elector of Saxony, used to say he had well discerned, that nothing could be propounded by human reason and understanding, (were it never so wise, cunning, or sharp,) but that a man, even out of the self-same proposition, might be able to confute and overthrow it. 'God's Word alone,' he said, " stood fast and sure, like a mighty wall which cannot be beaten or battered down.'"

The sad end of one who trifled with God.

"Albert, Bishop of Mentz, had a physician attending on his person who was a Protestant, and therefore the less in the bishop's favour. This man, being covetous and puffed up with ambition, recanted his religion, and fell again to papistry, uttering these words: — 'I will, for a while, set Christ behind the door, until I be grown rich, and then I will take Him to me again.' Such blasphemous words deserve the highest punishments, as befell that wicked dissembling wretch; for the same night he was found in his bed in a most shocking condition, with his tongue torn out of his mouth, as black as a coal, and his neck wrung in twain.* I myself," said Luther, " coming at that time from Frankfort to Mentz, was an eye witness of that just judgment of God. If," said he, " a man could bring that to pass, and at his pleasure could set God behind the door, and take him again when it

* There seems to be some exaggeration in this story, if correctly reported. The *moral* of it is exceedingly important.

suited him, then would God be his prisoner! They were the words of a cursed Epicure; and so, accordingly, he was rewarded."

A fearful Story.

"I knew a great doctor," said Luther, "who, in the year 1527, was chaplain to a great Popish bishop: he was, at the first, a great friend to the holy Gospel, insomuch that, contrary to his bishop's command, he received the holy communion in both kinds, according to Christ's institution; but when he felt himself disgraced with his master, and saw that many other Protestants in that place were driven away and banished, then he recanted, and forsook the Gospel. Afterwards, when he saw that the Protestants willingly suffered themselves to be thus cruelly banished, and with great joy set at nought this bishop's tyranny, then his conscience awoke, and sorely goaded him, because he had not suffered himself to be banished with the rest, but had forsaken and denied the truth. Upon this he fell into a great agony of mind, so that all comfortable admonitions and instructions concerning God's promises prevailed nothing at all with him. At length he fell into despair, and uttered these words: — ' Christ stands by His heavenly Father, and accuses me. He says, O Father, be not merciful to this man, neither do thou pardon him his sins of blasphemy; for he hath not confessed, but openly denied, both me and my Gospel before his bishop.' So ending his speech, he lamentably departed in despair.

"Here," said Luther, "we see the highest art of the devil, which is to make altogether the law out of the Gospel. If at all times I knew well how to make a difference of both doctrines, I would not care a fig for all the devices and temptations of the devil.

"This great doctor," said Luther, "at that time should have called to mind what St. Paul saith to the Romans;—' *Abundat gratia super peccatum, sic quoque major est vita quam mors,*'—Grace did superabound sin, as also life is above death; for God desireth not the death of a sinner, &c. God, through St. Paul, hath given his tempted ones a comfortable promise; namely, that He is faithful, and will not suffer us to be tempted above what we are able to bear, and will give a happy issue to our troubles: yet, notwithstanding, God permitteth it to come so near and hard upon us, that oftentimes we are able to hold out no longer."

Prince George and his Son.

"John Frederic, Prince Elector of Saxony, told me himself," said Luther, "that as Prince John (eldest son of Prince George of Saxony) was near the time of his death, he desired to receive the communion under both kinds. But when his father was informed of it, he sent an Austin friar to give him instruction for his soul's health, and to advise him to receive the sacrament under one kind, and that he should tell his son that he was very intimately acquainted with Martin Luther. The better to make the prince believe him, he said, that Luther himself had lately advised certain persons to receive the communion under one kind. Now, when this good and godly young prince was thus pitifully induced to give credit to the said friar's false information, he received the communion under one kind.

"But when the prince, his father, saw that his son

drew near to the last gasp, and needs must die, then he comforted his son with the article of justification by faith in Christ, and did put him in mind only to have regard to the Saviour of the world, and utterly to forget all his own works and deservings; that he should also banish out of his heart the invocation of saints.

"Now, when the son felt great comfort in his conscience by these his father's admonitions, he asked his father why he did not cause the same comfortable doctrine to be preached through all his country? His father answered and said, 'My dear child, we must say these things only to the dying, and not to the sound and healthy.' *

"Whereupon," said Luther, "I told the Prince Elector, that he must perfectly discern how wilfully our adversaries oppose the acknowledged truth. Albert, Bishop of Mentz, and Prince George do know and confess that our doctrine is God's word, and yet, because it proceedeth not from the Pope, they refuse it: but their own consciences do strike them down to the ground; therefore," said Luther, "I fear them not."

Henry VIII. King of England.

"I am lately advertised," said Luther, "that Henry, King of England, is fallen from the Gospel again; hath commanded, upon pain of death, that the

* Are there not many of Prince George's mind in England, among clergy as well as laity? such as would accede to the truth of the doctrine of justification by faith only (as in Art. 10.), for their own private comfort, but oppose the public preaching of it, for fear of its ill effects upon the minds of ordinary hearers. But Christ will have the truth of his Gospel preached, and be, Himself, answerable for the consequences.

people shall receive the sacrament under one kind; and that spiritual persons (friars and nuns) shall perform their vows, and tear in pieces their marriages; when formerly he had done quite the contrary.* At this the Papists will jeer, be joyful, and boast. Indeed," said Luther, " it is a great offence; but let it go. That king is still the old king, as in my first book I pictured him. He will surely find his judge. I never liked his resolution, in that he would kill the Pope's body, but preserve his soul, that is, his false doctrine."

Anno 1539, the 10th of July, Luther gave thanks to God that he had delivered our church † from that offensive King of England, who, with highest diligence, sought for a league with those of our part, but was not accepted. Doubtless, God, out of special providence, hindered the same; for that the king was always inconstant, and of a wavering mind."

Sir T. More.

Luther being asked whether Thomas More was executed for the Gospel's sake or not, answered, " No, in no wise; for he was a notable tyrant.‡ He was

* This refers to the famous Act of Six Articles, by which it was made a capital offence, 1. to deny transubstantiation; or to condemn, 2dly, communion in one kind; or, 3dly, the forced unmarried life of the clergy; or, 4thly, vows of chastity; or, 5thly, private masses; or, 6thly, auricular confession. The king, at the solicitation of the Romish party, obtained this act of parliament, and, for a short time, enforced its cruel penalties.

† *i. e.* The Protestant church in Germany.

‡ Luther had heard, from some of the English who resorted to Wittemberg, the account of Sir Thomas's treatment of some English Protestants.

the king's chiefest counsellor, a very learned and wise man. He shed the blood of many innocent Christians that confessed the Gospel: these he plagued and tormented with strange instruments, like a hangman or executioner. First he examined them in words under a green tree; afterwards with sharp torments in prison; at last he opposed himself against the edict of the king, and of the whole kingdom. He was disobedient, and so punished."

A Prince turned Friar.

"In the time of my living at Magdeburgh," said Luther, "a Prince of Anhalt became a begging friar, literally went about the city and begged bread; and although another strong, lazy, lout went with him, yet the prince himself always carried the sack: his aim was, by this means, to be esteemed humble. Thus were we fooled in Popedom. This example ought to be noted, *quia est notabile.*"

A merry Tale of two Friars.

Luther one day caught a sparrow, and holding it in his hand, said to it very gravely, " Thou barefooted friar, with thy grey coat, thou art the most mischievous bird." Then, addressing himself to the friends that were with him, " I could wish," said he, " that one would write a declamation on a subject that occurred at Erfurt when I was in the monastery there. It so happened," said Luther, " that a preaching friar and a barefoot * wandered at the same time

* A Dominican and a Franciscan. The out-door dress of the former was a black cloak and hood over a white cassock; that of the latter was a grey cloak, and they did not wear shoes.

into the country, to beg for the brethren, and to gather alms. These two coming together into the same place, played upon one another in their sermons with unprofitable words. The barefoot, preaching first, said, 'Loving country people, and my good friends, take heed of that bird the swallow; for it is white within, but upon the back it is black: it is an evil bird, always chirping, yet profitable for nothing, and when it is angered it is altogether mad; it pricketh the kine, and when it fouleth it maketh the people blind, as in the Book of Tobit ye read thereof.' This barefoot friar here intended to paint out the preaching friars, who wear white bandillions under a black coat. Now, as in the afternoon the preaching friar came into the pulpit, he played likewise upon the barefoot, and said, 'Indeed, loving friends, I neither can nor will defend the swallow; but the grey sparrow is a far worse and more mischievous bird than he, for he robbeth and devoureth all he can get — oats, barley, wheat, rye, apples, pears, cherries, &c.; moreover, he is a loose and licentious bird; the best thing he can do is to cry *Scrip, scrip*,' &c. Herewith," said Luther, " one beggar endeavoured to hinder another. A good rhetorician were here necessary, to amplify and enlarge this subject, and to explain it. But the barefoot friar ought to have painted out the preaching friar with better colours; for they are the haughtiest buzzards and most complete epicures, who go on in a particular style of pride. Again, the begging or barefoot friars, under the colour of sanctity and humility, are more proud and haughty than kings or princes, and have invented the most and greatest lies."

A shrewd Decipherer.

"Not long since,". said Luther, "King Ferdinand came into a monastery where then I was, in which, with very fair letters, were written on the wall as followeth:—

M. N. M. G. M. M. M. M.

The king stood looking upon these letters, musing what they might signify. Whereupon his secretary said, 'If your majesty would give me leave, and not be displeased, I persuade myself I can show what these letters mean.' The king gave him leave, and said it should be no prejudice to him. Then the secretary said, '*Mentitur Nausea* (who was then Bishop of Vienna); *Mentitur Gallus* (he was the king's court-preacher); *Mentiuntur Majores* (the Franciscans); *Minores* (the barefoot friars); *Minotaurii* (some friars so called, that dwell in the Alps).—They were liars all of them.' The king bit his lips, passed it over, and went away. This was a very courtier-like exposition of the secretary's," said Luther.

St. Bernard.

"St. Bernard," said Luther, "was the best friar, whom I love above all the rest; yet he dared to say, 'It were a sign of damnation if one quitted the monastery.' He had under him 3000 friars, among all which was not one damned, if his sentence were true: *sed vix credo*. St. Bernard lived in dangerous times, under the Emperors Henry IV. and V., under Conrad and Lothaire. He was an experienced and well-taught friar; but he gave an evil example. The state and calling of a true Christian (which God ordained and founded) consisteth in three hierarchies; namely, in domestic, temporal, and church government."

Prince Henry of Saxony.

"When God had laid hold," said Luther, "on Prince Henry of Saxon's elder brother, George, and punished him so that all his sons died before himself, he sent to his brother Prince Henry, who was then at Friberg, and showed him, that if he would forsake his faith, and become a Papist, he would make him heir of his dominions; if not, it was his intention to bequeath them, by will, to the emperor and others. Whereupon Prince Henry answered and said, 'By Mary (which was his usual word), rather than I will do so, and deny my Saviour Christ, I and my Kate, each of us with a staff in our hands, will beg our bread out of his dominions.' So constantly did he remain by God's word; and not long after, by the sudden death of his brother, he became a great and powerful prince. For most certain it is," said Luther, "that God will honour them who love and honour Him and His word."

The Landgrave of Hesse.

"Philip, Landgrave of Hesse," said Luther, "is a wonderful man. If he would forsake the Gospel, he might obtain what he pleased from both Pope and Emperor; but God hitherto hath preserved him steadfast. He hath a Hessian brain, and cannot be idle. He sent for me," said Luther, "and for Philip Melancthon, to Weymar, demanding our advice respecting his intended wars; but we, in the highest manner, dissuaded him from his enterprises; we made the best use we could of our rhetoric, and entreated him not to disgrace the Gospel, and trouble the peace of the empire by wars. Upon this he was greatly vexed, and grew very red, though otherwise he was of an upright mind.

"In the conference at Marpurg, in 1539, His Highness went disguised in mean apparel, so that no man knew him to be the Landgrave: he had, at the same time, high cogitations. Asking Philip Melancthon's advice in his affairs, he said, 'Loving Philip, shall I endure this, that the Bishop of Mentz driveth away my preachers of the Gospel?' Philip said, 'If the jurisdiction of those places belongs to the bishop, your highness may not resist him.' Then the Landgrave replied, 'I hear your advice, but I will not follow it.' At that time," said Luther, "I asked Beilnelburg (one of his nearest advisers) why he did not dissuade the Landgrave from his stratagems? He replied, 'Our admonition helpeth nothing; what he intendeth, from that he is not to be dissuaded.' When he was upon the march, resolved to set the Prince of Wirtemberg in possession again, every body desired him not to bring utter ruin upon Hesse: 'Be content,' he answered, 'let me go on; I will not bring it into any ruin at all.' The same he also performed," said Luther: " he shot into a castle 350 shot, and took it."

John, Elector of Saxony.

"In the year 1530, Emperor Charles V. summoned a Diet at Augsburg, intending to bring the differences in matters of religion to an agreement. He practised at that time, by all crafty means, to bring John, the Prince Elector of Saxony, from the profession of the Gospel; but the prince (disregarding all flattering friendships, all malice and threatenings,) would not yield, no, not the breadth of an hair, from the true religion.

and word of God, though he was compassed with many imminent dangers; but, on the contrary, he cheered up and comforted his learned divines (whom he brought with him to the Diet)*, as Philip Melancthon, Justus Jonas, George Spalatine, and John Agricola, and charged those of his council to tell his divines, 'That they should deal uprightly to the praise and honour of God, and regard neither himself, his countries, nor his people.' Therefore," said Luther, " this prince held constantly over God's word, with an excelling princely courage. If he had wavered, then all his council would have let go hands and feet, and have forsaken the Gospel. For even at that time, to appease the Emperor's wrath, his counsellors were ready to mediate, to tamper with, and to qualify *Gratiam Dei, et hominum salutem*. But the Prince Elector sent them word, and charged them once and again, not to look after his welfare in this world, but to speak and write that which was just and upright in the sight of God. He sent also for one of his chief privy-counsellors, named John von Minkwitz, and said unto him, 'You have heard my father say (running with him at the tilt), that to sit upright on horseback maketh a good tilter. If, therefore, it be good and laudable in temporal tilting to sit upright, how much more is it now praiseworthy in God's cause to sit, to stand, and to go, upright and just.' But the same," said Luther, " is the work of the Holy Ghost."

---

* Luther was not allowed to attend the Diet, but lived in the castle of Coburg during its sitting. His conduct there, and the letters of advice and encouragement which he wrote from thence to his associates at Augsburg, were truly admirable: very interesting notices of them may be seen in the first volume of Scott's continuation of Milner's Church History.

"I certainly do believe," said Luther, "that John, Prince Elector of Saxony, that good and godly prince, was endued with the Holy Ghost at Ausgburg, where (at the Imperial Diet) he would not suffer the preaching of the Gospel to be neglected or intermitted, notwithstanding Emperor Charles's strict command to the contrary. His Highness told the Emperor plainly, that he could no more do without God's word, than without meat and drink. And when at last Emperor Charles did by force cause the preaching of the Gospel to be silenced, then the Elector would rather have left the Diet, than be without the hearing of God's word. Insomuch that I held it then fitting to write unto His Highness, humbly entreating him to yield, for a time, in that respect, to the Emperor's pleasure, and to remain at the Diet, specially seeing that the city of Augsburg belonged to the Emperor. Upon the reading of this my letter, His Highness said, 'I know not whether I, or my Martin, playeth the fool.' His Highness, however, took my advice, and remained at the Diet. This letter of mine is printed in the fifth Jewish Tome."

"The admirable great constancy of John, Prince Elector of Saxony," said Luther, "is worthy of everlasting memory and praise; as he who for his person held stiffly and steadfastly over the pure doctrine of the Gospel, at the Imperial Diet at Augsburg, in 1530. And when the Emperor's final will and meaning was shown unto him, he said, 'Here are two ways, either to deny God or the world. Now, then, let every one consider which were best.'

"It was a miraculous thing, and special gift of God, that one only prince stood so steadfastly against all the rest; yea, against the emperor himself. Therefore," said Luther, " the acts and proceedings in the Augustinian Confession may not easily be described;—they are high things, large and spacious. This John, Prince Elector, had, attending continually upon him in his chamber, six pages of honour; these read to him every day six hours out of the Bible. Likewise in hearing sermons, he always had in his pocket writing-tables, and with his own hand wrote the sermons out of the preachers' mouths."

The Diet of Augsburg.

" God's word," said Luther, " is powerful; the more it is persecuted, the more and the further it spreadeth itself abroad. Behold the Imperial Diet at Augsburg, which, doubtless*, is the last trumpet before the dreadful day of judgment. How raged the world there against the word of God? O!" said Luther, " how fain were we then to pray the Pope and Papists that they would be pleased to permit and suffer Christ to live quietly in heaven! There our doctrine broke through into the light in such sort, that by the Emperor's strict command the same was sent to all kings, princes, and universities. This declaration of our doctrine forthwith enlightened many excellent people, scattered here and there in princes' courts, (of whom some were chosen of God to lay hold of this our doctrine,) like unto tinder, and afterwards kindled the same also in others."

* We are reminded how apt men are, in periods of great and general excitement on religious subjects, to exaggerate the importance of the events of their own times. There is peculiar need of caution in the application of prophecy to the times in which we live.

"Our Apology and Confession," said Luther, "with great honour came to light. The Popish confutations are kept in darkness, and do stink. O!" said Luther, "how willingly would I that their confutations might appear unto the world! then would I set upon that torn and tattered skin, and in such sort would baste it, that the flitches thereof should fly here and there about: but they shun the light. This time twelvemonth," said Luther, "no one would have given a farthing for the Protestants, so sure the ungodly Papists were of us. For," said Luther, "when my most gracious lord and master, the Prince Elector of Saxony, before other princes, came to the Diet, the Papists marvelled much thereat; for they verily believed that he would not have appeared, because (as they imagined) his cause was too bad and foul to be brought before the light. But what fell out? even this, that, in their greatest security, they were overwhelmed with the greatest fear and affrightments; for, inasmuch as the Prince Elector, like an upright prince, appeared so early at Augsburg, the Popish princes swiftly posted off from Augsburg to Inspruck, where they held serious counsel with Prince George and the Marquis of Baden, all of them wondering what the Prince Elector's so early approach to the Diet could mean, insomuch that the Emperor himself was astonished, and doubted whether he might go safely or not. Whereupon the princes were constrained to engage that they would set up body, goods, and blood, by the Emperor; one offering to maintain 6000 horse, another 6000 foot, &c. &c., to the end His Majesty might be the better secured: — a wonder among wonders it was to see how God struck the enemies of the truth with fear and cowardice! And although at that time the Elector was alone, and only the hundredth sheep, and they ninety and nine, yet it so fell out that they all trembled and feared. Now, when they came to the point, and began to take the business in hand, then there appeared but a very small heap that stood by the Word of God.

"But in truth," said Luther, "we brought with us a strong and mighty King,—a King above all kings and emperors,—namely, Christ Jesus, the powerful Word of God. Then all the Papists cried out, and said, 'Oh! it is insufferable that so small and silly a heap should set themselves against the imperial power.' But," said Luther, "the Lord of Hosts frustrateth the counsels of princes: Pilate had power to put our blessed Saviour to death, though willingly he would not; Annas and Caiaphas willingly would have done it, but they could not.

"The Emperor, for his part," said Luther, "is good and honest, but the Popish Bishops and Cardinals are undoubtedly knaves. And forasmuch as the Emperor now refuses to bathe his hands in innocent blood; therefore the frantic princes do bestir themselves, do scorn and contemn the good Emperor in the highest degree. The Pope also is ready to burst in pieces for anger, that the Diet should in this way be dissolved without bloodshed; therefore he sendeth the sword to the Duke of Bavaria to proceed therewith, and intendeth to take the crown from the Emperor's head, and to put it on Bavaria's: but," said Luther, "he shall not accomplish it.

"In this manner ordered God the business," said Luther, "that kings, princes, yea, and the Pope himself, fell from the Emperor, and that we joined with him, which was a great wonder of God's providence, in that he whom the devil intended to use against us, even the same God taketh and maketh use of for us. O wonder," said Luther, "above all wonders!"

———

"The Imperial Diet held at Augsburg, in 1530, is worthy of all praise; for then, there, and from thence, came the Gospel among people in other countries, contrary to the will and expectation of both Pope and Emperor: wherefore," said Luther, "what hath been spent there should be grievous to no man.* God," said Luther, "appointed the Imperial Diet at Augsburg that the Gospel might be spread further abroad and planted.

"Before that Diet was held, the Papists had persuaded the Emperor that our doctrine was altogether frivolous, and we ourselves most ungodly people, and led most wicked and detestable lives; and that we taught against the first and second of the commandments of God. They boasted also to the Emperor, that, when he came to the Diet, he should see that they would put us all to silence, so that none of us should be able to say a word in defence of our religion; but it fell out far otherwise, for we openly and freely confessed the Gospel before the Emperor and the whole Empire. At that Diet we confounded our adversaries in the highest degree. The Emperor," said Luther, "judged understandingly and discreetly, and conducted himself in a princely manner in this cause of religion. He found our confession to be

* The detention of the elector, with a numerous retinue, at the Diet was productive of great expenses; Luther probably refers to taxes levied to defray them.

very different from what the Papists had informed him; and he sent it, with our Apology, to all the universities. The Imperial Diet at Augsburg was invaluable," said Luther, " by reason of the Confession of faith and of God's word which on our part was there performed; for there our adversaries were constrained to confess that our Confession was upright and true."

Prince George's Reformation.

Anno 1538, the 4th of December, a written Reformation of the Popish Church under Prince George of Saxony was delivered to Luther; after reading of which he said, " These people intend to reform the church after their cogitations and human wisdom; whereas the same is too high a business for the enterprises and counsels of men. If our Lord God intended to have His Church reformed, it would have to be undertaken by divine, not by human, authority, as it was in the times of Joshua, the Judges, Samuel, the Apostles, and in our time. I mark well," said Luther, " the Papists are more afraid of Prince George than of me. They have invited him to be their gossip; and whereas they have made him drunken, so will he ere long spue in their bosoms, therefore they may wish they were rid of him again: for if his reformation take effect, then the Pope must lay down his state, and the Bishop of Mentz must ride with only four horses in his coach, and so on of the rest. I long to see," said Luther, " what sort of a reformation the Papists with Prince George will prepare, — whether according to the example of the church in the Apostles' days, or of the martyrs, or after the manner of the heretics' church: then they must read all the Fathers, and imitate them.

"Our Protestant church," said Luther, "is nearest and most like to the Apostles' church; for we have the doctrine pure, we have the catechism, the sacraments uprightly according to Christ's institutions; also, how we ought to make use of temporal and house government: God's word proceedeth and remaineth pure among us, which only maketh a true church. The Papists (who intend to prepare the church according to the Pope's Canons and Decretals) will make *concordantiam discordiarum*, an union of discords; they will force contrarieties, and make discords agree: and so, upon the confidence of human wisdom, sense, and reason, their labour will be lost and in vain."

Luther's Discourses on the Times.

"I will, God willing," said Luther, "provide and use diligence, that, after my departure, an upright church and schools be left to our posterity, to the end they may know how they ought, uprightly and Christian-like, to teach and govern: although the great unthankfulness of men, their wilfulness and contempt of God's word, maketh me to fear that this light will not stand nor shine long; for God's word hath always had its course.

"No greater mischief can ever happen to Christian people, than when God's word is taken from them and falsified; that they have it not pure and clear. God grant," said Luther, "that we and ours may not live to see such mischief take place!

"When we have God's word pure and clear, then we grow secure thereby, we are negligent, and do not regard it; we think it will always remain so. We do not watch and pray against the devil, who is ready to tear the word out of our hearts. It goeth with us as with travellers, who, as long as they are on the right road, are secure and careless; but when they go astray into woods or byways, then they are careful which way they take. Even so are we secure by the pure doctrine of the Gospel; we are sleepy and negligent, we stand not in God's fear, nor defend ourselves against the devil with prayer. But those that entertain errors are highly busied; yea, they are very careful and diligent how to entertain the same."

"When God is about to punish and destroy a people or a kingdom, then He first takes away from them good and godly teachers and preachers. He also bereaves them of wise, godly, and honest rulers and counsellors. He takes away good, upright, and experienced soldiers, and other good people. Then are the common people careless and merry; they go on in all wilfulness; they care no more for the truth and divine doctrine; yea, they despise it, and fall into blindness; they regard neither threatening, civility, nor honesty; they drive on all manner of shameful sins, out of which follows a wild, dissolute, and devilish kind of living, as now, alas! we see, and are, too, too well aware of, and cannot long endure. Therefore," said Luther, "I fear the axe is laid to the root of the tree, that it must soon be cut down. God of his infinite mercy graciously take us away, that we may not live to see such misery."

"The thanks which the world now giveth for the doctrine of the Gospel, is even that which they gave to Christ; namely, the cross:—the same must we expect, and nothing else. This year," said Luther, " is a year of *man's unthankfulness*; but the next that followeth will be a year of *God's revenge*. God must needs punish, though it be against His will, nature, and kind;—we ourselves are the cause thereof."

"Great and horrible are the punishments," said Luther, as he was conversing in the presence of the Prince Elector of Saxony, and other princes, "which will come and fall upon Germany; for the people are so wicked and stiff-necked, that they will suffer no discipline, correction, sermons of threatening, nor reformation. The world is grown very stubborn and headstrong since the revealing of the word of the Gospel.* Its sins and wickednesses are now grown

---

* Before the Reformation men were kept under the restraints of superstition and the fear of priestly power; and when, upon the revelation of the Gospel, it appeared that their ignorance had been imposed upon, those who were weary of papal bondage, and devoid of the fear of God, would submit to no control; they would be their own masters. These graceless characters were classed with the Protestants, and, by their lawless, abandoned conduct, brought a great reproach upon true religion.

But there is another and more general reason for that abounding of iniquity which Luther complains of. It is very reasonable to expect, from the known tendencies of human nature, that where true religion is making progress, there vice and irreligion will become more energetic, and, hence, more evident: the lives of true Christians will operate as an irksome reproach to ungodly people who witness their conduct; conscience will, consequently, make more frequent charges; and then, unless men are humbled to yield themselves to Christ, greater efforts must be made to master and to silence conscience. Some will try the methods of the hypocrite, others those of the libertine. Thus evils previously

so common and usual, that they are held no more for sins; therefore," said he, " let us pray, ' *Thy kingdom come;* ' *Deliver us from evil.*' Howbeit this is one comfort, it hath a better show with us than it had twenty years past:—we have now, God be praised! many godly learned people; so have we, moreover, fair schools, in which the youth are well taught and instructed. The gracious God give a blessing and furtherance thereunto; for much I fear that a horrible falling away will come after my decease."

" Oh!" said Luther, " how great is the presumption of the world, which, being so weak and small, yet dareth to set itself against Christ, and undertake to tread Him under feet. But that is not enough; it will be yet worse; for Epicurism by force will come and break in again. The world that despiseth God's word is nothing else than a preparation and an approaching of an Epicurish life before the last day of judgment, when people will neither believe that there is a God, nor a life eternal. Is it not, now, a fearful and an abominable thing, that such Epicures should be among the people of God; not only in secret, but openly among the preachers in the church, as the Sadducees among the Jews, who were also in the government, although they believed nothing of eternal life?

" Of the same kind are now our Papists, and such

---

existing are brought more openly to light; disguised unbelief becomes declared infidelity; and vice shows a bolder front.

We find Luther's complaints renewed in our own time and country; similar causes producing similar effects.

like also among ourselves. What the Bishop of Magdeburgh saith and doth, the same, of course, must be all good and well done. So it is likewise with the city of Lubeck. That city is drowned in such covetousness, that they take monthly upon usury one guilder in forty; yet all under colour of godliness; as if it were quite right and Christian-like: an act of tender love towards our poor neighbour, to help him, so that in lending him a hundred guilders, we receive for the same, upon use, yearly, forty-five. In ten years the use of one hundred guilders bringeth four hundred and fifty. Is not this very manifest Epicurism? Lubeck lies drowned in the sea of covetousness, deeper than the mountains lay in the deluge of Noah; they were covered but fifteen ells deep in the water, but that city lies fifteen miles deep in the waves of covetousness, and in the same state are all other usurers and covetous gluttons. Ah!" said Luther, "wicked times are at hand; our Epicures are worse than the cardinals in Italy[*]; and yet they say, We will teach others to be good and godly, but we ourselves will do what we please."

"Ah! Lord God," said Luther, one day, " the impiety and unthankfulness of the world is great indeed, so to contemn and persecute Thy unspeakable grace. And we ourselves, too, who boast ourselves of the Gospel, and do know that it is God's word, and acknowledge the same, and that the Father himself witnesseth from heaven, saying, ' *This is My Beloved Son,*'

[*] The Christian reader will be reminded of the Cretan church: " *They profess that they know God, but in works they deny him,*" &c. — Titus, i. 16.

&c.; we do as little regard the comfortable and sweet Gospel of Christ, that great and inestimable treasure, as we would a speech or sentence taken out of Terence or Virgil. I am not so much afraid of the Pope and tyrants," said Luther, "as of our own unthankfulness and contemning of God's word; the same, I fear, will help the Pope again into the saddle. When that comes to pass, I hope the day of judgment will soon after follow."

"The prebendaries at Wartzburg, Mentz, and Cologne have the best days[*]," said Luther; "they live in idleness, they spend and waste; they have all manner of good things provided them beforehand, without any care; they have here what their hearts can desire, and afterwards they go to that heaven where it hisseth. The popish bishops have not such good days; for they are in the government, and have other business[†] to do of greater weight than to meddle with God's word. Dr. Eck, a man of great understanding, and of a ready memory, but very impudent, shameless, and ungodly, during his stay at Rome saw so many good examples of Epicurism, that never since hath he regarded either Papistry or the Gospel. Such fruits are reaped in Rome. Twenty years ago, I did not suppose that now, in the Christian church, there

---

[*] "Thou, in thy lifetime, receivedst thy good things."—Luke, xvi.

[†] A great many of these bishops were employed in civil offices, and lived about the king's courts. It was so rare a thing for bishops to "meddle with God's word," that Latimer, speaking in his own way upon the subject, said, in one of his sermons, "that there was a large department in hell, reaching across as far as from London to Calais, full of unpreaching prelates."

were any Epicures, when the truth is that almost all Popedom is drowned in the life of Epicurism. They trouble themselves neither about God nor the conscience. These are abominable times, in which Epicurism goeth on in full sway and flourisheth. This life is the main object; for this is Epicurism—to lead from the heavenly and everlasting life, to the earthly and the temporal. A nobleman of Vienna, in Austria, in the time of my abode there," said Luther, "made a great feast, and, in the midst of his joy and pleasure therein, he spake these words;—'If God would leave me my riches, with a thousand years of life to enjoy them in, then would I willingly leave to God His heaven.'

"God, of His mercy, preserve us from such Epicurean meanings and opinions," said Luther.

"God's word, by us," said Luther, "is in the highest degree contemned; by the Papists it is blasphemed; and so, both ways, there are most abominable sins against the first table of God's commandments. It is an evil sign; and, if God in his great mercy prevent not, we are utterly lost.

"But I am comforted again, first, because the great pride of the Turk (who dependeth upon his strength and power) will be a means of drawing God's anger, in some measure, from us upon him. For God's nature and manner is, to 'put down the mighty from their seat.'

"Secondly, I am comforted," said Luther, "in that the Pope and the French king do invite and instigate the Turk to invade us and our country. Therefore, assuredly, God will help us; and although the Turk should come and they some never, yet he must leave Hezekiah and Isaiah behind him."*

———

"The nobility, the gentry, citizens, farmers, &c. are now become so naughty and ungodly, that they regard not ministers nor preachers, and," said Luther, "if we were not somewhat holpen by princes and other great personages, we could not long subsist; therefore that is a good word of Isaiah. — ' Kings shall be thy nursing fathers, &c.' Isaiah. xlix. 23.)

———

"Worldly and outward peace," said Luther, "is one of the highest gifts of God; but we abuse it too much; every one lives after his own will and pleasure, against God and the magistrate. O! how soundly will our gentry and farmers in Germany pay for this, before one hundred and fifty years come to an end (as already they have done in Hungary and Austria); but afterwards God will restore them again, and beat down Popedom. Let us not cease to pray."

———

"How exceeding glorious was the deliverance out of Egypt, the dividing of the Red Sea, the cloudy pillar, the bread from heaven, &c. The Jews were wearied and cloyed with these wonderful glorious actions, because they had and saw them daily. Even so," said Luther, "is it now with us; for, at the first, baptism was held a great, an excelling, a glorious treasure, at which every one wondered; but we are now so used to it, that we regard it nothing at all, but rather will run to behold a tilting, a horse-race, or other fooleries. Let us but consider the small de-

* Luther refers to 2 Kings, xix. 1. &c.

sire that people have now in reading the Psalter, and whether they admire and esteem it as much as they do Terence and Cicero."

"Noblemen conceive themselves to be wise: from whence they contemn God's ministers. Well, on!" said Luther; "God will contemn them again. A nobleman thinketh he understandeth the Gospel better than St. Paul."

"The Lord Marshal," said Luther, "is a great Thraso, a roarer and boaster, who bawleth and crieth out with high prancing words; but the great, upright, and true noblemen and brave captains, carry themselves far otherwise: they are silent; they do not brag and boast; their manner sets off and commends their actions. Such a nobleman is Lord Bernard of Mela, an excellent man, indeed. He hath a lion in his heart, but in his words and demeanour is modest and unassuming.

"Our nobility are ashamed to study*," said Luther; "therefore they are unfit to govern: their greatest diligence and study is in the riding of great palfreys, in feasting, playing, hunting, and in vexing and troubling their subjects with unnecessary taxation. They would willingly rule, but they know not how to govern."

"Whoso, after my death," said Luther, "shall condemn the authority of this school here at Wittemberg (if both church and school remain as at present), the

* England should acknowledge it as no common distinction, that this cannot be said of a great proportion of her nobility.

same is a heretic, and a perverted human creature; for in this school God first revealed * and purified His word. This school and city (both in doctrine and manner of life) may justly be compared with any others: howsoever, we are not altogether complete, but still are faulty in our kind of living. The highest and chiefest divines in the whole empire do hold and join with us, as Amsdorff, Brentius, and Rhegius; they all desire our friendship, and salute us with their learned and loving letters.

"A few years back," said Luther, "nothing was of any value but the Pope; *ecclesiæ gemebant, clamabant, suspirabant;* i. e., the churches mourned, cried, and sighed: these knocked and wakened up our Lord God in heaven, as in the psalm God saith, '*Propter miseriam inopum, et gemitum pauperum, nunc exsurgam,*' &c.; 'for the oppression of the poor, for the sighing of the needy, I will now arise.' *Gemitus pauperum,*" said Luther, "is a great matter before our Lord God; for when *gemitus* goeth forth, then let the devil and the world take heed. Our nobility do now exhaust people and countries with usury, insomuch that many poor people are constrained to starve for want of food, and are not able to come *ad conjugium,* to wedlock; so that a forced *cælibatus,* or single life, will hence ensue. This is not good," said Luther; "these wicked courses will squeeze out the sighs and cries of the poor, which will awaken and rouse up God and the heavenly host; wherefore I say — Germany beware. I make oftentimes my account," said Luther, "and always I find that I come nearer and nearer to forty

---

* i. e. discovered its truth to the minds and hearts of men, after it had been so long darkened under the reign of Popery.

ars; then I think with myself, now cometh an alteration: for St. Paul preached not above forty years; St. Austin the same; and always when forty years had expired (wherein God's word was purely preached), then it ceased, and great calamity ensued."

Luther's Prayer for a gracious Rain, and the Success thereof.

In the year 1532 was a great drought throughout all Germany; the corn in the fields, in lamentable sort, began to wither. On the 9th of June, in the same year, Luther called together the whole assembly into the church, and directed his prayer, with deep sighs, to God, in manner following:—

"O Lord, attend unto our prayers, for Thy mercy's sake. We have prayed, and our hearts have sighed; but the covetousness of the rich farmers doth hinder and hem in Thy blessing; for seeing that, through Thy Gospel, they are unbridled, they think it free for them to live and to do what they please. They now fear neither hell nor purgatory; but say*, I believe, therefore I shall be saved: they become haughty and pitiful mammonists, and accursed covetous cut-throats, that suck out land and people. Moreover, also, the usurers among the gentry in every place deal wickedly, insomuch as (it seemeth) Thou, O Lord, wilt visit both with the rod. Still, O Lord, Thou hast the means to maintain those that are Thine, although Thou sufferest no rain to fall upon the ungodly."

* They were of the same character with those reproved by St. James in his day, who "*said* they had faith," but without any works to prove the truth of their assertion. A *profession* of faith will save no man.

And as he said thus, he lifted up his eyes towards heaven and prayed, saying, — " Lord God, Thou hast always, through Thy servant David, said, *' The Lord is nigh to all them that call upon Him in truth.'* How is it, Lord, that Thou givest no rain, seeing we have cried and prayed so long unto Thee? Thy will be done, O Lord! We know that although Thou givest not rain, Thou wilt give us something better — a still, quiet, and peaceable life. Now, we pray, O Lord, from the bottom of our hearts. If Thou, O Lord, wilt not be pleased to hear, and give us rain, then ungodly people will say Christ Thy only son is a liar: for He saith, — ' *Verily I say unto you, whatsoever ye shall ask the Father in my name, He will give it you:*' so that they will give Thy Son the lie. I know, O Lord, that we do cry to Thee from our heart with yearning and sighing; why, then, dost Thou not hear us?" Now, even the same day, and within the space of half an hour after the people went from church, it began to rain so sweet and mildly (and continued in that moderate temper a whole fortnight), that the grounds thereby were changed and refreshed in most marvellous manner. This was in June, 1532.

CHAPTER II.

CONTAINING DIVERS WEIGHTY SENTENCES OF DR. MARTIN LUTHER TOUCHING THE HOLY SCRIPTURES, AND THE PROFITABLE STUDY THEREOF.

"Let us not lose the Bible," said Luther, "but with all diligence, and in God's fear, read and preach the same; for if that remaineth, flourisheth, and be taught, then all is safe; she is the head and empress of all faculties and arts: if Divinity falleth, then whatsoever remaineth besides is nothing worth."

"The Holy Scripture," said Luther, "is such a wisdom as no man is able to learn and study out; we must continually remain scholars therein: for we cannot sufficiently sound out the depth of one word in Holy Scripture; we have only the first-fruits; and when we think we have learned much therein, then have we scarcely learned the A B C. Let those Epicures, those proud and insolent worldly wise men, who contemn and scorn the Holy Writ, thinking they have studied out the same, as Dr. Jacob Schenck, and Michael Cochlæus, who are a plague and a poison to religion, and whose fruits and end of their contemning of God's word will be madness and blindness, Ah! Lord God," said Luther, "how dare we presume to deal so wickedly in Thy holy sanctuary, and cast under feet Thy Holy Scripture, to master and wrest the same after our carnal wisdom and understanding? How can we be so cold and slow in Thy Divine Word, while the Gentiles, in their false religion, were so fervent and zealous, that the women and matrons would even sweep their temples with the hair of their heads!"

"I intended many times," said Luther, "well and thoroughly to search and find out the Ten Commandments; but when I began at the first words,—'*I am the Lord thy God*,' there stuck I fast; the very first word (*I*) brought me to a nonplus. Therefore, he that hath but one only word of God to his text, and out of that one word cannot make a sermon, will never be a good preacher. I am content," said Luther, "that I know, though but a little, what God's word is; and take great heed that I murmur not at such my small knowledge, which God hath given me.

"I have grounded my preaching upon the literal word; whoso pleaseth may follow me; he that will not may choose. I challenge St. Peter, St. Paul, Moses, and all the saints, who were not able, fundamentally, to understand one only word of God, on which they had not continually to learn; for the Psalm saith, '*Sapientiæ ejus non est numerus;*' His wisdom and understanding is infinite. True it is, the saints do know God's word, and they can speak thereof, but the practice will not follow; therein we are, and remain always, scholars.

"The school divines," said Luther, "gave a fine comparison touching the same. It is therewith, say they, as with a sphere or round globe, which, lying on a table, toucheth upon it with but one point; while, notwithstanding, the table supporteth the globe wholly and altogether. I," said Luther, " am-an old Doctor of Divinity, yet to this day I am not come out of the children's learning; that is, the Ten Commandments, the Creed, and the Lord's Prayer. I confess seriously that I understand them not yet as well as I should: for if I rightly understood and did believe only these few words,— ' *Our Father which art in heaven;* ' that God, who made heaven and earth, and created all creatures, and hath all things in His hand and power, were my father: then should I certainly conclude with myself, that I am (in a manner) a lord of heaven and earth; that Christ is my brother; that Gabriel is my servant, and Raphael my coachman; that all the angels in my necessities are my attendants; for they are given unto me of my Heavenly Father to keep me in all my ways: in short, it must needs follow that every thing is mine.* But, to the end our faith may be exercised and confirmed, our Heavenly Father suffereth some of us to be cast into the dungeon, some to be drowned in water, &c. Then we see and find how finely we understood these words, and how faith quivereth and striveth, and how great our weakness is: then we begin to think and to say, ' Ah, who knoweth whether that be true or not which is written in the Scriptures?'"

Luther (two days before his death, at Isleben) wrote these Latin lines following, and left them on his table, which John Amisfaber copied out; and Dr. Justus Jonas took the paper on which they were written away with him.

* 1 Cor. iii. 21, &c.

1. *Virgilium in Bucolicis nemo potest intelligere nisi fuerit quinque annis pastor.*

Virgilium in Georgicis nemo potest intelligere, nisi fuerit quinque annis agricola.

2. *Ciceronem in Epistolis (sic præcipio) nemo integrè intelligit nisi viginti annis sit versatus in republicâ aliquâ insigni.*

3. *Scripturas sanctas sciat se nemo degustasse satis, nisi centum annis cum Prophetis, ut Elia, Elisæo, Johanne Baptistâ, Christo et Apostolis, ecclesias gubernavit.*

Hoc: ut ut dicamus, Euclits texta
—— Sol occiduis proclus abire.

Hæc est verum. 16º Februarii, anno 1546.

" The wise of the world, and the great ones," said Luther, " understand not God's word, but God hath revealed it to the poor, contemned, simple people, as our Saviour Christ witnesseth, where he saith, ' *I thank Thee, O Father, Lord of heaven and earth, that Thou hast hid these things from the wise and prudent, and hast revealed them unto babes,*' &c. from whence St. Gregory saith well and right, ' that the Holy Scripture is like a water wherein an elephant swimmeth, but a little sheep goeth therein upon his feet.' "

" Upon these words of Christ, ' *If a man loveth me he will keep my word, and my Father will love him, and we will come unto him, and make our abode with him,*' I say thus," said Luther : " Heaven and earth, the castles and palaces of all emperors, kings, and princes, are in nowise sufficient to make a dwelling-place for God : yet, in a simple human creature that keepeth His word, He will dwell. Isaiah calleth heaven His *seat*, and earth His *footstool*, but not His

* Matt. xi. 25, 26.

dwelling. Therefore when we long to seek after God, we shall find Him with them that hear and keep His word; as Christ saith, '*He that keepeth my word, I will come and dwell with him.*'"

"A man could not speak more simply, and, in a sort, more childishly, than Christ spake; and yet therewith he confoundeth all the wisdom of the worldly wise. To speak in such a manner," said Luther, "is *in sublimi non in humili genere.* If I had to teach a child*, I should teach in this sort: 'He that loves me will keep my word.'"

"When I read in the Psalter," said Luther, "I do much admire that David had such a spirit. Oh! what a high enlightened people were among the Jews. This David was a married man; he was a king, a soldier, and a preacher; he was busy with temporal affairs, yet nevertheless he wrote such an excellent surpassing book. The New Testament was also

---

* The wisdom of God is, indeed, very strikingly displayed, in the simplicity, plainness, and variety which so peculiarly distinguish the Holy Scripture. Learned and clever people, who are disposed to censure and slight the Bible, because it does not realise their idea of what the Word of God should be, will do well to remember, that *they* (the learned and the clever) are an exceedingly small portion of our species; that the Bible was not written for them, but for the mass of mankind; and that what might suit *them*, would be utterly lost to almost all the female sex, as well as to children, servants, and, in fact, to all but themselves. Hence it is, that so much *historical* matter is found in the Bible: it abounds in incidents which arrest the attention, and instruct the mind, and affect the heart of ordinary people, far more than any mere statements of truth, or arguments about it. 'Tis very well that God did not consult with man about the writing of His word.

written by men that were Jews, and the Apostles were Jews — of a nation greatly despised, yet greatly honourable. God would signify thereby, that we should adore His Word, — that we should preciously esteem thereof, reverence, and love the same."

"We Gentiles have no book that ruleth in the church; therefore we are not comparable to the Jews: from whence it is that St. Paul maketh a very fine distinction between Sarah and Hagar, and the two sons, Isaac and Ishmael. Hagar was also a wife, but nothing near like Sarah; therefore," said Luther, "it is a great pride, presumption, and wilfulness of the Pope, in that he, being a human creature, will presume (without Scripture) to set himself against the Scripture, and will exalt himself above the same."

"I desire and truly admonish every good Christian," said Luther, "that he take not offence at the plain and simple manner of speech which is written in the Bible, and not to make doubt thereof, how slight and mean soever it appeareth; for they are altogether words, works, acts, and judgments of the high majesty, power, and wisdom of God. For the Bible is the book[*] that maketh fools of the crafty and wise of the world, and is understood only by the plain and simple, as our Saviour Christ saith: therefore," said Luther, "away with thy natural good sense and reason, and esteem of this book as of the most high and precious holy relique, and the right fountain which can never be exhausted. In this book thou findest the swaddling clothes, and the manger in which Christ lieth, to which the angels directed the poor and simple shep-

[*] See 1 Cor. i. 18. Isaiah, xliv. 25. Matt. xi. 25.

herds; indeed," said Luther, "they seem to be mean, poor clouts; but dear and precious is the treasure that lieth therein.

"Moses," said Luther, "mentioneth nothing of the creating of Angels; first, because he would only describe the creating of the visible world, and the creatures that are therein; secondly, he would not give us occasion to speculate of needless things: nevertheless he remembereth the Angels in the history of Abraham and Lot (Gen. 18 and 19.) So doth the Scripture in other parts also speak of Angels.

"Therefore God hath done exceeding well, in that He hath not caused many things to be written; otherwise we had cast them in the wind, and scorned to learn and consider that which we have now expressed in the Scriptures, and which serves for our salvation; and instead thereof we should have undertaken to search out that which is too high for us, with which we should be nothing bettered."

"A world were to be given," said Luther, "that we might have the acts and legends of the Patriarchs (if it were possible) that lived before the Deluge; for therein a man might see how they lived and preached, and how they suffered, &c.: But it pleased our Lord God to overwhelm all their acts and legends with the Deluge; because He knew that those who should come after would not regard, much less understand them: therefore God would keep and preserve them till they came together in the life to come. Then will the loving patriarchs (who lived after the Deluge), as Abraham, Isaac, Jacob, &c., also the prophets and apostles, their posterity, and other holy people whom, at their lifetime, the devil would not leave unmolested, these will view into the Patriarchs that lived before the flood, and will give them a great sum of pre-eminence in acceptance of divine and continual honour, and will say:—"Ye loving and most venerable Patriarchs, I have lived a short time in regard of you, greatest but a few years, and suffer God's word thereof, and therefore did suffer my crosses, &c.—What is it at all to compare with the great tedious, innumerable labour and anguish, tempests and pains, which ye, holy fathers, endured before the Deluge, some 700, some 900 years and longer, from the devil and the wicked world?"

"It is one of the devil's master-pieces and chief deceiving tricks," said Luther, "that we, through other temporal affairs, suffer ourselves so pitifully to be drawn away from the word: we think that they are of greater weight than the hearing, reading, and considering of God's word, wherein, notwithstanding, all our welfare and salvation, both temporal and eternal, consisteth."

"St. John the Evangelist speaketh majestically, with very simple, few, and plain words; as where he saith, '*In the beginning was the Word, and the Word was with God, and the Word was God, the same was in the beginning with God. All things were made by Him, and without Him was not any thing made that was made. In Him was life, and the life was the light of men, and the light shineth in darkness, and the darkness comprehended it not.*'

"Behold," said Luther, "how he describeth God the Creator, and also the creatures, with very plain and simple words, as with lightning. If one of our philosophers and highly learned persons should have described the same, what wonderful swelling and high-trotting words would he have breathed forth, and prattled *de ente et essentia*, of a self-being thing, and of celestial strength and power, &c., insomuch that no man should, or could, have understood any thing what he meaned. Hereby we see," said Luther, " and experience teacheth us, how mighty and powerful Divine Truth is: she presseth through, though she be hemmed in; the more she is read, she moveth and taketh possession of the heart."*

" John," said Luther, " was simple, and spake also simply; but we ought seriously to regard what such a one speaketh. Every word in John weigheth two tons; as when he saith, (ch. iv.) ' *He came into a city of Samaria, named Sychar, and spake with a woman, and said, If thou knewest*,' &c. Also, ' *The Father honoureth the Son*,' &c. (ch. v.) These seem, indeed, to be sleepy words; but when they are wakened, uncovered, and diligently considered, then they are of great value. I am persuaded," said Luther, " that this simplicity of John much offendeth Erasmus of Rotterdam; surely he thinketh that John speaketh not like Jerome and Virgil, nor like one of us; insomuch that he censureth according to human reason and understanding: but God judgeth otherwise."

" The Bible, or Holy Scripture," saith Luther, " is like a fair orchard, wherein all sorts of trees do grow,

* Let it be thy endeavour, good reader, so to search and study Holy Scripture, that thy heart may be moved and *taken possession of* thereby.

from which we may gather divers kinds of fruits; for in the Bible we have rich and precious comforts, doctrines, admonitions, warnings, promises, and threatenings, &c. There is not a tree in this orchard," said Luther, " on which I have not knocked, and have shaken at least a couple of apples or pears from the same."

" That the Bible is the Word of God," said Luther, "the same I prove as followeth. All things that have been and now are in the world; also, how it now goeth and standeth in the world, the same was written altogether, particularly, at the beginning, in the first book of Moses. And even as God created it, even so it was, even so it is, and even so doth it stand to this present day. And although King Alexander the Great, the kingdom of Egypt, the empire of Babylon, the Persian, Grecian, and Roman monarchs, the Emperors Julian and Dioclesian, &c., most fiercely did rage and swell against This Book, utterly to suppress and destroy the same, yet could they prevail nothing; they are all gone and vanished, but This Book from age to age hath still remained, and will remain, unremoved, in full and ample manner as it was written at the first. But who kept and preserved it from so great and raging power? or who defendeth it still? Truly," said Luther, " no human creature, but only and alone God Himself, who is the rightful owner thereof; and how great is the wonder that it has been so long preserved, the devil and the world being such grievous enemies unto it ! The devil, doubtless, hath destroyed many good books in the church, as he hath rooted out and slain many saints, concerning whom we have now no knowledge; but (no thanks to him) the Bible he was fain to leave unmeddled with. In like manner baptism, the sacrament, and the office of preaching, have remained amongst us against the power of many tyrants and heretics who have opposed the same. These our Lord God hath kept and maintained by His special strength."

On the Study of Divinity.

"The chief lesson and study in divinity," said Luther, "is well and rightly to know Christ; from hence, St. Peter saith, '*Grow up in the knowledge of our Lord Jesus Christ;*' and Christ himself also teacheth, that we should learn to know Him only out of the Scriptures, where He saith, '*Search the Scriptures, for they testify of Me.*'

"Now we ought not to measure, censure, and understand the Scripture according to our own natural sense and reason; but we ought diligently, by prayer, to meditate therein, and search into the same. Again, without trials and temptations we shall not understand any thing thereof to purpose; no, though we diligently read and hear the same. The devil, therefore, and temptations do give occasion to our learning the Scriptures better, and having experience touching the same. Moreover, the Holy Ghost must be the only master and tutor to teach us therein; and let youth and scholars not be ashamed to learn of this tutor. When I," said Luther, "find myself in temptation, then I quickly fasten upon some text in the Bible, which Christ Jesus layeth before me, — as, namely, that '*He died, the just for the unjust, that He might bring us to God,*' — from whence I have and receive comfort."

"Whoso is armed with the text, the same is a right pastor; and my best advice and counsel is," said Luther, " that we water out of the true fountain; that is, diligently to read the Bible. He is a learned divine that is well grounded in the text; for one text and sentence out of the Bible is of far more value than many writings and glosses, which are neither sound, strong, nor armour of proof. As when I hear that text of St. Paul, ' *Every creature of God is good, and nothing to be refused, if it be received with thanksgiving,*' &c.* This text showeth that what God hath made is good. Now, eating, drinking, marrying, &c. are of God's making; therefore they are good: but the glosses of the Fathers are against this text; for St. Bernard, Basil, Dominic, Jerome, and other holy fathers have written far otherwise of the same. But," said Luther, " I prefer the text before them all; and it is far more to be esteemed of than all their glosses: yet, notwithstanding, in Popedom, the glosses of the Fathers were in higher regard than the bright, clear text of the Bible, through which great wrong is often done to the Holy Scriptures; for even the good Fathers, as Ambrose, Basil, and Gregory, have oftentimes written very cold things touching the Divine Word.

* Such a text as this sets the conscience free from the supposed necessity of observing the Romish ordinances; their compulsory fasting and abstinence from animal food, — the celibacy of the clergy, — and the rules of monastic discipline. The writings of those who commended such things were held in so great authority in Luther's time, and formerly by Luther himself, that nothing but the supremacy of God's word, above all the judgments of men, could effectually release the consciences of those who were religiously disposed from their unhappy bondage.

Of the School Divines, and their vain speculating Divinity.

"The art of the School Divines," said Luther, "with their speculations in the Holy Scripture, are merely vain and human cogitations, spun out of their own natural wit and understanding, of which I have read much in Bonaventura; but he had almost made me deaf. I fain would have learned, out of that book of his, how God and my sinful soul might be reconciled together; but of that there was nothing to be found therein. They talk much of the union of the will and understanding, but all is mere fantasy and fondness. The right and true speculation," said Luther, "is this: — believe in Christ; do what thou oughtest to do in thy vocation, &c. This is the only practice in Divinity. Also *Mystica Theologia Dionysii* is a mere fable, and a lie, like to Plato's fables. *Omnia sunt non ens, et omnia sunt ens;* all is something, and all is nothing; and so he leaveth all hanging in frivolous and idle sort.

"True and upright Divinity consisteth in the practice, use, and exercise; her foundation is Christ; she taketh hold, by faith, on His passion, death, and resurrection. All those," said Luther, "that concur not with us, and have not this doctrine before their eyes, the same do feign unto themselves a speculative Divinity, according to their carnal sense and reason, and as they use to determine in temporal causes; for no man can divert them from these opinions, — Whoso doeth good works, and leadeth an honest, civil sort of life, the same is an upright Christian, and he is well and safe. But they are therein far deceived; for this is the truth indeed,— Whoso feareth God, and trusteth in Him, the same will most surely be well and safe at last.

"Therefore," said Luther, " these speculating divines belong directly to the devil in hell; they follow only their cogitations, and what with their own five senses they are able to comprehend. And such is also Origen's divinity. But David is of another mind: he acknowledgeth his sins, and saith, ' *Miserere mei, Domine;*' God be merciful to me, a sinner. At the hand of these sophisticated divines, God can scarcely obtain that He is God alone, much less can He find this favour of them — that they should allow Him only to be good and just; very hardly will they yield that He is an immortal God."

"To the understanding of the worldly wise," said Luther, "there is no lighter and more easy study than Divinity, and to understand God's word; for the children of the world (and almost every man) will be looked upon as experienced people in Divinity: but they shoot far from the mark. I," said Luther, "would give all my fingers, three excepted, on condition that I could find Divinity so easy as they take it to be. The cause which maketh people think Divinity so easy and light, and so soon to be learned, is this — they are soon weary of the same; they are quickly filled and cloyed therewith. And even so we found it in the world; and even so we must leave it and let it remain; *sed in fine videbitur cujus toni.*"

"There is but one rule and article in Divinity — he that knoweth not the same well is no divine — namely, upright faith and confidence in Christ. In this article all others do flow and issue forth again, and without this article the others are nothing. The devil," said Luther, "hath opposed this article from the beginning of the world, and would, long since, willingly have foisted in his craft. Sorrowful, broken, vexed, and tormented hearts," said Luther, "do well relish this article, and they only understand the same."

"Although a man knew, and were able to do, as much as an angel in heaven, yet all this would not make him a Christian, unless he knew Christ and believed in Him: therefore God saith, '*Let not the wise man glory in his wisdom, neither let the mighty man glory in his might; let not the rich man glory in his riches; but let him that glorieth glory in this, that he understandeth and knoweth Me, that I am the Lord which doth exercise loving-kindness, judgment, and righteousness in the earth,*' &c. (Jer. ix.)

"The Sacred Scriptures," said Luther, "will have humble hearts, that hold God's word in honour, love, and worth, and that pray continually, '*Lord, teach me thy ways and statutes.*' But the Holy Ghost resisteth the proud, and will not dwell with them. And although some for a time diligently do study in Holy Scripture, do teach and preach Christ uprightly and pure, yet so soon as they become proud, God excludeth them out of the church; therefore every proud spirit is a heretic, though not as yet in act and deed, yet *de jure* before God.

"But it is a hard matter that such a one (that hath some particular gift and quality above others) should not be haughty, proud, and presumptuous, and not continue so. Therefore God suffereth them that have great gifts to fall many times into heavy tribulations, to the end that they may learn this; viz., when God draweth away His hand, then they are of no value. St. Paul was obliged to bear on his body the sting, or thorn, of the flesh, to preserve him from haughtiness. And if Philip Melancthon were not plagued now and then in the way that he is, so would he have strange conceits and fancies."

"In the psalm it is said, '*In omnem terram exivit sonus eorum;*' their voice went out into the whole world: but St. Paul to the Romans giveth it thus, in the German tongue, 'Their sound went out in all the earth;' which is all one. There are many sentences in the Bible wherein St. Paul observeth the translation of the Seventy Interpreters; for he contemned them not: and whereas he was preacher to the Grecians, therefore he was constrained to preach as they understood.

"In such sort did he use that sentence, 1 Cor. xv., '*Death is swallowed up in victory;*' whereas in the Hebrew it is written, *in finem*. Yet it is all one, *in finem, in eternum,* that death *in victoriâ* will not come again; *id est, vita vincit.* St. Paul was very rich, flowing in words; one of his words containeth well three of Cicero's orations. Oftentimes Paul speaketh one word which pierces through the whole of Isaiah and Jeremiah. O!" said Luther, " St. Paul was an excellent preacher; he is not in vain named *vas electum.* Our Lord God saith, I will give a preacher to the world that shall be precious; there was never any that understood the Old Testament so well as St. Paul, except only John the Baptist: St. Peter excelleth also. Indeed, St. Matthew and the rest do well and diligently describe the histories, which are very necessary; but *res, et verba, et vim verborum, Veteris Testamenti*, they never mention what sticketh therein.

"St. Paul translated much out of Hebrew into Greek, which none besides were able to do; he so handleth sometimes one chapter, that he expoundeth four, five, and six chapters. O! he dearly loved Moses and Isaiah; for they, together with King David, were the chief prophets. The words and things of St. Paul were extracted out of Moses and the prophets.

"Therefore," said Luther, "young divines ought to study Hebrew, to the end they may be able to compare Greek and Hebrew words together, and discern the properties, natures, and strength of the same.

"If I were young," said Luther, "and intended to be a high divine, so would I confer Paul, *cum Veteri Testamento:* he was a powerful logician and rhetorician."

"He that now intendeth to be a good divine hath a great advantage; for, first, he hath the Bible, which I have so clearly translated out of the Hebrew into the High German tongue, that every one may read it without hinderance. Afterwards he may read also *Locos Communes Philippi Melancthonis:* let him read the same with diligence, in such sort that he hath the same altogether in his memory. When he hath these two pieces, then he is a divine against whom neither the devil, nor any heretic, can be able to take any advantage; for the whole of divinity lieth open before him, so that he may read what and when he will, *ad ædificationem*. Then he may also read *Philippi Melancthonis commentarium in Epistolam Pauli ad Romanos*. Then also let him read my commentary on the Epistle to the Galatians, and on Deuteronomy;—

then also let him attain *eloquentiam et copiam verborum.*

We find no book where the sum of religion, or whole divinity, is more finely compacted together than in Philip Melancthon's common-places; all the Fathers and sententiaries are nothing comparable thereto: *non est melior liber, post sanctam Scripturam, quam ipsius Loci Communes.* Philip Melancthon," said Luther, " is straiter tied than I am: *Ille pugnat et docet.* I am more of a rhetorician, or a talker. If the book-printers would be ruled by me, they would print those books of mine which have doctrine; as *Ad Galatas, in Deuteronomium,* also the sermons out of the four chapters of the Evangelist St. John: my other books may be read *pro cognoscendâ historiâ revelati Evangelii,* that they may see how the doctrine went forward at the first; for then it was not so clear as now it is."

" I," said Luther, " did not learn my divinity all at once, but was constrained to search deeper and deeper; to which my temptations brought me: for no man without temptations can attain to the true understanding of the Holy Scriptures. St. Paul had a devil that buffeted, and with temptations drove him diligently to study the Holy Scriptures. I," said Luther, had hanging on my neck the Pope, the universities, all the deeply learned, and with them the devil himself; these hunted me into the Bible, wherein I diligently read, and at length (God be praised!) attained to the true understanding of the same. Without such a devil we are (I often say it) only speculators of divinity, and, according to our vain cogitations, dream that so also it must be, like the monks and friars in monasteries.

"The Holy Scripture of itself is certain and true enough; but God grant me the grace that I may catch hold on the right use thereof; for when Satan disputeth with me in this sort, namely, 'Whether God be gracious unto me or no?' then I must not meet him with this text, 'Whoso loveth God with all his heart, and soul, and strength, the same shall inherit the kingdom of God;' for then the devil presently objecteth and retorteth upon me thus, 'But thou hast not loved God,' &c. &c., which, indeed, is true, and my own conscience beareth witness against me: at such a time, therefore, I must arm myself, and encounter him, in a different manner; as thus, that ' Jesus Christ died for me, and through Him I have a gracious God and Father;' 'Christ is sacrificed, and hath made an atonement for us;' and, as St. Paul saith, '*He is of God given unto us for wisdom, and righteousness, and sanctification, and redemption.*'

"Tyrants, sectaries, seducers, and heretics, do nothing else but drive us into the Bible, and make us read more diligently therein, and with more fervency to sharpen our prayers."

"I believe," said Luther, "that the words of our Christian Belief were in such sort ordained by the apostles, who were together, and made this sweet *symbolum*, so briefly and comfortable. It is a work of the Holy Spirit to describe those great things with such strong, brief, and weighty words. No human creature, beside the apostles and the Holy Ghost, had been able to comprehend them in such manner: no, not although ten thousand worlds had studied to make them. Therefore the words therein ought to be well considered. I," said Luther, "cannot sufficiently admire the same."

"When I was a friar," said Luther, "I was a master in spiritual significations; then I was altogether in my allegories; there was nothing in me, but altogether art; but, afterwards, when, through the Epistle to the Romans, I came a little to the acknowledgment of Christ, I saw that allegories were vain. Before that time I turned every thing into an allegory; yea, even the *cloaca*. But, afterwards, I considered the histories, how difficult and heavy a matter it was, that Gideon fought with the enemy in the way that the Scripture showeth; those were no allegories, nor spiritual significations; but the Holy Ghost, in that passage, saith simply this, that faith, with 300 men, beat so great a multitude of the enemies. St. Jerome and Origen (God forgive it them) were the occasion of allegories being in such esteem. In all Origen is not so much as one[*] word of Christ. Now I have shaken off all that folly," said Luther, "and my best art is, '*Tradere Scripturam simplici sensu*,' that is, to deliver the Scripture in its plain sense; the same doth the deed: therein is life, strength, doctrine, and art; in the other is nothing but foolishness, let it lustre and shine how it will. When men will aim at that mark," said Luther, "and will make tropes, then we that are Christians have lost.

"Muntzer, in that manner, played his tropes with the third chapter of John. '*Except a man be born again of water*,' &c. *Water*, said that man, here signifies *affliction*, as in that place, '*Many waters*

---

[*] *i. e.* Of the true doctrine of salvation by Him only.

entered into my soul.' The meaning, therefore, is, that by tribulations we must enter into the kingdom of heaven. Thus did Muntzer; but St. Austin gave the right rule, *i.e.* ' That figures and allegories prove nothing at all, but history, words, and grammar.' "

CHAPTER III.

SAYINGS OF DR. MARTIN LUTHER TOUCHING THE KNOWLEDGE OF GOD.

"The philosophers and learned heathen," said Luther, "have described God, that he is like a circle, the centre of which is every where, but the circumference nowhere. Herewith they would show that God is all, and yet is nothing. And, indeed, our Lord God is every where, and yet he can nowhere be fastened upon, nor comprehended, in his high majesty. I," said Luther, "find Him not only at Jerusalem in the temple, and in that manner as He hath figured Himself unto me; but I find Him also in every place, — in the baptism, in the manger at Bethlehem, in the sacrament, &c. &c.; but, in His majesty, He is nowhere.

"Ah! good God," said Luther, "how wonderful art Thou, that so puttest to shame the wise of the world! It were pains and labour enough for us that we attained unto the knowledge of A, B, C, concerning these high divine mysteries. When the ungodly, out of their own thirst and insolence (according to their natural sense and reason), will conclude any thing without God, or, against God, then God presently doth turn the same so about, that it goeth backward: for if God did not so, He would lose His honour, His glory, and majesty.

The Trinity.

"That Three are One, and One Three," said Luther, "goeth beyond all human sense, reason, wit, wisdom, and understanding. No arithmetician, no philosopher, lawyer, Jew, nor Turk, can fasten upon and comprehend it. Neither doth that comparison, or similitude, of the corporal father and son serve any thing to the purpose, for it is a very weak picture or likeness, in which is shown only the difference of the two Persons, namely, that those two Persons are an undivided substance, which is not to be comprehended or understood by any human creature."

"In the Gospel of St. John, chap. iii., is plainly and directly shown the distinction of the Persons, in the highest and greatest work that God accomplisheth with us, poor human creatures; for there it is plainly written of the Father, that He loved the world, and hath given to the world His only begotten Son: these are two several Persons; the Father, the Son. The Father loveth the world, and giveth unto it His Son. The Son suffereth himself to be given to the world, and, as Christ clearly saith, He suffereth himself to be lifted up on the cross, as the serpent was lifted up in the wilderness, that whosoever believeth in Him should not perish, but have everlasting life. To this work cometh afterwards the third Person, the Holy Ghost, who kindleth faith in the heart, through the waters of baptism, and regenerateth us into God's kingdom.

"This article," said Luther, "although it be handled most clearly in the Scripture, hath always been assaulted and opposed in the highest degree, insomuch that the histories do show that St. John wrote his gospel for the confirmation of this article. Then came presently that heretic Cerinthus, who taught, out of Moses, that there was but one God, concluding thereupon, that Christ could not be God, neither could God become man. In such manner he prated, out of human reason and understanding, and thought it must needs be just so as he concluded it.

"But," said Luther, "we ought to keep close to God's word, to what in these cases the Holy Scripture saith; namely, 'That Christ is true God with God the Father, and that the Holy Ghost is true God, and yet there are not three Gods, nor three substances* (as three men, three angels, three sons, three windows, &c.). No: God is not separated nor divided in such manner in His substance, but there is only and alone one Divine essence and no more.

"Now," said Luther, "although this article seemeth strange or foolish, what matter is it? Here is no dis-

---

* Luther's meaning is this, that we must beware of conceiving of the Three Persons in the unity of the Godhead, as we should of three distinct *created beings;* a remark deserving of deep and serious consideration. When we speak of three men, three angels, or three windows, we may declare, from real knowledge and experience, that they are essentially distinct, and that the three, except in a very restrained sense, cannot possibly be one. Our faculties are so fully capable of judging upon this subject, that it becomes, in a manner, a question of arithmetic. But when we come to speak about God, our Creator, whose glory (as the Scripture speaks) is above the heavens, it is mere folly, with our most imperfect, infantine conceptions of the mode of our Creator's existence, to judge of Him as one would of one's fellow-creatures; and to say it is impossible that the Three Divine Persons should be One God. It is a subject (as Luther hints above) beyond the reach of the arithmetician's calculation; one that he cannot comprehend.

puting whether it be so or no. The question is, whether the same be grounded on God's word or no? If it be God's word, as most surely it is, then let us make no doubt thereof. He will not lie; therefore let us keep close to God's word, and not dispute how Father, Son, and Holy Ghost can be but one God. For we, as poor wretches, cannot know how it cometh that we laugh; or how, with our eyes, we can see a high mountain ten miles off; or how it cometh when we sleep, that in body we are dead, and yet we live. This small knowledge we cannot attain unto; no, not although we took to help the advice and art of all the wise in the world; we are not able to know these least things which concern ourselves, and yet, like foolish devils, we will clamber up with our poor wit and wisdom, and presume to fasten and comprehend *what* GOD *is in His incomprehensible majesty.*"

How to find out God.

"If," said Luther, "thou wilt be sure and certain of thy conscience and salvation, then abstain from speculating, and searching to know and to seek God the Lord, as well what His essence is, as also His will, according to thine own sense, reason, and carnal cogitations, — for without His word, and His Son, Christ, He will not be found. Thou must learn to take hold on God by such means as He is expressed to thee in Holy Scripture, concerning which St. Paul saith: — '*For after that, in the wisdom of God, the world, by wisdom, knew not God: it pleased God, by the foolishness of preaching, to save them that believe. For the Jews require a sign, and the Greeks seek after wisdom, but we preach Christ crucified; to the Jews a* stumbling block, and to the Greeks foolishness; but unto them that are called, both Jews and Greeks, Christ the power of God and the wisdom of God.'

"Therefore," said Luther, "begin thou to seek God there where Christ himself began; namely, where he was conceived in the womb of his mother, the Virgin Mary, where he lay in the manger at Bethlehem, sucking at his mother's breasts, &c.; for He came from heaven, was born a natural human creature, he walked with us of mankind on earth, he preached, wrought miracles, suffered, was crucified, died, and rose again from the dead, only for this end, that he might place himself in such a manner before our bodily eyes, as thereby to draw the eyes of our hearts, that is, all our thoughts and senses unto Him; so as to debar us from that presumptuous speculating and searching out the majesty of God in heaven.

"We can seek, find, and understand, the heavy temptations of that everlasting predestination, which terrifies many people, nowhere better," said Luther, "than in the wounds of our Saviour, Christ Jesus, of whom the Father hath commanded, saying, '*Hear ye Him*.' The Father, in His Divine majesty, is far too high and great for us; we cannot take hold of Him; therefore He showeth to us the right way by which we may certainly come to Him, namely, Christ, and saith, 'Believe on Him, depend on Him, so shall ye easily find who I am, and what my will and essence is.' But," said Luther, "the wise of the world, the mighty, the high learned, and the greatest company in the world, by no means do this. Therefore God is, and remains, unknown to them, notwithstanding they have many cogitations, and do dispute and talk much of God; for it is a short and sound conclusion, that without

Christ God will not be found, known, nor comprehended."

"I have said it often, and do say it still," said Luther, "he that, without danger, will know God, and will speculate of Him, let him first look into the manger; that is, let him begin below, and let him first learn to know the Son of the Virgin Mary, born at Bethlehem, that lies and sucks in his mother's bosom; or let one look upon Him hanging on the cross. Afterwards he will finely learn to know who God is. Then shall he have a knowledge that will not affright, but be most sweet, loving, and comfortable. But take good heed, I say, in any case, of high climbing cogitations, of clambering up to heaven without this ladder, namely, the Lord Jesus Christ, as He is simply, plainly, and most excellently, described in the word. Only do thou rely upon Him, and suffer not thyself to be drawn from Him, with thy wit, human sense, and reason: so shalt thou take a right hold of God.

Concerning the Attributes and Proceedings of the Almighty.

"All the works of God," said Luther, "are unsearchable and unspeakable; no human sense can rightly find them out; faith alone takes hold thereof, without any human power or addition. No human creature can apprehend God in His majesty; and, therefore, He hath set himself down in the simplest manner, and was made man; yea, was made sin, death, and weakness. He was simple, indeed, and mean enough, when He took upon him the quality of a servant, as St. Paul saith to the Philippians. But," said Luther, "who can believe it? we think that the Turkish Emperor is much more mighty; Erasmus, of Rotterdam, much more learned; a friar far more good and godly, than God himself is.

"We may see, in all things," said Luther, "in the least things, and even in their members, God's almighty power, and great and wonderful wisdom, clearly shining. For what man (how powerful, wise, and holy soever) can make out of one fig a fig-tree, or another fig? or, out of one cherry-stone another cherry, or a cherry-tree? or, what man can so much as know how God preserveth all things, and makes them grow.

"Neither," said Luther, "can we conceive or know how the apple of the eye doth see; or how understanding words are spoken distinctly and plainly by the motion of the tongue within the mouth; all which are natural things, which we daily see and do. How then should we be able to comprehend the secret counsel of God's majesty, or to search it out, with our sense, reason, and understanding?"

Philip Melancthon asked Luther, one day, if this word, "*hardened*" (in Rom. ix.), were to be understood directly as it sounded, or in a figurative and coloured sense? To which question Luther answered and said, "We must understand it properly, and not operatively, for God worketh and doth no evil; but through His almighty power he worketh all in all, and as He findeth a man, so he worketh in him. So in the case of Pharaoh, God found him evil, he continually proceeded to be wicked, and to do evil, which was his nature. But he was hardened, because that God, with His spirit and grace, did nothing hinder his ungodly proceedings, but suffered him to go on and have his mind. Now the reason why God did not hinder nor restrain, is a point which we have no business to enquire into; for this word ' *quare,' why?* hath misled and destroyed many souls; it is too, too high for us to enquire into. Therefore God saith to us, ' Why I do this, thou shalt not know. Look thou upon the word, believe thou in Christ, and pray: be sure that I do things well enough without thy understanding why. * If God shall be asked at the last day," said Luther, " why He suffered Adam to fall, then will He answer and say, ' Because my goodness might be known and seen towards the generation of mankind, in that I gave to the world my Son to be a Saviour."

" God scorns and mocks the devil, in that he sets under the devil's nose a poor weak human creature, that is dust and ashes (yet hath the first fruits of the Spirit), against whom the devil can do nothing, although he is so proud, subtle, and powerful a spirit. We read in histories," said Luther, " that a mighty powerful king of Persia was utterly routed at the city of Edessa, through a wonderful host sent of God, namely, through an innumerable multitude of flies and gnats. Even so God takes pleasure to overcome and triumph, not through power, but through weakness. Flies and gnats shall beat and overcome great kings, and drive away powerful armies of chariots and of horsemen. Also a weak human creature shall bid defiance to the devil, and overcome that prince and god of the world, only through faith.

---

* How well were it for many if they could only digest that one sentence, — " Be sure that God does things well enough without thy understanding why He does them."

"As lately I lay very sick," said Luther, " and so sorely sick that I thought I should have left this world, many cogitations and musings I had in my weakness. 'Ah!' thought I, 'what may that eternity be? What joys may it have?' &c. Methought," said Luther, " if I had been with God Almighty before He created the world, I could not have given Him counsel that out of nothing he should make such a round ball or globe, that He should create the firmament and set therein such a spangle, the sun, which through his swift course giveth light to the whole circle of the earth, or that he should in such manner make man, woman, &c.;—all these things God made for us without any advice or thought of ours. Therefore ought we justly to give Him the honour, and to leave to His divine power and goodness the new creation of the life to come, and not to presume to speculate and search out the same. Meanwhile, I know that that same eternity is already ours; through Christ it is given and prepared for us, if we can but believe. There it shall all be opened to us; but here we shall not know that new or second creation, seeing that even the first creation we understand not."

Dr. Jonas, inviting Luther to dinner, had caused a bough with ripe cherries to be hung up over the table, where they dined, in remembrance of the creation, and thereby to put his guests in mind to praise the glorious God for creating, preserving, and bestowing such fruits, &c. Upon which Luther asked him " why he did not rather remember the same by his children, who were the fruit of his body? for," said he, " they are far more excellent creatures than all the fruit of trees; by them we see God's power, and great skill and wisdom, who hath made them all out of nothing, and hath given them in one year life and all members, and, having so exquisitely created, will maintain and preserve the same. Yet," said he, " we do but very little regard this; nay, in such gifts of God, we are, commonly, so blind and covetous, that it often happens that people when they have children, grow worse and more covetous; they rake and rend all they can, to the end that enough may be left for their children. They little know that before a child comes into the world and is born, it hath its lot. It is already determined and ordained, what and how much it shall have, and what shall become of it.

" In the state of matrimony we learn and find, that begetting and bearing of children stand not in our wills and pleasures; for the parents can neither see nor know whether they shall be fruitful or not, nor whether God will give them son or daughter. 'All this is done without our ordaining, thinking, or foreknowing. My father and mother did not think that they should have brought a *superintendent*[*] into the world: it is all God's creation, which we cannot rightly understand or conceive. I believe," said Luther, "that in the life to come we shall have nothing else to do but to meditate upon our Creator, and on His celestial creatures, and to wonder at the same."

" God's power is great," said Luther, "who upholdeth and nourisheth the whole world; and it is a hard article where we say and acknowledge, '*I believe in God the Father,*' &c. He hath created all things sufficient for us. All the seas are our cellars, all the

[*] A name given by the German Protestants to their bishops.

woods are our huntings, the earth is full of silver and gold and of innumerable fruits, which are created all for our sakes;—the earth is a corn-house, and a larder for us," &c.

———

One evening Luther saw cattle going along a pasture-field. "Behold," said he, "there go our preachers;—there are our milk-bearers, butter-bearers, cheese and wool bearers, which do daily preach to us faith towards God, that we should trust in Him, as in our loving Father, who careth for us, and will maintain and nourish us."

———

"No man," said Luther, "can calculate the great charges God is at only in maintaining the birds and such creatures, which, in a manner, are nothing, or of little worth. I am persuaded," said he, "that it costeth God more yearly to maintain the sparrows alone, than the whole year's revenue of the French king! What, then, shall we say of the rest of his creatures?"

———

"God," said Luther, "could be exceeding rich in money and in temporal wealth, if He pleased; but He will not. If He were but to come to the Pope, to the Emperor, to a king, a prince, a bishop, to a rich merchant, a citizen, or a farmer, and were to say, 'Except thou givest me a hundred thousand crowns thou shalt die this instant.' Then every one would presently say, 'I will give it with all my heart if I may but live.' But now we are such unthankful slovens, that we give Him not so much as a *Deo Gratias*, although we receive from Him richly, and overflowing, so great benefits, merely out of His goodness and mercy. Is not this a shame? Yet, notwithstanding such our unthankfulness, our Lord God and merciful Father doth not suffer Himself thereby to be scared away, but continually doth show to us all manner of goodnesses. But," said Luther, " if in His gifts and benefits He were more sparing, and in imparting the same to us were more close handed, then might we learn to be thankful. If, for example, He caused every human creature to be born into the world with only one leg or foot, and, seven years afterwards, gave him the other leg; or in the fourteenth year gave one of the hands, and in the twentieth the other, then we should better acknowledge God's gifts and benefits; we should then also value them at a higher rate, and be thankful to Almighty God for the same. But now, since God heaps upon us these and the like His blessings, we never regard the same, nor show ourselves thankful to Him.

" Then again," said Luther, " God hath given to us in these days a whole sea full of His word; He giveth unto us all manner of languages, and good, free, liberal arts: we buy, at this time, for a small price, all manner and sorts of good books; moreover He giveth unto us learned people, that do teach well and orderly, insomuch that a young youth (if he be not altogether a dunce) may learn and study more in one year now, than formerly in many years. Arts are now so cheap that they almost go about begging for bread. Woe be to us," said Luther, " that we are so lazy and improvident, so negligent and unthankful.

" But God, I fear, will shut up His liberal hand and mercy again, and will give unto us sparingly enough, so that we shall have again sects, schisms, preachers of lies, and scoffers of God, and then we shall adore and carry them upon our hands, seeing that now we do contemn His word and servants."

"The greater God's corporal gifts and wondrous works are, the less," said Luther, "they are regarded. The greatest and most precious treasure of this kind that we receive of God is, that we can speak, hear, see, &c. Yet who is there that feels these to be God's gifts, or gives Him thanks for them? Men value such things as wealth, honour, power, and other things that are of less worth; but what costly things can they be that so soon do vanish away? A blind man (if he be in his right wits) would willingly miss of all these, if he might but see. The reason," said Luther, "why the corporeal gifts of God are so much undervalued, is this, that they are so common, and God bestows them upon the senseless beasts as well as upon us people, and often in greater perfection. But what shall I say? Christ made the blind to see. He drove out devils, raised the dead, &c.; yet must He be upbraided by the ungodly hypocrites who gave themselves out for God's people, and must hear from them that He was a Samaritan, and had a devil. Ah!" said Luther; "the world is the devil's, wheresoever it be. How, then, can it acknowledge God's gifts and benefits? It is with God Almighty as it is with parents and their children which are young: they regard not so much the daily bread, as an apple or a pear, or other toys."

"The wicked and ungodly," said Luther, "do enjoy and use the most part of God's creatures; for the tyrants have the greatest power, lands, and people in the world; the usurers have the money, the farmers have eggs, butter, corn, barley, oats, apples, pears, &c.; but good and godly Christians must suffer and be persecuted, must sit in dungeons, where they can have neither sun or moon, but must be thrust out into poverty, be banished, plagued, &c. But certainly it must be better one day; it cannot always remain so: let us have but patience, and steadfastly remain by the pure doctrine, and notwithstanding all this misery, let us not fall away from the same."

"Whoever can humble himself before God, earnestly and from the heart, hath certainly gained. For God can do nothing but be merciful towards them that humble themselves. For if God should always be stern and angry, I should be afraid of Him," said Luther, "as of the executioner. And seeing that I must stand in fear of the Pope, of the Emperor, of the papistical bishops, and of other tyrants, which are God's enemies, to whom then should I fly and take my refuge, if I should also be afraid of God?"

"God styleth himself in all the Holy Scriptures a God of life, of peace, of comfort, and joy, for the sake of Christ. Therefore I am an enemy to myself," said Luther, "that I cannot believe it so constantly and surely as I ought to do. No human creature can rightly know how mercifully God is inclined to those who steadfastly do believe in Christ."

"When God took away his word from the Greeks, then, instead thereof he gave them Mahomet and the Turk. God," said Luther, "for a heavy punishment, hath given to us Germans, and to the Italians, the Pope, with whom we have all manner of abominations, as the denial of the true faith, &c. No greater plague could come from God unto us, than to suffer us to be bereaved of His word. We might rather wish unto ourselves all manner of plagues and punishments, than to be without God's word, and to have it impure and falsified."

Of Christ — God manifest in the Flesh.

"The articles of faith are too high for the children of this world; — that three Persons is one only God; that the true Son of God was made man; that in Christ are two natures, divine and human, &c. At these things they are offended, nay, they hold them for fictions and fables. For to human sense and reason it seemeth as likely for a stone and a man to be one person, as for God to be made man, or for the divine and human natures to be united in the one person of Christ.[*] St. Paul understood an excellent

[*] Luther felt very powerfully the truth of the declaration of St. Paul, that " *No man can say that Jesus is the Lord, but by the Holy Ghost:*" that to believe in Christ, therefore, is a special *gift of God*. (Phil. i. 29. Eph. ii. 8.) We have a striking illustration of the peremptory manner in which this article is rejected by men, in the conduct of the chief priests and elders at Jerusalem, who having asked Jesus, then standing as a prisoner at their bar, whether He was the Christ, the Son of the Blessed One; upon receiving his answer in the affirmative, the cry instantly arose from them all, that there was no need of calling witnesses to prove him guilty of the vilest blasphemy. Yet these men had the prophecies of Isaiah, and, very probably, had read the ninth and the fifty-third chapters. But as he was evidently a *man*, and yet presumed to make himself *God*, (John, x. 33.) it *stood to reason*, they would say, that he must be a blasphemer of the worst kind: which He

piece thereof, although he took not hold of all. Thus, he breaketh forth to the Colossians, and saith, '*In Christ dwelleth all the fulness of the Godhead bodily;*' also, '*In Him lie hid all the treasures of wisdom and knowledge.*' His meaning is, Whoso findeth not God in Christ, the same shall never find Him, let him seek where and how long he will, much less shall he find out what God's will and essence is.

"But we acknowledge all in Christ, the whole Godhead and manhood; that is, we see in Him the highest strength and power, together with the highest weakness: we see in Him both life and death, righteousness and sin, God's grace and anger.

"Ah!" said Luther, "what shall we say? that God was made man? truly it is a very high and hard article, above and against all human sense and reason; but how very few do seriously meditate the same!"

"If," said Luther, "Christ be not God, then neither the Father nor the Holy Ghost is God; for our article of faith, according to the Scripture, speaketh thus: — that Christ is God with the Father and the Holy Ghost. Many there are," said Luther, "that talk much of the Godhead of Christ (as doth the Pope and others), but they discourse thereof as a blind man speaketh of colours. For myself, when I hear Christ speak, and say, '*Come unto me, all ye that labour and are heavy laden, and I will refresh you,*' then do I be-

---

certainly would have been, had it not been true that He was indeed, what He professed to be, and what Zechariah foretold that He should be, "*The man who was God's fellow;*" or, as St. Paul explains it, who "*thought it not robbery to be equal with God;*" and "*in whom dwelt all the fulness of the Godhead bodily.*"

lieve steadfastly that the whole Godhead speaketh in an undivided and inseparate substance. Wherefore let him that will picture and preach such a god to me as died not for me the death upon the cross, that god will I neither have nor receive."

———

"Now, he that hath this article hath the chief and most principal article of faith, although to the world it seem very silly and ridiculous. Christ saith, the Comforter which I will send shall not depart from you, but will remain with you, and enable you to bear all manner of tribulations and evil. When Christ saith, '*I will pray the Father*,' then He speaketh as a human creature, as very man; but when He saith, I will do this or that, as above, '*I will send the Comforter*,' then He speaketh as very God. In this manner," said Luther, "do I learn my article, That Christ is both God and man."

———

"That Christ is God and man," said Luther, "is against human reason and understanding. For when we are taught to bring the two natures of Christ (the divine and the human) into one person, then immediately the wit, wisdom, and common sense, of man, do, as it were, startle, and say, how can this be? I understand it not. O!" said Luther, "no thanks unto thee for this confession; for it is not written to that end and purpose, that thou shouldest understand and comprehend it with thy natural sense and wisdom; but thou must yield thyself captive, and believe the word of the Gospel, through the operation of the Holy Ghost, and give God the honour that He is true. Christ saith (John, xiv. 13.), '*Whatsoever ye shall ask the Father in my name, that will I do, that the Father may be glorified in the Son.*' Here Christ speaketh as one that hath all things in His hand and power, to give every thing that a man prayeth to Him for in faith. Is it not, then, most sure, that He hath a boundless, an immeasurable, almighty power, equal with the Father?

"Christ bringeth, also, peace," said Luther; "but not as the apostles bring it; namely, through preaching; but He giveth it as a Creator, as His own proper creature. The Father createth and giveth life, grace, and peace; even so giveth the Son the same gifts. Now, to give grace, peace, everlasting life, forgiveness of sins; to justify, to save, to deliver from death and hell, surely these are not the works of any creature, but of the Majesty of God alone; and these things the angels can neither create nor give."

"Although no religion seemeth more foolish to the world than the Christian religion, yet, notwithstanding, I believe in that God who is the Son of the heavenly Father; namely, in Christ Jesus. In no other God will I believe, as the infidels and idolaters do; for they are rejected, and given over to a reprobate mind. I, Martin Luther, neither do, nor will take notice of any other God, but only of Him, that hung on the Cross, Christ Jesus, the Son of God, and the Virgin Mary."

"We cannot vex the devil more," said Luther, "than when we teach, preach, sing, and speak of Jesus and His humanity, &c. Therefore I like it very well," said Luther, "when with loud voices, and fine, long, and deliberately, we sing in the church, '*Et homo factus est: et Verbum caro factum est.*' The [illegible] that the whole Gospel [illegible] and [illegible] that will [illegible] and preach [illegible] the death upon the [illegible] neither [illegible]."

[illegible] as that hath this article [illegible] article of faith, altho[illegible] silly and ridiculous [illegible] which I will send shall [illegible] remain with you, and en[illegible] of tribulations and evil. [illegible] the Father,' then He [illegible] as very man; but wh[illegible] as above, 'I wi[illegible] speaketh as very G[illegible] I learn my [illegible] man."

[illegible] is God and [illegible] reason and [illegible] creed [illegible] Saviour Christ [illegible] crucified [illegible] should [illegible]

[illegible] This [illegible] whole [illegible] Christ [illegible]

167

...l, nor the
oath, that
the Priest.
...ur refuge to
bishop of our
of His hand.

...t a crafty and
...ight, and, with
...ood and godly
...mfort, and begin
...erning Christ,—
...t complaineth of
...hop of their souls,
...c. Therefore the
...d not in vain warn
...atch, and should be
...rewith to resist the
...nes. v.)"

...thine enemies.' These
...port, that Christ must
... which we preach and
...d world; yea, and He
...tes of Hell. We Pro-
...d the Papists do dwell
...will be God's people, and
...ill not yield to the other;
...must yield; the ungodly to
...and the apostles, together
...der one roof. Now, as the
...well and **thoroughly plagued**,
...lain the **Christians, and, at**
...all away; **insomuch that they**

were now well rid of those wicked wretches; then came the Romans, and made an utter ruin of the Jews.

"Even so," said Luther, "will it go with us and the Papists: when they have made an end of their raging persecutions, of their blaspheming and condemning Christ and his doctrines; of shedding the blood of Christians, &c., then (no thanks unto them) must they yield to this our party; for, to the world's end, they that do hold and acknowledge Christ for their everlasting King and High Priest, do confess and preach His doctrine, and do comfort themselves in His prayers, who hath offered up Himself for their sins, Christ neither can nor will leave them without help or comfort."

———

"He that hath Christ for his king and God, let him be assured that he hath the devil for his enemy; who will work him much sorrow, and plague him all the days of his life. But," said Luther, "let this be our comfort and great glory, that we poor people have the Lord of life, of death, and of all creatures, clothed with our flesh and blood, sitting at the right hand of God His Father, who ever liveth and maketh intercession for us, defendeth and protecteth us."

שֵׁב לִימִינִי. *Sheb limini.*

"*Sheb limini;* that is, '*Sit thou on my right hand.*' This *sheb limini,*" said Luther, "hath many and great enemies, which we poor small heap must both find and feel; but it is no matter: this I know for certain, that many of us must suffer and be slain by their fury and raging; yet let us not be dismayed, but, with a divine resolution, let us engage and venture ourselves, our bodies and souls, upon this His word and promise:—

'*Because I live, ye shall live;*' and '*Where I am, there shall ye be also.*'

"Christ oftentimes carrieth himself in such a manner as if He took not the parts of us His poor troubled and persecuted members; therefore," said Luther, "He is not to be comprehended in this life. For the world rewardeth His best servants very evil; they persecute, they condemn and kill them as the most wicked, mischievous heretics and malefactors; and Christ holdeth His peace, and suffereth the same to be done, insomuch that I sometimes have such thoughts as these upon the subject:—'Who will tell me whereabouts I am, and whether I preach right or no?' Even this also was one of St. Paul's trials and temptations, touching which he spake not much, neither could (as I think), for who can tell me what those words do import, where he saith, '*I die daily.*'" *

"Christ is our bridegroom," said Luther, "and we are His bride. What He, the loving Saviour, hath (yea Himself) is ours; for *we are members of His body, of His flesh, and of His bones*,' as St. Paul saith. And again, what we have, the same is also His: but," said Luther, "how exceedingly unequal is the change! for He hath everlasting innocence, righteousness, life, and salvation, and this He giveth unto us to be our own. On the contrary, what we have is sin, death, damnation, and hell; and these we give unto Him, for He hath taken our sins upon Him, He hath delivered us from the power of the devil, hath crushed his head, hath taken him prisoner, and cast him down to hell,

* 1 Cor. xv. 31.

so that we may now with St. Paul undauntedly say,— '*Death, where is thy sting?*'

"Also, when He ascended into heaven, then He took us all likewise to the right hand of the Father (Eph. ii. 6.), and hath removed us also (us that are members of His body) into the heavenly places, seeing that we also with Him shall be lords of all things (1 Cor. iii. 21.), yet so that he remaineth '*the first-born among many brethren.*'"

"Is it not a wonder beyond all wonders," said Luther, "that the Son of God (whom the heavenly hosts do worship, and at whose presence the whole earth quaketh and trembleth,) should sit there among those wicked wretches, and should suffer Himself to be so lamentably tormented, scorned, derided, and set at naught? They spit in His face, and strike Him on the mouth with a reed, and say, 'O! He is a king, He must have a crown and a sceptre.' The sweet blessed Saviour," said Luther, "complaineth not in vain, in the psalm, *diminuerunt ossa mea;* in such sort did they vex and harass Him. Ah! our suffering," said Luther, "is not worthy to be called a suffering. When I consider my crosses, tribulations, and temptations, I shame myself almost to death, thinking what they are in comparison of the sufferings of my blessed Saviour, Christ Jesus. And yet we must be conformable to the image of the Son of God. And what if we were conformed to the same? yet were it nothing. He is *Filius Dei*, we are poor creatures; although we should suffer everlasting death, yet were the same of no value."

"The wrath is fierce and devouring which the devil hath against the Son of God, and the generation of mankind. I beheld once," said Luther, "a wolf tearing a sheep in pieces; it pitied me much to see it. When the wolf cometh into a sheepfold, he devours none till he has killed them all; then he begins to eat, thinking he shall devour all. Even so it is also with the devil. 'I have now,' thinketh he, 'taken hold of Christ, and in time also I will snap his disciples;' but the devil's foolishness is this:—he seeth not that he hath to do with the Son of God; he knoweth not that in the end it will be his bane. It will come to that pass," said Luther, "that the devil must be afraid of a child in the cradle; for when he only heareth the name *Jesus* uttered out of a true faith, then he cannot stay, for he thinketh 'I have murdered Him.' The devil would rather run through fire, than be where Christ is: therefore it is justly said, '*Semen mulieris conteret caput serpentis;*'—the seed of the woman shall bruise the serpent's head. I ween, indeed," said Luther, "that He hath so crushed his head, that he can neither abide to hear, nor to see, Christ Jesus. I oftentimes delight myself," said Luther, "with that similitude in Job, of an angle hook. The fishermen use to put on the hook a little worm, and then cast it into the water; by-and-by cometh the fish and snatcheth at the worm, and getteth therewith the hook in his jaws, so that the fisher pulleth him out of the water. Even so hath our Lord God dealt with the devil: God hath cast into the world His beloved Son (as the angle), and upon the hook hath put Christ's humanity (as the worm); then cometh the devil and snappeth at the man (Christ), and devoureth Him, and therewithal he biteth the iron hook, that is, the Godhead of Christ, which choketh him, and all his power is overthrown to the ground. This is called Divine Wisdom."

"The conversation which Christ held with His disciples, when He took His leave of them at the last supper, was doubtless most sweet, loving, and friendly; when Christ talked with them so lovingly, like a father with his children, when he is obliged to depart from them. He took their weakness in good part, and did bear with them, although, now and then, their discourse was very gross and full of simplicity. As when Philip said, '*Show us the Father,*' &c.; and Thomas, '*We know not the way,*' &c.; and Peter, '*I will go with thee unto death:*' these were all collations and table discourses, where each of them freely and undauntedly gave utterance to the cogitations of his heart. Never since the world stood," said Luther, "was there a more precious, costly, sweet, and amiable banquet, feast, conversation, and discourse, than this."

"Touching the sweating of blood," said Luther, "and other high spiritual sufferings which Christ endured in the garden, the same no human creature can know nor imagine. If one of us should but begin to feel one of the least of those sufferings, then surely he must at once die. Ye know there are many people who die *ægritudine animi*,—for grief of mind;—for sorrow of heart is death itself. If a man should feel such anguish as Christ hath, and the soul, notwithstanding, should remain in the body, and endure the same, it were impossible but that soul and body must part in sunder. In Christ only it was possible, and thereupon there issued from Him that bloody sweat.

"Christ," said Luther, "had neither riches, nor an

earthly kingdom; for these He gave to kings and princes. But He reserved one thing peculiarly to Himself, which no human creature nor angel could undertake to do, namely, to be a conqueror over sin, death, devil, and hell; and in the midst of death to deliver, and save those who believe in Him through His word."

"Truly," said Luther, "the prophets did well foresee in the Spirit, that Christ would become the greatest sinner that ever came upon the face of the earth. For inasmuch as He is a sacrifice for the sins of the whole world, He is now no more an innocent person and without sin; He is not now the Son of God in glory; but He is a notorious sinner, and for a while forsaken, and hath lying upon His neck the sins of all mankind. He hath now loaded upon Him the sins of St. Paul, who was a blasphemer of God, and a persecutor of His church. He hath also upon Him St. Peter's sins, who denied Christ; in like manner David's sins, who was an adulterer and a murderer, and caused the name of the Lord to be blasphemed among the heathen. To conclude, He is now that person who hath loaded himself with all the sins that have been, are, and hereafter shall be committed, by the whole generation of mankind. Not that He Himself committed those sins, but that He hath taken upon His body the sins from us, which we have done and committed, to the end He might make satisfaction for the same with His own most precious blood."

"The riding of our blessed Saviour into Jerusalem," said Luther, " was altogether a poor and beggarly kind of riding, where Christ (the King of heaven and earth) sitteth upon a poor, simple ass, which was not His own, nor even hired with His money;—His saddle was the disciples' clothes, which they laid over the ass's back. This was a very strange kind of riding for so powerful a potentate, as the prophet Zechariah showed: for as He came from Bethany to Bethphage to the Mount of Olives, which was not a quarter of a league from Jerusalem, and when He had raised Lazarus from the dead, and that a multitude went before, and followed after Him, then sent He His disciples away to fetch the ass. He would needs ride thus, to fulfil the Scriptures. But," said Luther, "this riding of our Saviour Christ, was, notwithstanding,—if we consider the purpose and intent of it,—exceeding stately and glorious, though outwardly to the world it must needs seem poor, contemptible, and beggarly."

"The communion or fellowship of our blessed Saviour," said Luther, "was doubtless most loving and familiar; for though He held it for no robbery to be equal with God, He humbled Himself to be made man like unto us, yet without sin. He served and waited upon His disciples as they sat at table (just as my servant doth to me). The good disciples (as plain, simple people) were so used to it, that they were even content to let Him wait. In such manner hath Christ sufficiently fulfilled His office, as it is written,—'*He came not to be ministered unto, but to minister.*' Ah!" said Luther, "it is a high example, that He so deeply humbled Himself and suffered, who, nevertheless, had created the whole world, heaven and earth, and all that is therein; and who with one finger could have turned it upside down, and destroyed it."

"Let this religion which we profess seem to the world never so foolish, yet, notwithstanding, I," said Luther, "do and will believe in that one only Jew, who is called Jesus Christ, who is the only beginning of all my divine reflections, which I have, or may have, day and night continually. Nevertheless, I do find, and freely confess it, that I have scarcely attained to a small and weak beginning of the height, of the depth, of the breadth, of this immeasurable, incomprehensible, and endless wisdom, and have hardly gotten or brought to light any thing but a few stumps and fragments out of this most deep and precious profundity."

"Is it not a plague," said Luther, "that we will always be afraid of Christ? whereas there never was, in heaven, or on earth, a more loving, familiar, mild man, both in words, works, and demeanour, specially towards poor, sorrowful, and tormented consciences. From hence, the prophet Jeremiah prayeth, '*O Lord, grant that we be not afraid of Thee.*'"

"'The deaths of many people are forgotten,' said once a Jew; 'and cannot the death of Jesus be forgotten?' This was a devilish speech," said Luther "O! no, sir devil; it is written, — '*Sit thou on my right hand, until I make thine enemies thy footstool;*' therefore we must and will preach and teach of Jesus Christ, of His passion and death, so long as the world endureth."

"We should not take the whole world," said Luther, "for this knowledge, that we know that Jesus Christ is *Christ*, that He is our only Saviour, our High Priest, our Lord and King. This did not I know," said he, "so long as I lived a friar in the monastery. Now, although the case should so fall out that we should lose our lives for the sake of this acknowledgment, yet Christ liveth, and, if He liveth, then shall we also live most certainly; for our sentence standeth fast, and so will for ever, against the gates of hell, where He saith, '*Because I live, ye shall live also.*' Now Christ, whom we preach, is God; therefore the whole world, in comparison of this Christ, is nothing.

"All the wise of the world," said Luther, "do scoff and scorn that we take Christ's cause in hand with such fervency*; but at the last their scoffing and scorning will fall into their own bosom."

"The prophets," said Luther, "did know that Christ should and must be true and natural God, to the end He might deliver from the everlasting curse those who should believe in Him, as their prophecies do clearly declare. Isaiah, in chap. vii., calleth him *Immanuel*, that is, *God with us*. Jeremiah, in chap. xxiii., saith, '*He shall be called, The Lord our Righteousness.*'

"But as touching the particular circumstances, how and in what manner He would deliver the generation of mankind from the eternal curse, I believe," said Luther, "that all the prophets did not know the same; but I rather think that they and other godly hearts among the children of Israel, were preserved in their faith, in the same way as our children are, who simply and plainly do believe that Christ is our God

---

* The name "fanatic," or "enthusiast," or some term indicating a defect in judgment, is, to this day, applied to those who discover a lively interest in the cause of Christ.

and Saviour, and that they had also joyful, comfortable reflections concerning the same."

———

"The greatest work of wonder which ever was done on earth," said Luther, "is, that the only begotten Son of God died the most contemned death upon the cross. It is to us a wonder above all wonders that the Father should say to His only Son (who by nature is God), 'Go thy way, let them hang Thee on the gallows:' yet, notwithstanding, the love of the everlasting Father was immeasurably greater towards His only begotten Son, than the love of Abraham was towards Isaac; for the Father witnesseth from heaven (Matt. iii.), '*This is my beloved Son, in whom I am well pleased;*' yet was He cast away so lamentably like '*a worm and no man; yea, a scorn of men, and an outcast of the people.*' At this," said Luther, " the blind wisdom and understanding of man stumbleth; it thinketh, 'Is this the only begotten Son of the everlasting Father?' how, then, dealeth He so unmercifully with Him? He showeth Himself more kind and friendly towards Herod and towards Pilate, than towards this His only beloved Son. The Jews, saith Paul, are offended at this sermon; so are also the seeming holy workers, and the wise of the world,—these hold it altogether foolish; but to us true Christians," said Luther, "it is the greatest comfort; for we thereby acknowledge and certainly believe, that the merciful Lord God our Father in such manner loved the poor condemned world, that He spared not His beloved Son, but gave Him up to the most ignominious death for us all, '*that whosoever believeth in Him should not perish, but have everlasting life.*' We, therefore, hold this sermon for our highest comfort and wisdom, for the true golden art, and for a divine power, through which we shall be saved."

"A believing soul," said Luther, "ought to speak with our Saviour Christ in this manner:—'Lord! I am Thy sins, Thou art my righteousness; therefore am I joyful, and do boldly triumph, for my sins do not overbalance Thy righteousness; neither will Thy righteousness suffer me to be or remain a sinner. Blessed and praised be Thy holy name, sweet Jesus, for evermore.'"

"Christ once appeared visible here on earth, and showed His glory, and, according to the foreordained counsel of God, He finished the work of the redemption of mankind. I," said Luther, "do not desire that He should thus appear again; neither would I that He should send an angel unto me; and although an angel should come, and appear before mine eyes from heaven, yet would I not believe him; for I have of my Saviour Christ Jesus bond and seal; that is, I have His word and sacraments; upon these I depend, and desire no new revelations.

"To confirm me," said Luther, "the more steadfastly in this resolution to remain by God's word alone, and not to give credit to any visions and revelations, I will tell you what lately befell me. I being, on Good Friday last, in my inner chamber in fervent prayer contemplating with myself how Christ my Saviour hung upon the cross, how he suffered and died for our sins, there appeared suddenly upon the wall a bright shining vision, in which there was a glorious form of our Saviour Christ with the five wounds, steadfastly looking upon me, as if it had been Christ himself corporally. Now at first sight thereof I thought it had been some good revelation; yet I bethought myself again, that surely it must needs be the juggling of the devil, for Christ appeareth unto us in His word, and in a meaner and more humble form, therefore I spake unto the vision in this manner:—' Avoid, thou confounded devil; I know no other Christ but Him that was crucified, and who is pictured and preached unto me in His word.' Upon which the image vanished, showing plainly whose work it was."*

"It is written in the legends of St. Peter, that Peter always wore a linen cloth about him, with which he wiped his eyes, which at length became very red, as," said Luther, "I can well believe to be true. Being asked why he wept so often, he said, ' *Si recordaretur illius dulcissimæ consuetudinis Christi cum apostolis, tum se non posse continere lacrymas:*' — If he

---

* Some may think this vision merely the effect of a distempered brain; and it is not to be denied that so it *may* have been: but, seeing that there are such beings as evil angels, and that the imagination is that faculty of the human mind upon which they act (it would seem) most powerfully; it is not at all unreasonable to suppose that an impression of this kind was made, by means of the imagination, upon the senses of Luther. Nor is it unscriptural to believe that the devil, when thus resisted, fled from him (James, iv.), unable to support the illusion any longer. No one could well be further removed from enthusiasm than Luther, who brought all his feelings, and every irregular impression made upon his imagination or his senses, to the test of God's Holy Word. Luther knew what that meant, in Isaiah, viii. 20., "To the word and to the testimony," &c., and looked, as is well known, with great jealousy, upon all pretences to inspiration derived from dreams and visions. — See Milner's Church History, vol. v. pp. 47. and 70.

thought on that sweet society of Christ with His apostles, then he could not refrain from tears. Our Saviour Christ doubtless was an exceeding amiable, mild, and friendly man, and so He is with us to this day; but we know it not. Oh!" said Luther, " how willingly would I have been once with our Saviour Christ here on earth, at such a time when He was merry."

" Christ said to the heathenish woman, '*I am not sent but unto the lost sheep of the house of Israel;*' yet He afterwards helped both her and her daughter. It might seem from hence," said Luther, " as if Christ at that time spake against his conscience.

" The truth is this: — Christ was not sent to the Gentiles; but when the Gentiles came to Him, He would not reject nor put them from Him. In person, He was sent to the Jews only, and therefore He preached in the land of the Jews; but, through His apostles, His doctrine went into the whole world. Indeed," said Luther, " it is a glorious name and title which Moses giveth to the Jews, — '*Tu es gens sancta;*' Thou art a holy nation. But David, in his psalm, afterwards promiseth Christ to the Gentiles: — '*Praise the Lord all ye Gentiles,*' &c. The good and loving apostles hardly understood this sentence; they thought they should be made great persons: they had already shared the people to themselves; as where the two disciples, on the road to Emmaus, said, '*We hoped that He should have delivered Israel.*' But this their conceit and opinion must be mortified. The good fellows were possessed with such carnal cogitations; yet our Saviour Christ dealeth mildly, and hath patience with them and their weakness."

"Christ, our blessed Saviour," said Luther, "forbore to preach and teach until the thirtieth year of His age; neither would He openly be heard: no, notwithstanding He heard and beheld so many impieties, abominable idolatries, heresies, blasphemings of God, &c. It was a wonderful thing that He could abstain and endure all this with patience until the time came that He was to appear in His office of preaching."

Of the Holy Ghost.

"The Holy Ghost," said Luther, "is an everlasting God, as we acknowledge and believe in our Christian faith. Our Saviour Christ giveth sundry names and titles to the Holy Ghost:— first, He nameth Him a Reprover, or Convincer,— '*He shall convince the world of sin,*' &c. — 2dly, a Comforter; 3dly, a Spirit of Truth; 4thly, that He proceedeth from the Father, and therein that He is, with the Father and the Son, true and eternal God; 5thly, that He witnesseth of Christ," &c.

Luther, being asked, wherefore the Holy Ghost hath the name of Comforter, answered thus:— "The world, saith our Saviour Christ, will excommunicate and kill you as heretics and rebels, and will think that they do right therein; yea, and that in this killing and persecuting of you, they are doing God good service. Ye, my people, must be held in the wrong; so that every one will say, 'O! these heretics are served well and rightly. Who would wish them better?' And then ye will be weak in your consciences, and often times ye will think with yourselves, 'Who knoweth whether we have done well and rightly, or no? Surely we have gone too far;' insomuch that ye will be censured by the world, and, at times, even in your own consciences.

"Wherefore (saith Christ) forasmuch as I know already how it will go with you; namely, that you shall find comfort neither in the world, nor from yourselves, therefore I will not forsake you, nor suffer you to stick in such a need, neither will I lead you so far into the mire that ye shall sink therein; but when all comfort from the world is gone, and when ye are terrified and dismayed, then I will send unto you the Holy Ghost, who is called, and is, the true Comforter; He shall cheer up your hearts again, and say, 'Be of good comfort, and faint not; do not be careful about the censures of the world, nor what your own troubled thoughts may be; but hold ye fast on that which I say.' The Holy Ghost," said Luther, "is a Comforter, and not a breeder of sorrow; for where sorrow and heaviness are, there the Holy Ghost (the Comforter) is not at home. The devil is a spirit of fear, and of frighting; but the Holy Ghost is a Comforter."

"Indeed," said Luther, speaking of the bold and hearty zeal which the Holy Ghost wrought in the apostles, "such a spirit was very necessary at that time for the apostles and disciples: even so, at this day, He is also needful for us; for our adversaries do now accuse us, as they then did the apostles, for rebels, for disturbers of the union and peace of the church. What evil soever happeneth, they say that we are the cause of it. Our slanderers now cry out, 'Before, in Popedom, it was far better with us, than since this new doctrine came in; now we have all manner of mischiefs, deaths, wars, and the Turks.'

"All the fault," said Luther, "they put on our preaching; and if they could charge us with being the cause of the devil's falling from heaven, yea, and that we had crucified and slain Christ, they would not omit it.

"Therefore the Whitsuntide Sermons of the Holy Ghost are very needful for us, that thereby we may be comforted, and may boldly contemn and slight such blasphemy, and obtain from the Holy Ghost such strength and courage in our hearts, that we may stoutly thrust ourselves forward, let who will be offended, boldly and freely acknowledging and preaching Jesus Christ.

"It is the nature of the Gospel," said Luther, "to be a ridiculous and offensive preaching, which, in all places of the world, is rejected and contemned. If it were not so," said Luther; "if the Gospel were such a doctrine as offended and angered neither citizen nor countryman, neither prince nor bishop, then it would be a fine and acceptable preaching, and might be well tolerated, and people would hear and receive it with pleasure. But seeing it is such a kind of preaching as maketh people angry, (especially the great and high powerful persons, and such as will be deep learned ones in the world,) so needeth there truly a divine constancy, a courage of the Holy Ghost, to those that intend to preach the same.

"What an undaunted courage it was," said Luther, "in the poor beggars and fishers (the apostles) to stand up and preach in such sort as to bring down upon their backs the wrath and displeasure of the whole government, of both the spiritual and temporal estates, yea, of the Roman Emperor himself; and (which is more) to open their mouths so wide, and to say, Ye are all traitors, murderers, &c. Truly the same could not have been done without the Holy Ghost.*

"A great wonder it was," said Luther, "that the high priests, together with Pontius Pilate, did not cause those preachers to be put to death. For it sounded much of rebellion that the apostles stood up and preached of the crucified Jesus of Nazareth against the spiritual and temporal government; yet, notwithstanding, both high priests and Pilate must be struck with fear, as, indeed, they deserved well to be made afraid, even 'where no fear was,' to the end that God might show His power in the simple apostles' weakness.

"This is the manner and proceeding of Christianity," said Luther; "it goeth on in apparent weakness, and yet, in such weakness, there is so great and mighty strength and power, that all the worldly wise and powerful thereat may stand amazed and be in fear."

Luther said, in Dr. Hennage's † presence, that the Holy Ghost is the certainty itself in the Word, making us so sure and certain of the Word, that, without all wavering or doubting, we certainly believe that it is even so, and no otherwise than as God's Word declareth. Dr. H. objected, that people of all sects

---

* It was not the making such charges against the rulers which marked the power and presence of the Holy Ghost in the apostles, but that, being men in low estate, and naturally timid and faint-hearted, they had the courage, calmly and deliberately, to say such things in such an assembly, with nothing to support them in it but a sense of the duty they owed to their God and Saviour, whose witnesses they were.

† At that time rector of the university of Wittemberg.

might then claim the gift of the Holy Ghost, seeing they be so positive of the truth of their own tenets. Luther replied to him briefly, and then continued:—
" A true and godly Christian (while others doubt) saith thus,—' I regard nothing these doubtings; I neither look upon my holiness, nor my unworthiness; but I believe in Jesus Christ, who is both holy and worthy; and whether I be holy or unholy, yet am I sure and certain that Christ giveth Himself (with all His holiness, worthiness, and whatsoever He is and hath) to be mine own. For my part, I am a poor sinner, and that I am assured of out of God's word.'

" Therefore the Holy Ghost alone is able to say * Jesus Christ is the Lord. The Holy Ghost teacheth, preacheth, and declareth Christ; all others do, in one way or another, blaspheme Him.

" The Holy Ghost," said Luther, " goeth first and before in what pertaineth to teaching; but in what concerneth hearing, the Word goeth first and before; and then the Holy Ghost followeth after. For we must first hear the Word, and then afterwards the Holy Ghost worketh in our hearts; He worketh in the hearts of whom He will, and when He pleaseth. To conclude, the Holy Ghost worketh not without the Word."

* i. e. in the heart of the Christian, 1 Cor. xii. 3.

CHAPTER IV.

TOUCHING CERTAIN PRINCIPAL DOCTRINES OF THE CHRISTIAN RELIGION.

Concerning Justification.

"THIS article, how we are saved, is the chiefest of the whole Christian doctrine. All divine disputations must be directed to it. All the prophets agitated this question, and thereabout turmoiled themselves. For when this article, concerning the salvation of our souls, is kept fast and sure by a constant faith, then all other articles draw on softly afterwards, as that of the Holy Trinity, &c. God," said Luther, "hath declared no article so plainly and openly as this, that only by Christ we are saved. And although he spake much of the Holy Trinity, yet resteth He continually upon this article of the salvation of our souls; other articles are of great weight, but this surpasseth all.

"Where this article remaineth pure and clean, there remaineth also the church pure; but if the same be falsified, then the church is made a whore, and is gone, as we have well seen, in Popedom.

"It is a mischievous thing," said Luther, "that we, miserable sinful wretches, will upbraid God, and hit Him on the teeth with our works, and think to be justified thereby before God, but God will not allow thereof. My own conscience telleth me," said Luther, "that I cannot be justified by works, yet the Papists will not believe it. We ought," said Luther, " to say, with the fifty-first psalm, '*Against thee only have I sinned, and done this evil in thy sight, that Thou mightest be justified in Thy sayings.*' We should remember that it is said, '*Forgive us our debts.*' We ought to say at once, We neither will, nor desire to be, righteous before the judgment-seat of God; but, much rather, willingly to confess ourselves sinners. What could we more easily say than this, We, poor creatures, are sinners, but Thou, O God, are righteous? Then," said Luther, "the case with us would be clear (1 John, i. 8, 9.): but we are our own hangmen, and tormenters of ourselves. The spirit ought, indeed, to say, 'I am righteous and just*;' but the flesh † must say, 'I am a sinner; Thou, O God, art righteous, *ut justificeris in sermonibus tuis.*'"

"The nature of an upright and true faith (which holdeth itself only in Christ) is," said Luther, "not to be disputing whether thou hast done many good works, whereby thou mightest be saved, or whether thou hast committed many sins, whereby thou mightest be damned; but it concludeth, in most simple and plain manner, for certain, that although thou hast done many good works, yet thou art not thereby righteous before God; and, again, although thou hast committed great sins, yet that thereby thou art not damned.

"But," said Luther, "I will herewith not dishonour nor blaspheme good works, much less will I applaud

---

* *i. e.* in Christ, in whom I believe. — 2 Cor. v. 21.
† In which "dwelleth no good thing."— Rom. vii. 18.

sin; but this I say, *He that will stand before the judgment-seat of God*, and be found a child of grace, he shall and must only and diligently have regard how he may take and keep hold on Christ through faith; lest Christ be made unprofitable unto him, in that he relies upon the Law, trusting to be justified and saved by it."

Anno 1539, the 21st of January, an English doctor, named Antony Barnes, asked Luther, "If an upright Christian and fearer of God, who already was justified by faith in Christ, deserved or merited any thing by reason of his works which follow after his justification; for," said he, "this question is very frequent in England." Luther answered him and said, "First, we must know that we are still sinners, yea, after we have been justified; and, therefore, pray for the remission of sins, in this life — '*Forgive us our trespasses*,' also, '*Enter not into judgment*,' &c. This meaning and sentence is sure, that we are all sinners, and do all live under grace, and the forgiveness of sins.

"Secondly, God promiseth recompense and reward to those who are good; therefore (may you say) we deserve, then, and merit something. Well," said Luther, "be it so; that God recompenseth and rewardeth people's good works, but the same is done altogether under the forgiveness of sins; for seeing heaven, *i.e.* seeing righteousness is under grace, how much more are the stars under grace? for like as the stars make not heaven, but only do trim and adorn it; even so, the works do not merit heaven, but adorn and beautify that faith which justifieth.

"We ought, simply and plainly, to believe the word; and when we are justified, and do such works as God hath commanded, then are we like the stars.

"To conclude, the article of justification is *Christ* solveth all*; for if Christ hath merited my justification by His passion and death (which is most sure and certain), then," said Luther, " can I never merit it; in Christ are gifts, not deserts. Now, seeing that the head and principal righteousness is nothing, therefore, the accidental righteousness can be nothing. *Justitia substantialis* is the righteousness of faith; *accidentalis justitia* are the gifts; but God crowneth no gifts, but only those which are His gifts."

The question being moved, Whether a man be justified and accepted before God, first, through faith, but afterwards is accomplished or finished off by works? "I," said Luther, "answer the question thus:— A creature being already created, it cannot be said of it, that it shall be created, seeing it is created already; even so, it cannot be said of one who is justified, that he shall be justified, because he is justified already.

"It were senselessly spoken to say, We are at first justified by faith, but afterwards justification must be

---

* Coloss. iii. 23, 24., may serve very well to explain this; "*Whatsoever ye do,*" says St. Paul, addressing himself to Christian servants, "*do it heartily, as to the Lord, and not unto men; knowing that of the Lord ye shall receive the reward of the inheritance, for ye serve the Lord Christ.*" (John, xii. 26.) It is, in a sense, a reward, we see, yet so as to be an *inheritance*. A father leaves an inheritance to his son, because he is *his son;* but if he be a *good* son, (as the Lord makes all His good, Eph. ii. 10., see also 1 Peter, i. 1—5.) then saith he to him, "Thou hast been a dear good child to me, and I leave thee my estate, the reward of the inheritance."

finished and settled by works. I hold this, and am certain," said Luther, " that the true meaning of the Gospel and of the apostles is, that we are justified before God, *gratis**, for nothing, only by God's mere mercy; wherewith, and by reason whereof, He imputeth righteousness unto us in Christ.

" We can attribute to works in themselves no righteousness before God; although they adorn the justified, and make illustrious by a certain and sure recompense, yet they do not themselves justify the person. For we are all justified after one manner, in and by one Christ: We are altogether acceptable and pleasing to God, according to the person; yet one star excelleth another star in brightness; nevertheless God loveth the star, Saturnus, no less than He loveth the sun and moon.

" A faithful person," said Luther, "is a '*new creature,*' a new tree. Therefore all those speeches which in the Law are usual belong not to this case. To say a faithful person *must* do good works, is about as correctly spoken as to say, the sun *shall* shine, a good tree *shall* bring forth good fruit, three and seven *shall* make ten. For the sun shall not shine, but it *doth* shine, by nature, unbidden; it is thereunto created. Likewise, a good tree bringeth forth good fruit without bidding. Three and seven are ten already, and shall not be, &c.

" If we were speaking of a *pretended* faith, or of a mock sun, we might use this kind of language against it.† It is a sun, therefore it must shine; thou art a

* Compare Rom. iii. 28. 24. with Rom. iv. 16. and Eph. ii. 8, 9.

† It is the case of a pretended faith that St. James refers to, where he says, " If a man say he hath faith, and have not works,

faithful person, therefore thou must do good works; to speak so of the upright faith, or of the true sun, would be ridiculous.

"We understand, then, that as the sun (if it be the sun indeed) of necessity shineth, not by reason of any law, but by nature (as I may say), by reason of the immutability, for thereunto it is created, on purpose to shine; even so, one that is justified and regenerated doth good works, not by reason of any law, or by compulsion (for no * law is given to one that is justified), but † out of unchangeable necessity; for St. Paul saith, ' *We are God's workmanship, created in Christ Jesus unto good works, which God hath before ordained that we should walk in them.*' "

Concerning the Law and the Gospel.

"The Law is, and teacheth, what we should do; but the Gospel is what God will give unto us. The

---

what does it profit?" If he say true, and he hath faith indeed, then works will prove the truth of his saying; if there are not works (called also "fruits") answerable to his profession of faith, it is a pretence. A man presents a counterfeit sovereign; it has the right colour, shape, size, image, and superscription, but it wants *weight*, it is not *gold*. What is the use of coin of that description? So a man's works are the test of his faith. It is a common thing to " *hold the truth in unrighteousness;* " to profess an orthodox creed, and have an unsanctified heart, and an ungodly life.

* 1 Tim. i. 9. The law is not given to *enforce* the obedience of a righteous (*i.e.* a justified) person, but only to *direct* it.

† Rom. vi. 1, 2. 1 John, iii. 9.

first we cannot fulfil; the second we take hold of by faith; for God worketh by and through the Word and Sacraments."

"The cause," said Luther, "that St. Paul now and then speaketh so scornfully of the Law is, not that we should contemn the Law; no, in no wise; but will rather that we should esteem it very precious.

"But whereas St. Paul, in those places of Scripture, teacheth how we become justified before God; therefore it was very necessary for him to speak disdainfully of the Law; for it is another thing, when we dispute how we may be justified before God, and when we deal in a general way about the Law. When we are in hand with the righteousness that justifieth before God, then we cannot sufficiently undervalue the Law. The reason, in this case, is," said Luther, "that the conscience must have regard to nothing but Christ; for which cause we must, with all diligence, endeavour to remove Moses*, with his law, far from us, and out of sight, when we intend to stand justified before God, and neither to receive

---

* Luther, whose conscience had been grievously harassed by his vain attempt to justify himself, according to the tenets of the Romish church, by works of righteousness which he should do, was in the habit of speaking of the law of God, by the name of Moses, who delivered it to Israel. When he had learned the true way of salvation through the all-sufficient sacrifice and obedience of Christ, Moses (the Law), from whom he had ignorantly expected his justification, was made to take his proper place. In the matter of justification Moses has nothing to do but to let the sinner see and feel how entirely he needeth Christ. (Gal. iii. 21 – 25.)

nor to entertain any thing, but only the promise in Christ."

"When," said Luther, "we are not in hand with the righteousness and justification, wherein we stand as righteous and just before God, then we ought to have great and high esteem of the Law; we must extol and applaud it in the highest degree; we must (with St. Paul) call it holy, and just, and good, and spiritual, and divine, as, in truth, it is: for in that it affrighteth and killeth, that is not the fault of the Law, but of our evil and (by the devil) poisoned nature.

"Therefore we must in no case suffer the Law to be mingled with the righteousness which availeth before God, seeing it hath cost our Saviour Christ so much to rid the conscience of its tyranny; for on this account He became a curse himself, that He might deliver us from the curse."

"If," said Luther, "the Law be rightly understood, then it amazeth; it maketh faintness of heart, and produceth despair. But if it be not understood, then it prepareth and maketh hypocrites.

"When the Gospel is not rightly understood, it maketh careless and rude people, who use it to carnal freedom: but when it is well and rightly understood, then it maketh upright, godly, and true Christian people."*

"The Law and the righteousness thereof," said Luther, " is like a cloud without rain; it raiseth great hopes, but disappointeth them: for the Law promiseth

* Ps. cxxx. 4.   1 Tim. vi. 3.   Titus, ii. 11, 12, &c.

K

salvation, but giveth it not; neither can the Law give salvation; for the Law was not given to that end, as St. Paul saith in Gal. iii."

"The Gospel," said Luther, "is a comfortable messenger; it bringeth good news; namely, that the Son of God is made man; that He died for us, rose again from the dead, &c. The Gospel preacheth nothing of works. Therefore he that saith that the Gospel* exacteth works necessary to salvation, I say, flat and plain, he is a liar.

"Nothing that is good," said Luther, "proceedeth out of the works of the law, except grace be present; for what we are forced to do, the same goeth not from the heart, neither is acceptable. The people under Moses were always in a murmuring state and condition; they would needs stone him; they were rather his enemies than his friends."

"Never was a more bold and harsh sermon preached in the world," said Luther, "than that which St. Paul preached, wherein he quite abolisheth and taketh away Moses, together with his law, which is nothing else than to take away the religion and the temporal government. Who now with patience could endure this? From thence arose the continual dissension and strifes which St. Paul had always with the Jews. And if Moses had not cashiered and put himself out of his office, and had not taken it away with these

* The Gospel useth no harsh language; it saith not, "Thou must and shalt do this." It speaks, as in Romans, ch. xii. 1., "I beseech you, brethren, by the mercies of God," &c.; and, again, Eph. v. 1., "Be ye, therefore, followers of God as *dear children*," &c.

words, where he saith, '*A prophet shall the Lord your God raise up from among you like unto me; Him thou shalt hear.*' Who, then, would or could have believed the Gospel, and forsaken Moses?"

"Not long since," said Luther, "a learned divine at Wittemberg made his complaint to me, that he could by no means make the right distinction between the Law and the Gospel. I answered him, and said, 'I believe you well: if you were able to do that, then I would hold you for a learned doctor indeed.' We flatter ourselves, that so soon as we have heard a sermon, we understand it thoroughly; but therein we deceive ourselves.

"I," said Luther, "thought so myself, that I had it at my fingers' ends, seeing I had written so much concerning the same; but truly I found myself far to seek therein at such times when I stood most in need thereof, when the devil began to school me. But when, by his frequent assaults, I gained better experience of his devices and temptations, then (thanks be given to God!) I jeered him with his arguments, even in the teeth, with unspeakable joy and comfort to my troubled conscience.

"The Law and the Gospel," said Luther, "are the two chief articles of the doctrine in the church of God. Through the Law, God will keep off and affright the ungodly, the wild, rude people, and sinners, from blaspheming. He will also thereby teach the proud hypocrites, and the invocators of saints, the folly of their imagined *overplus** of works. But the Gospel comforteth the sad and sorrowful conscience, &c. It

* Works of supererogation.

comforteth all those of whom the prophet Isaiah speaks (chap. lxi.), and saith to them, '*Be of good comfort, for I do forgive you your sins.*' What could God do more for us?" said Luther.

"St. Paul saith, '*What the law could not do, in that it was weak through the flesh, God (sending his own Son in the likeness of sinful flesh, and for sin) condemned sin in the flesh, that the righteousness of the law might be fulfilled in us,*' &c. (Rom. viii.) That is," said Luther, "Christ is the sum of all. He is the right pure meaning and contents of the Law. Whoso hath Christ* (1 John, v. 12.), the same hath rightly fulfilled the Law. But to take away the Law altogether (which sticketh in nature, and is naturally written in our hearts), that is a thing impossible, and against God. For whereas the law of nature is but darkly written, and speaketh of works only in a general way; therefore the Holy Ghost, by Moses, more plain and clearly doth declare and expound it, and shows (as they say) *in specie,* by naming those works which God will have us to do, and to leave undone. From hence Christ also saith, '*I came not to destroy the law.*' We would willingly," said Luther, "give that man great, yea, royal, entertainment in this world, who could make it out that Moses, through Christ, is utterly taken away. O! then we should quickly see what a fine kind of life

---

* He *hath* Christ who believes in Him. As the manna in the wilderness became the property of him who gathered it, so Christ (the true bread, John, vi. 35.), the gift of God (John, iv. 10.), becomes the property of those who receive Him for the purposes for which He was given by the Father (1 Cor. i. 30.). Christ is *theirs*, with all His saving benefits; their "wisdom, righteousness, sanctification, and redemption."

there would be in the world! But God forbid, and keep us from such errors, and suffer us not to live to see the same!*

"The cause that I," said Luther, "at the first spake and wrote so harshly against the Law, was this: — the Christian church was altogether laden and overheaped with manifold superstitions and false believings, and Christ was altogether darkened and buried. Therefore I was desirous, through God's grace and the word of the Gospel, to deliver and set free good and godly hearts from such tormenting of conscience; but I never rejected the Law."

Anno 1541, certain propositions were brought to Luther, as he sate at dinner, importing that the Law ought not to be preached in the church, because we are not justified thereby: at the sight whereof he was much moved to anger, and said, "Such seducers do come already among our people while we yet live: what will be done when we are gone?"

---

* The heart of man is naturally so averse to the pure and spiritual obedience which the law of God requires, that one who knows something of its holiness, and has not, through the effectual working of the Spirit ("*the spirit of life in Christ Jesus*," Rom. viii. 2.), the love of holiness, must needs wish to be rid of the law altogether. This Luther considers to be the spring of Antinomianism. The Christian who believes that he is "*justified by Christ*," (Is. liii. 12. Gal. ii. 16. Rom. v. 19.), and being "*sprinkled with his blood*," has also received the "sanctification of the spirit unto obedience." (1 Peter, i. 2.) — the Christian is thankful to have the law as "*the lantern to his feet*." Such a one claims *both* the grand privileges of the New Covenant, — sins fully, freely, and for ever, forgiven; and the laws of God written in the mind and heart. He responds to each of the commandments as they are solemnly pronounced, "*Lord, have mercy upon me: and incline my heart to keep this law.*"

"Let us," said he, "give Philip Melancthon the honour due unto him; for he teacheth exceeding well and plainly of the right difference, use, and profit of the Law and Gospel. I, also, teach the same; and have thoroughly handled that point in the Epistle to the Galatians. I doubt his prophecy will prove true which he wrote to me; namely, that a Muntzer * was lurking somewhere. For he that taketh the doctrine of the Law out of the church, doth rend and tear away both political and household government; and when the Law is cast out of the church, then there is no more acknowledging of sins in the world: for the Gospel reproveth not sin, except it maketh use of the office of the Law, which is done spiritually in describing and revealing sins that are committed against God's will and command."

Philip Melancthon demanded of Luther, whether the opinion of Calixtus were to be approved of; namely, that the Gospel of God's grace ought to be continually preached? " for thereby doubtless," said Melancthon, " people would grow worse and worse." † Luther answered him, and said, " We must preach *Gratiam* notwithstanding, because Christ hath commanded it: and although we do, long and often, preach of grace, yet, at the hour of death, they know but little thereof. It nearly concerneth God's honour to preach of grace; and, although men should grow the worse thereby‡, yet

---

* Thomas Muntzer, infamous for his practical Antinomianism.

† We find that, even at the beginning of the Gospel, in the Apostles' days, there were those who abused the grace of God to gratify their sinful desires; using it as " an occasion to the flesh, for a cloak of licentiousness, and even of maliciousness."

‡ 2 Cor. ii. 15, 16.

we must not leave God's word unpreached. But, after that *, then we diligently drive on also with the Ten Commandments, in due time and place.

"The ungodly," said Luther, "suck out of the Gospel only a carnal freedom, and become worse thereby: therefore, not the Gospel, but the Law, belongeth unto them. Even as when my little son John offendeth, if then I should not whip him, but call him to the table, and give him sugar and plums; thereby, indeed, I should make him worse: I should quite spoil him.

"The Gospel is like a mild, fresh, and cool air in the most extreme heat in summer time †; that is, a solace and comfort in the anguish of the conscience: not in the winter time, when it is cold enough already; that is, in the time of peace, when people are secure, and purpose to be justified by their own works.

"But as this heat is produced by the sun, so likewise the troubling and alarming of the conscience must be produced by the preaching of the Law; to the end that we may consider and know that we have offended and transgressed, not against the laws of men, but against the Law of God. The celestial refreshing air likewise (which must raise up the conscience again) must quicken and comfort the same;

---

* As St. Paul, in all his Epistles, layeth the foundation of sound doctrine; after which he exhorteth to a diligent attention to those good works "which God hath fore-ordained that His people should walk in them."—" *Preach thou,*" saith he to Titus, "*the things which become sound doctrine,* that the aged men," &c. &c. — Tit. ii. 1. &c.

† "The shadow of a great rock in a weary land."—Is. xxxii. 2.

not through the comfort of any human works and deservings, but through the preaching of the Gospel.

"Now," said Luther, "when, in this manner, the strength is refreshed and quickened again by the cool air of the Gospel, then we must not be idle, lie down, and snore; that is, when our consciences are settled in peace, quieted, and comforted, through God's Spirit, then we should show also and approve our faith by such good works as God has commanded. But so long as we live in this vale of misery, we shall be plagued and vexed with flies, beetles, vermin, &c.; that is, with the devil, with the world, and with our own flesh: yet we must press through, and not suffer ourselves to recoil."

Concerning Sins, and the Confession and Forgiveness of the same.

"The greatest sins which are committed against God," said Luther, "are those which the four first commandments do contain; those which are committed against the First Table. No man understandeth nor feeleth these sins, but he only that hath the Holy Ghost:—therefore all people are secure and heedless. And although such offenders do draw down God's wrath upon them, and are the devil's own; yet they think and flatter themselves that they are in God's favour: and although they falsify the word and commandments of God, persecute and condemn the same; yet they think in their minds they do that which is pleasing to God, and God's special service.

"Of this Paul affordeth us a notable example; who, being a young man, wanting neither understanding, learning, wisdom, nor power,—having a wonderful zeal and diligence in his religion, and possessing the respect of all the learned, understanding, and seeming holy people, and of all the high authorities in church and state,—yet must he be struck on the ear," said Luther, "so that he fell to the ground, and must hear, 'Saule, Saule, quid persequeris me?' And what must he do now? He must creep to the cross,—must be ashamed of his proceedings, and say, 'I have not rightly understood the law of God:' he must acknowledge and confess his great sins, his unjust dealing, his misbelief, his corrupt understanding, and blindness of heart: he must pronounce his own sentence over himself, and say, 'I am served right.' Therefore, also, he saith, 'Lord, what wilt thou have me to do?' Mark," said Luther; "this man was a master in the law and Moses, and yet now asketh what he should do.

"Over and above these greatest and most grievous sins," said Luther, "we have much upon us which is against our Lord God, and which justly displeaseth Him. There is anger, impatience, covetousness, care and carping for the belly, incontinence, wicked lust, hatred, malice, and other vices. These are great, horrible, and deadly sins, which, every where in the world, go on with power, and get the upper hand. Yet these sins are nothing, compared with the abominable contempt of God's word, which is so common and so great, that, in truth, all the sins before named are not so common; yea, all those sins would remain uncommitted, if we did but love and reverence God's word. But, alas! the whole world in this sin is drowned. No man giveth a fillip for the Gospel, but all do snarl against it;

and although they contemn and persecute it, they hold it for no sin.

"In like manner I behold my wonder in the church, that, among the hearers, one goeth this way, another that way; and, among so great a multitude, there are scarcely ten or twelve who come there with a mind to mark what is delivered in the sermon. Moreover, this sin is so common, so fearful, hellish, and devilish a sin, that people will not acknowledge it to be like other sins; every one holdeth it for a small and light matter to be inattentive at the sermon. Nay, the most part go away, and think that the wine tasteth even as well at the sermon as at other times. Men seem not to make a conscience in the slighting and disregarding of God's word. This is not the case with other sins, as murder, adultery, thieving, &c.: for after these sins, if not at present, yet in due time, doth follow gentleman Grief; so that the heart becomes affrighted, and wishes they had not been committed: but not to hear God's word with attention and diligence, of this no man maketh reckoning. Therefore it is a sin so fearful, that that land and people where it is committed must and will be destroyed. For seeing it remaineth unacknowledged, there can follow no repentance, no remission, nor amendment. And even so it went with Jerusalem, Rome, Greece, and other kingdoms.

"And the same," said Luther, "will fall upon Germany, if we do not repent in time: for our sins do continually cry up to heaven, and will not suffer God to rest, but that of necessity He must be angry, and say, ' I have presented you with my well beloved Son (my most precious and highest treasure), and He would willingly talk with you, would teach and instruct you to everlasting life; but I have no creature that will hear Him: therefore, I must needs let my punishment proceed and go on.' As the Lord himself witnesseth (John, iii.), '*This is the condemnation; that light is come into the world, and men loved darkness rather than light, because their deeds were evil.*'

" As if He would say, ' All other things I will willingly conceal; but this is the condemnation and the break-neck of the world; namely, that I have sent my Word, and they have not regarded it. They are full of other sins beside this, of which I would willingly help and cure them through my word, but they refuse to be helped. Therefore, seeing they will not hear my word, let them hear the devil's word; and they will find at last what they have gotten thereby.'

" In this way went it with the Christians towards the East, in those excellent, great, and fair countries which the Turk hath now brought under his rule. Hungary, also, is now almost gone, where God's word hath been and is contemned: therefore they must now hear the Turk with his Alcoran. For seeing that this is the highest and greatest sin, there belongeth to it the greatest and sharpest punishment."

" Christ well knew," said Luther, " how to make a distinction between sins: for we see finely in the Gospel how harsh He was towards the Pharisees, by reason of their great hatred and envy against Him and His word. How mild, on the other hand, and how friendly, He showed Himself towards the woman who was a sinner. This gentleman, Envy, will needs rob Christ of His word: he is a bitter enemy unto Christ, and persecuteth, and, in the end, killeth Him, But the woman, as the greatest sinner, taketh hold on the word, heareth Christ, and believeth that He is the only Saviour of the world. She washeth his feet; anointeth and strengtheneth Him with a costly water: from whence Christ said to the Pharisee which invited Him, '*Thou gavest me no kiss*,' &c. Therefore let us acknowledge ourselves to be sinners, and humble ourselves; and not be sinners, proud and puffed up."

" The sins of common simple people are nothing, compared with such as are committed by great and high persons that are in spiritual and temporal offices.

" What are the sins done by them, that, according to law and justice, are hanged; or the offences of a poor whore, to be compared to the sins of a false teacher, who daily maketh away with many poor people, and killeth them both in body and soul? But sins committed against the First Table of God's Ten Commandments are not so much regarded by the world, as those which are committed against the Second Table.

" But what is sin * ?" said Luther. " Sin is called a burden, which troubleth and maketh heavy the conscience before God; which taketh one captive, and condemneth him to eternal death. Such are not sins which are devised and feigned by the Pope and his jugglers, the bishops; as eating flesh on forbidden days, &c. Those are new devised sins and righteousnesses, which belong not to Christ's government; neither do

* " *Sin* is the transgression of the law" of God; *guilt*, or consciousness of sin, which Luther here speaks of as a burden, is the sense and feeling which a man has of the punishment which his sin deserves, and to which it is liable at the hand of God.

they condemn any creature: for God hath nowhere forbidden or commanded the same."

"When David sinned with Bathsheba, committed adultery, and slew Uriah, then he went on securely; he troubled not himself much about it, for the sin slept; yea, it was altogether dead in him: but when Nathan came, and struck thunder into his heart, and said, '*Thou art the man,*' then the sin began to live, to stir, and to be quick in David's heart. But he was comforted again by Nathan, who said unto him, '*Thou shalt not die.*' Therefore to the forgiveness of sins belongeth also *conscientia peccati*, that we feel our sins, acknowledge and confess the same."

"The punishments of sins are not alike," said Luther; "some are greater and heavier than others. Our Saviour Christ declareth the same. It is altogether an ungodly opinion of those who allege all sins are alike (as Sebastian Franck teacheth). I, Martin Luther, say, the sins of Paul were different from the sins of Nero.

"Christ himself," said Luther, "instituted this office (Absolution), through which all the sins in the whole world shall be forgiven, so far forth that they be right sins, be confessed, and the word believed: for no Absolution can be pronounced to those that make foolish and fanciful sins; nor to such in whose hearts the sins do not live, which are slumbering and sleepy sins; nor to those who regard them not. Thou, therefore, whosoever thou art, must sing that psalm which David sung:—'*I acknowledge my transgressions, and my sin is ever before me. Against Thee only have I sinned, and done this evil in Thy sight.*'"

"The forgiveness of sins is declared only in God's word; and there we must also seek for it: for the Absolution is only grounded on God's promises. God forgiveth thee thy sins, not because thou feelest them, and art sad and sorry, for that the sin itself produceth; and it cannot, as the Pope teacheth, deserve any thing at all: but He forgiveth thy sins, because He is merciful, and because He hath promised to forgive sins, for the sake of Christ, His dearly beloved Son, and causeth His word of absolution to be pronounced over thee; namely, '*Be of good cheer, thy sins are forgiven thee.*' Believest thou this? then hast thou, most certain, the forgiveness of sins.

"Therefore," said Luther, "hold thee fast to the word: for it is decreed that we can make no atonement for sins, nor overcome them with our works, with sorrow, confession, penance, or satisfaction; but when we have done all that we possibly can, yea, though we tormented ourselves to death, yet all is vain and labour lost, as in Popedom hath been well found. Now, he that cometh not to that word which includeth therein the forgiveness of sins, then must he come to the word wherein they are detained.

"Christ," said Luther, "laid them both in the Apostles' mouths. If now thou wilt have forgiveness of sins, then thou must fetch it out of the apostles' mouths, out of the mouths of preachers, or of Christ*:

---

* How did the paralytic (Matt. ix.) receive forgiveness of sins? Out of the mouth of Christ, saying, "*Be of good cheer, thy sins be forgiven thee.*" So also the sinful woman in Luke, vii. How received the gaoler forgiveness? Out of the mouth of Paul, who testified, "*Believe in the Lord Jesus Christ, and thou shalt be saved.*" How received Paul forgiveness? Out of the mouth of Ananias.— How the Æthiopian? Out of the mouth of Philip.— How the saints

if thou dost not fetch them from thence, then thou obtainest not forgiveness of sins, although thou performest the best works; yea, though thou sufferest thyself to be slain, yet are thy sins detained: therefore take now which way thou wilt."

The Character of God's People.

"God will have His servants to be repenting sinners, such as stand in fear of His anger, of the devil, death, and hell, and that do believe in Christ. 'Therefore,' saith David in the Thirty-fourth Psalm, '*The Lord is nigh unto them that are of a broken heart, and saveth those that are of a humble spirit.*' And in Isaiah, lxvi., '*I dwell with him that is poor, and of a contrite spirit, and that trembleth at my word.*' The same doth the poor sinner on the cross. St. Peter did so when he had denied Christ; Mary Magdalene, that was possessed of the devil; St. Paul, the persecutor, &c. All these were sorrowful for their sins; and such shall have forgiveness of their sins, and be God's servants. The great prelates," said Luther, " the puffed-up saints, the rich usurers, the oxen-drovers, who seek such unconscionable gain, &c.,—these are not God's servants, neither were it good they should be; for then no poor people could have access to God for them: neither were it for God's honour that such should be His servants; for they would ascribe all honour and praise

---

at Colossæ? Out of the mouth of Epaphras, who declared to them, "*the word of the truth of the Gospel.*" In each case faith received the forgiveness from the mouth of Christ, or of those who were intrusted by Him with "*the ministry of reconciliation.*"

to themselves, and say, '*We are they*,' &c. Nevertheless, there are some great kings and princes that do call upon God, and serve Him from their hearts. These, although they be rich and powerful, rule over land and people, yet are they poor in spirit; that is, they acknowledge themselves, in good earnest, to be poor sinners, praying with David, that great king, '*Miserere mei, Domine*.' Also they implore and say, '*Enter not into judgment with thy servant, O Lord*.'"

"The Scripture nameth the faithful a people of God's saints. It is sin and shame," said Luther, "that we should forget this glorious name and title. From hence it is that the Papists are such upright sinners; they will not be sinners. And again, they will not be saints, nor held so to be. And in this way it goeth, on both sides, untowardly and crossly with them; so that, in fact, they neither believe the Gospel which comforteth, nor the Law which punisheth.

"But here one may say, 'The sins which we daily commit do offend and anger God: how, then, can we be holy?' To this," said Luther, "I answer: A mother's love to her child is much stronger than her aversion to the child's scurf and excrements. Even so, God's love towards us, His people, is far too strong to be overcome by our filthiness and uncleanness. Therefore, although we be sinners, yet we lose not, on this account, the childhood, neither do we fall from grace by reason of our sins.

"Yea, one may say again, 'We sin without ceasing; and where sin is, there the Holy Spirit is not: therefore we are not holy, because the Holy Spirit, who maketh holy, is not in us.' To this," said Luther, "I answer again: the Text saith plainly, '*The Holy Ghost shall glorify me; for He shall receive of mine, and shall show it unto you.'* Now where Christ is, there is the Holy Spirit. But Christ is in the faithful*, although they have and feel sins, and do confess them, and with sorrow of heart mourn over them: therefore sins do not separate Christ from those who believe."

"The God of the Turks helpeth no longer, nor further (as they think), than when they be good people; and it is the same with the God of the Papists. But when Turk and Papist begin to feel their sins and unworthiness (as is the case in times of trial and temptations, and in death's need), then they tremble and despair. This is the faith of the Pope and of the Turk.†

"But a true Christian saith, 'I believe in Jesus Christ, my Lord and Saviour, who gave Himself for my sins, and is at God's right hand, and intercedeth for me. Fall I into sin? (as, alas! oftentimes I do,) so am I sorry for it; I rise again, through hope of mercy, and am an enemy unto sin, &c.: for faith giveth the honour to God, that He can and will perform what He promiseth; namely, to make sinners righteous.' (Rom. iv.)

"But is it not to be lamented," said Luther, "that we are so wavering and weak in faith? Christ giveth Himself unto us with all that He is and hath: He offereth unto us His celestial, everlasting wealth; as,

---

* Luther asserts this as an admitted truth, as, indeed, it must be by all who seriously submit themselves to the authority of Scripture. Compare John, xv. 4. 6. and Luke, xxii. 32., also 2 Cor. xiii. 5., with 1 John, i. 8. 10. and ii. 1, 2.

† It need hardly be added,—and of every ignorant misguided Protestant;—the inference is too plain to be mistaken.

His grace, remission of sins, everlasting righteousness, life, and salvation: He nameth us His brethren and co-heirs; yet, nevertheless, we are, in time of necessity, affrighted, and do flee from Him, when we have most need of His help and comfort.

"This putteth me in mind," said Luther, "of a thing that happened to me in my youthful time. At Shrovetide (as was usual), myself and another boy went about to sing before people's doors for puddings. On one of these days, a certain townsman, merrily disposed, came towards us, crying out, 'What do these rascal boys want?' and with such words he ran towards us, having in his hands two puddings, which he offered us. But we, being scared by his first gestures in running and calling, ran and flew from him, who, all the while, intended us no harm, but intended to do us good. Afterwards, seeing our mistake, and that he might not fail of his kind purpose, he called to us with a mild voice; so that, at last, we turned to him, and received his puddings.

"Even thus do we carry ourselves towards our loving Lord God, who spared not His own Son, but gave Him up for us, and with Him hath given us all things;—we fly from Him, and think He is not our gracious God, but a stern and severe judge."

"Upright and true saints are all the servants of the church, temporal princes and magistrates, parents, children, masters and mistresses of families, house servants, and what state or calling else is instituted and ordained by God; who, first of all, do hold and believe that Christ is their wisdom, righteousness, sanctification, and redemption; and who, afterwards, do perform in their vocation what God commandeth and layeth upon them, and do abstain from the lusts and sins of the flesh.

"But inasmuch as all are not alike strong, and that in some still many faults, weaknesses, and offences, are seen and found, this doth neither hurt nor hinder them of their sanctification, so far forth as they sin not of evil purpose and premeditation, but only out of weakness. For a Christian, indeed, doth feel the lusts of the flesh, but he resisteth them from being accomplished; and although now and then he doth oversee, stumble, and fall into sin, yet it is forgiven him when he riseth again, and holdeth himself on Christ, who will '*not have the lost sheep hunted away, but sought after.*' (Luke xv. Ezek. xxxiv.)"

CHAPTER V.

TOUCHING THE CHURCH, AND THE MINISTRY THEREOF; AND HEREIN CONCERNING PREACHING.

Of the Church, and its Condition and Appearance in this World.

"THE great and worldly-wise people," said Luther, "take offence at the poor and mean form of the Church, which is subject to many offences, transgressions, and sects, wherewith she is plagued; for they dream that the Church is altogether pure, holy, blameless, that she is God's dove, and therefore, &c. True it is," said Luther, "that the Church, in the eyes and sight of God, hath such an esteem; but in the sight of men she is like unto her bridegroom, Christ Jesus, '*whose visage*,' saith Isaiah, '*was marred more than any man's:*' she is hacked, torn, spitted on, derided, and crucified.

"The similitude of the upright and true Church is a poor silly sheep; but the similitude of the false and hypocritical church is a serpent, a poisonous adder, which now we find by experience: for how bitter is the hatred which the Popish adversaries bear towards the upright, true, and pure religion. Cocleus wrote first unto me," said Luther, "and encouraged me in the Gospel; but afterwards he himself became an adder."

"The form and aspect of the world," said Luther, on another occasion, "is like a paradise; but the true Christian Church, in the eyes of the world, is foul, deformed, and offensive: nevertheless, in God's sight, she is precious, she is high, and dearly esteemed of. Aaron, the high priest, appeared gloriously in the temple, with his ornaments and rich attire, with odoriferous and sweet-smelling perfume; but, on the contrary, Christ appeared in a most mean, simple, and contemptible aspect.

"Wherefore," said Luther, "I regard nothing at all, I am by no means troubled, that the world hath so base an esteem of the Church. What do I care," said Luther, "if the usurers, the nobility, gentry, citizens, country people, covetous paunches, and roaring companions, contemn me, and esteem of me as of dirt; I shall in due time esteem of them as little. We must not suffer ourselves to be deceived, nor troubled at what the world think of us. *Virtus est placuisse bonis.*"

"God beholdeth not in His Church and assembly aught that is evil, or that hath a deformed aspect; for He beholdeth therein only His dearly beloved Son, Christ. Him He loveth so entirely, that, by reason of such love, He beholdeth in his bride, for which he gave Himself, altogether that which is amiable and full of beauty; for he hath cleansed her with the washing of water by the word. (Ephes. v.)

"Nothing less is seen by men in the Church, than that which is written of her; namely, that she is the spouse of Christ: therefore," said Luther, " we must open the eyes of the heart, and lift them up on high, and look upon the Church, — not according to the outward view, or according to our natural sense, wisdom, and understanding (for we are sensible of our sins and the devil's affrightings),— but we must judge touching these celestial blessings according to God's word and promise."

" If any enquire why the Church is in misery here on earth, I answer: First, to put us in mind and admonish us that we are exiled servants, banished out of Paradise for Adam's sake; secondly, that we may always bear in mind the misery of the Son of God, who was made man for our sake, took upon Him our flesh and blood (yet without sin), walked in this vale of misery Himself, suffered for us, died and rose again from the dead, and so brought us again to our paternal home, from whence we were driven; thirdly, that we may be reminded, that our habitation is not in this world, but we are here only pilgrims, and that there is another, an everlasting life, prepared for us."

" The upright and true Church," said Luther, " is distinguished from the false in this manner: the true Church teacheth that sins are forgiven merely out of God's grace and mercy, only for Christ's sake, without our works and merits, to those who from their hearts do confess their sins, and with their hearts do steadfastly believe in Christ; but the false church ascribeth all to the works and merits of people, and teacheth that they must always stand in doubt of the remission of their sins and of their salvation. Therefore," said Luther, " let us pray in the Church, with the Church, and for the Church: for there are three things * which support the Church, and properly pertain to it; first, to teach truly; secondly, to pray diligently; and thirdly, to suffer patiently."

" We tell our Lord God plainly," said Luther, " that if He will have His Church, He must look how to maintain and defend it: for what can we do to protect or uphold it? And then, if we were able to do so, we should become the proudest asses under heaven. But God saith, *I* say it, *I* do it; it is God only that speaketh, and doth what he pleaseth: He doth nothing according to the fancies of the ungodly, nor which they hold for upright and good."

" It is," said Luther, " impossible that the Christian and true Church should be supported without shedding of blood, for her adversary the devil is a liar and a murderer; but the Church groweth and increaseth through blood, she is sprinkled with blood, she is spoiled and bereaved of her blood. Tertullian, the ancient teacher, saith, exceeding well, ' *Cruore sanctorum rigatur Ecclesia.*' Therefore, saith the psalm, " *We are as sheep appointed to be slain;*' that is, who daily are slaughtered for Christ's sake. And truly," said Luther, " it would grieve me if I should carry my blood into the grave.

" I much marvel," said Luther, " that the Pope boasteth and extolleth his church at Rome to be the chiefest, when the church at Jerusalem is plainly the mother; for there the doctrine was first revealed and set forth by Christ the Son of God himself, and by His Apostles. After this church was the church at

* 1 Tim. iii. 15. Luke, xviii. 7. Luke, xxi. 19. Rev. i. 9.

And truly

I should car

Luther,

church at R

at Jerusalem

ctrine was

Son of God

church was

AND THE MINISTRY THEREOF.

[...]: for there are three things which support [...], and properly pertain to it; first, to teach [...], to pray diligently; and thirdly, to suffer [...]

[...] our Lord God plainly," said Luther, "that [...] have His Church, He must look how to [...] defend it: for what can we do to protect it? And then, if we were able to do so, we [...] the proudest asses under heaven. But [...] say it, I do it: it is God only that standeth [...] he pleaseth: He doth nothing according [...] of the ungodly, nor which they hold for [...] good."

[...] Luther. "Impossible that the Christian [...] should be supported without shedding [...] adversary the devil is a liar and a mur[derer]. [...] Church groweth and increaseth by [...] sprinkled with blood, she is spread and [...] her blood. Tertullian, the ancient teacher, [...] well, Cruore unctorum reparatur Ec[clesia]. [...]fore, saith the psalm, "We are as [...] to be slain"; that is, who daily are [...] for Christ's sake. And truly," said Lu[ther] [...] grieve me if I should carry my blood [...]

[...]vel," said Luther, "that the Pope [...] extolleth his church at Rome to be the [...] the church at Jerusalem is plainly the [...] the doctrine was first revealed and by [...] the Son of God himself, and by Christ [...] After this church was the church at [...]

15. Luke, xviii. 7. Luke, xxi. 18. Acts i.

how that *A. B.* hath been admonished; first, by myself in private, afterwards also by two chaplains, thirdly, by two aldermen and churchwardens, and those of the assembly, yet notwithstanding he will not desist from his sinful kind of life. Wherefore I earnestly desire you to assist and advise, to kneel down with me, and let us pray against him, and deliver him over to the devil,' &c.

"Hereby," said Luther, "we should, doubtless, prevail so far, that people would not live in such public sin and shame; for this would be a strict excommunication (not like the Pope's money-bulls), and profitable to the church. But when such a person were converted, and became better, then we might absolve him again.

"These are the keys of the church, wherewith sinners are bound and loosed again."

Of the Sacrament of the Lord's Supper.

"The operative cause of this sacrament," said Luther, "is the word and institution of Christ who ordained it. The substance is bread and wine; the form is the true body and blood of Christ, which is spiritually received by faith; the final cause of instituting the same is the benefit and fruit, in that, being strengthened in faith, we doubt not that Christ's body and blood were given and shed for us, and that our sins, by Christ's death, are certainly forgiven. Now these graces and benefits we have obtained, in

---

* 1 Cor. v. 4, 5. 1 Tim. i. 20.

that He is our Saviour, not a stern and angry judge; our Redeemer and Deliverer, not an accuser, or a bailiff that hath taken us prisoners. For in Adam we are altogether sinners, and guilty of everlasting death, and condemned; but now, by the blood of Christ, we are redeemed, justified, and sanctified. Let us therefore only take hold of this by faith."

Question was made, in the course of conversation, touching the words, "*Given for you*," &c., whether they were to be understood of present administering, when the sacrament was held and distributed, or when it was offered and accomplished on the cross. Luther gave his opinion thus:—"I like it best when it is understood of the present administering; though it may be understood as fulfilled on the cross. It hindereth not, that Christ saith, ' *Which is given for you*,' when He should have said, ' Which shall be given for you;' for Christ is *hodie et heri*—to-day and yesterday. ' I, saith Christ, ' am He that doth it.' Therefore I like it well, that ' *is given* ' be understood in such a manner as to show the use of the work." It was also demanded whether honour and reverence were to be shown to the sacrament of the altar. Luther answered and said, " When I am at the altar and do receive the sacrament, I bow my knees in honour thereof; but in bed I receive it lying. The elevation*," said Luther, " is utterly to be rejected by reason of the adoring thereof. Some churches have seen that we have put down the

---

* The elevation is the lifting up of the consecrated wafer, or host, after the priest has said the words, " *Hoc est corpus meum*," to be adored, as the present God, by all beholders.

elevation, and have followed our example, which giveth us great satisfaction."

Dr. Justus Jonas asked Luther, how he should conduct himself towards certain persons in his congregation, who in the space of twenty years had not received the holy communion? Luther said, "Let them go to the devil*, and when they die in that manner, let them be buried under the gallows." He asked further, if they were to be forced to do it? Luther said, "No: for that were papistical: let them be admonished. Will they hearken and do it, well and good; if not, let them alone."

"These words, '*Drink ye all of it*,' do concern (say the Papists) only the priests. Then," said Luther, "these words must also concern only the priests, where Christ saith, '*Ye are clean, but not all;*' that is, not the priests."

---

* Were Luther judged, in this instance, according to the first expression of his feelings, he would receive, from many, a hard sentence. Luther is like a painter, sketching rapidly the bold outline of his first conceptions. Sometimes he would (as here) fill up and soften the picture: sometimes he would leave it unfinished. His hearers, if familiar with him, would quickly apprehend his meaning, or come at it (like Dr. Jonas in this case) by a second question. Others might think over it, and, if they would, might learn.

Viewing his friend's question in relation to the offence, and the contempt put upon the Lord by those who thus neglected His ordinance, Luther made his first answer; considering it in its reference to the offender, and the discipline of the church, he made the second.

OF THE MINISTRY OF THE CHURCH, PREACHING, &c.

Luther giving Orders.

On Sunday, April 22. 1540, Luther gave orders to Benedict Casilio; on which occasion he read the sentence in Acts, xiii., how the hands were laid upon the apostles Paul and Barnabas: also in Acts, xx., how St. Paul warned the bishops and ministers at Miletus to take heed of wolves, &c. He likewise read 1 Tim. iii. and Titus, i., how a bishop should be called and qualified. After which he said, "My loving brother Benedict, thou art by God ordained to be a true servant of Jesus Christ at Torgau, to further His holy name through the pure doctrine of the Gospel, to which, through God's power, we call and send thee, as God hath called and sent us. Therefore watch earnestly, be diligent, pray to God to keep and preserve thee in this high vocation, and that thou mayest not fall away, not be seduced by false doctrine, by heresies and sects, nor through thy own cogitations; but may begin the same in God's fear, true diligence, and continual prayer, and finish it aright in Christ." Afterwards he laid his hands upon him, and, kneeling, he prayed aloud the Lord's Prayer. Then rising up again, he lifted up his eyes to heaven and said, "Lord God, heavenly, merciful Father, who hast commanded to pray, to seek and to knock, and hast promised to hear us when we call upon Thee in the name of Thy Son. Upon these Thy promises we depend, and pray Thee to send this servant of Thy word, Benedict, into Thy harvest; to

elevation, and have followed our ... ...nce, to open the
us great satisfaction." ...urse of Thy word,
...aised, Thy kingdom
...grow. Amen. There-
Dr. Justus Jonas aske... ...ish thee happiness and
conduct himself towards ... ...r, and in confidence in the
gregation, who in the ... "Now pray we the Holy
received the holy c... ...
them go to the d... ...
manner, let them ... ...
asked further, i... ...yer for Ministers.
Luther said, " ... ...come to that pass in Germany," said
be admonish... ...in Spain and France, where no preachers
and good; ... ...nners up and down, as in former times
... ...ioners were; these went up and down the
"The ... ...d preached one week in the time of Lent
the P... ... n, wherewith the people were fain to con-
"the... ...elves for a whole year. That town which
whe... ...gave a friar a hundred guilders to preach the
not ... Lent. Therefore, loving brethren, let us pray
...this great office, and for those engaged therein,
...e see with what earnest zeal Christ prayed, before
...called the apostles. Satan, through tyrants, se-
...cers, and false brethren in this last time, layeth hold
...the ministers with earnest power. Therefore pray
...that our Lord would show His strength and power in
...our weakness. It is high time to pray."

"An upright shepherd and minister must, by edifi-
cation, increase his flock, and also must resist, and defend; otherwise if resisting be absent, then the wolf
devoureth the sheep: the rather where they be fat
and well fed. Therefore," said Luther, " St. Paul
earnestly presseth Titus, that a bishop should be able,

by sound doctrine, both to exhort and to convince the gainsayers; that is, to resist false doctrine. A minister must be a soldier and a shepherd together."

A Minister's Honour.

Anno 1541. Luther discoursed much concerning the ambition of certain ministers, and said, " God oftentimes layeth upon the necks of such haughty divines all manner of crosses and plagues, thereby to humble them; and such are well and rightly served, for they will have honour, which belongeth to our Lord God alone. When we are found true in our vocation, then we have reaped honour enough, though not in this life, yet in that to come: there we shall be crowned with the unchangeable crown of honour, which, as St. Paul saith, ' *is laid up for us*.' But here on earth we must seek for no honour, for it is written, ' *Woe unto you when all men shall speak well of you.*' We belong not to this life," said Luther, " but are called to another far better. The world loveth that which is their own, but we must content ourselves with what they bestow upon us; namely, with scoffing, flouting, and contempt. For myself," said Luther, " I desire no honour nor crown, here on earth, but I will have retribution from God, the just Judge, in heaven. It is said to this day concerning us preachers, ' *Retribuunt mihi mala pro bonis.*'"

" From the year of our Lord 1518, to this day," said Luther, " every Maundy Thursday, at Rome, have I been excommunicated and cast into hell by the Pope, yet live I still. For every year on Maundy Thursday (*quando Christus instituit cœnam*) all heretics are excommunicated at Rome, among whom I am always the first and chiefest. This do they on that blessed, sanctified, day, when they ought rather to be rendering thanks to God, for the great benefit of His holy supper, and for His bitter death and passion. This is the honour and crown which we must expect and have in this world. God sometimes can endure honour in lawyers and physicians; but in divines He will in nowise suffer ambition or greediness of honour, for a boasting and ambitious preacher soon contemneth Christ, who with His blood hath redeemed the whole world."

A Minister's Spirit.

"He must be of a high and great spirit," said Luther, "that undertaketh to serve the people in body and soul, while nevertheless he suffers the highest unthankfulness from them, and the greatest trouble. Therefore Christ said to Peter, '*Simon, son of Jonas, lovest thou me?*' He repeated it three times together; afterwards He said, '*Feed my sheep:*' 'twas as if he had said, 'Wilt thou be an upright minister and shepherd?' then *love* alone must do it: *thy love to me* must do the deed, otherwise it is impossible; for who can endure unthankfulness? to study away his wealth and health, and afterwards to lay himself open to the greatest danger and unthankfulness of the wicked world; therefore He saith, 'It is very needful that thou lovest me.'"

The right Etymology of the Word "Bishop."

"The office and charge of a bishop," said Luther, "is a great business; it is a matter of high importance for one to have committed to his custody and only a herd, not of goats or swine, not of silver or gold, but the herd and sheep of Christ. In the high German tongue I can find no word that plainly and properly expresseth this word Bishop. As for the Greek word σκοπεω, it means, *to have regard, to have a care, or diligently to mark;* from whence ministers and preachers are named Curates, *i. e.* Carers, or Sorrowers, for the Souls, Stewards, and Shepherds. It is originally not unfitly translated *bishop,* that is, *by sheep;* because they ought always to be *by the sheep,* continually to look unto them," &c.

Scandalous Ministers.

"Preachers and ministers that give offence, ought to be imprisoned," said Luther, "and put from their office. I have obtained of the Prince Elector that a prison shall be built for the punishment and discipline of offensive ministers and preachers."

Concerning the due and honourable Maintenance of Church Ministers.

"Some," said Luther, "out of a mere devilish hate, do calumniate and blaspheme the office of preaching, because some certain honourable stipends and wages are bestowed upon the ministers of the church, being made and ordered according to the ability of the church's revenue. If we rightly considered and furthered the good and profit of the church, should we not rather try to provide an honest maintenance for the church officers, than allow things to be as they are in some places, where they can hardly defend themselves and theirs from hunger. For such misery affrighteth many (especially the best wits among young and toward people) from the ministry.

"It is not every one that hath the gift, with joy, courage, and constancy, to be content to take the wages of unthankfulness, of hate, and hunger, for the hardest and most heavy labour. Nothing can be more grievous and intolerable to an honest housefather," said Luther, "than to see his wife and children suffer hunger, who otherwise (if he had betaken himself to some other calling) might have lived better, and with more credit.

"It will surely come to pass," said Luther, "that the church must be wasted, through such want and misery as her ministers endure, and must be served with unlearned asses. Of this there are already very evident examples; for we see how the pure doctrine is darkened through the government of unlearned people, and all liberal arts growing into contempt.

"Therefore no man should stumble, or be offended, that now and then good and godly rulers do well and sufficiently provide for the church's true ministers, and honestly maintain them. Nay, we ought much more to complain, to bewail, and sigh, that the greatest part of princes and rulers do not seriously regard the true and pure religion, nor provide for posterity, who, through such miserableness, will have either the most unlearned church rulers and ministers, or else none at all.

"Therefore we are in duty bound to give unto good, true, and Christian teachers and church servants their wages, and honestly to provide for and maintain them. But to abuse the office of the ministry in seeking only honour, favour, wealth, and easy days, the same is justly to be condemned. It is against such false teachers, who flatter sinful great princes and others for filthy lucre's sake, that the prophet uttereth that sharp sentence:—' *The priests thereof teach for hire, and the prophets thereof divine for money.*' (Micah, iii. 11.) Otherwise, no man ought to cast it in a preacher's teeth that he taketh wages; for the Scripture saith, '*The labourer is worthy of his hire*' (Luke, x. 7.); and, moreover, certifieth us that it is the very ordinance of the Lord, ' *That they which preach the Gospel should live of the Gospel.*' " (1 Cor. ix.)

There came one day to Wittemberg a minister from Isenach, who complained to the professors of his great poverty and misery. Philip Melancthon said unto him, " Loving brother, have patience for a time: hitherto we have striven concerning ministers' matrimony; and, having obtained that, we intend now to strive for the honour and dignity, and afterwards we will also strive and labour to secure the livings." *

* Even in England the church property was very greatly diminished at the Reformation; and what is at present employed in the maintenance of church ministers is but a portion of the immense wealth amassed by the Roman Catholic clergy, and which, but for the statute of mortmain, would have been greater still. When we consider that the church lands, independent of tithes, were situated in the most fertile and cultivated districts, and that the greater part of what is now in cultivation was then unimproved and unproductive, there may be more truth than is commonly supposed in the statement, that the church revenues were nearly a third of those of the whole kingdom. It is said by those who desire to degrade the Protestant Establishment, that the revenues of the church were formerly employed to support the poor; and, no doubt, they did support many poor, and *made* many poor by supporting them, as it may be seen in Roman Catholic countries to this day, where multitudes live upon the broken victuals from

Whereupon Luther said, "To the poor the Gospel is preached; for the rich regard it not. If the Pope did not maintain us with that which he hath gotten (though much against his will), we might even starve. The Pope hath swallowed down stolen goods, and he must spew them all up again, as Job saith. He must give the same to those to whom he wisheth nothing good: although scarcely the fiftieth part is used to the church's profit, the rest he lavisheth away; we obtain little more than fragments under the table. But we are assured of better wages after this life; and if our hope were not fixed thereon, then were we the most miserable wretches of all people."

A Minister's Learning.

"One knife," said Luther, "cutteth better than another; so likewise one that hath learned languages and good arts, can better and more distinctly read and teach than another. But in that many of them (as Erasmus of Rotterdam and other learned men) are well skilled in languages and good arts, and yet do err very grievously, we must distinguish and separate the

---

the tables of the monks. But when it is remembered, that the population of England, in Elizabeth's reign, was estimated, by Guicciardini, the historian, at no more than 2,000,000, we may conclude, that the poor, sturdy beggars and all, might be supported at little more cost than that of furnishing the monks with a fresh and abundant meal daily, enough and to spare. It was, indeed, a very different state of things from what we have in England now, when its population has increased to 14,000,000, and the whole income of the church, would not, perhaps, pay half the poor rates.

thing from the abuse of it, even as Job distinguished, when he answered his wife who troubled him:—'*Thou speakest*,' said he, '*as one of the foolish women speaketh.*' This speech pleaseth me well," said Luther; "because he made a difference between the creature and the abuse."

OF PREACHING.

The best Preachers and best Hearers.

"I," said Luther, "esteem those to be the best preachers who teach the common people and youth most plainly and simply, without subtlety, screwed words, or enlargements. Christ taught the people by plain and simple parables. In like manner, those are the best hearers that willingly do hear God's word simply and plainly; and, although they be weak in faith, yet they are to be helped forward; for God will bear with weakness, if it be acknowledged, and that we creep again to the cross, and pray to God for grace, and amend ourselves."

Of powerful Preaching.

Doctor Forstemius asked Luther from whence it was that some sermons were spoken so powerfully, that both god-fearing and ungodly men were moved thereby, and laid them to heart. He answered and said, "It proceedeth from the first commandment of God,—'*I am the Lord thy God;* Against the ungodly

I am a strong and a jealous God; and towards the good and godly, I am a merciful God; I do well to them, and show them mercy.' For this will have us preach hell fire to the proud and haughty, and paradise to the good and godly; to reprove the wicked, and to comfort the good, &c. The instruments and worktools of God are different, and not alike; even as one knife cutteth better than another. The sermons of Dr. Cordatus and Dr. Cruciger are taken more to heart than the preaching of many others."

Luther's Preparation of a Sermon.

Luther preached at Dresden before the Prince Elector, the Prince of Anhalt, and other princes, out of 1 Tim. i., a sermon which was afterwards printed. Philip Melancthon, being then present, asked Luther, " If he had comprehended in his memory every point of that sermon before he preached it? for," said he, " it was a most excellent admonition to the highest service of God,—the hearing of His word." Thereupon Luther answered and said, " I use not to collect and fasten every point in particular, but only the chief and head points, on which the contents of the whole sermon depend; as, for example, in this sermon, I directed the admonition to the hearing of God's word, as His chief service. Afterwards, in speaking, such things fall into my mind as before I never thought of; for if I should comprehend every word which I deliver, and should speak of every point in particular, then I should not so briefly run through. I much commend the expertness of Dr. Gaspar Cruciger, who excellently comprehendeth and catcheth up his words. I hold," said Luther, " that he goeth far beyond me."

Long Sermons.

"I would not have preachers torment their hearers," said Luther, " and detain them with long and tedious preaching; for the delight of hearing vanisheth, and the preachers hurt themselves by it. Dr. Pommer ought to be reproved by reason of his long sermons; howsoever I know that he useth it not of purpose, but only from an erroneous custom."

Rambling Preachers.

Luther's wife said unto him, "Sir, I heard your cousin John Palmer (who attended on Luther) preach this afternoon in the parish church, and I understood him better than I do Dr. Pommer, who is held to be a very excellent preacher." Whereupon Luther made her this answer, " John Palmer preacheth as ye women use to talk; for what cometh into your minds the same ye also speak. A preacher ought to remain by the propounded text*, and should deliver that which he hath before him, to the end the people may well understand the same. But such a preacher as will speak every thing that cometh to his mind, I liken to a maid that goeth to market, when another maid meeteth her, then they make a stand, and hold together a goose-market, &c. Even so likewise do those preachers, *qui*

---

* Some preachers seem to choose a text to suit their sermon; so that in the delivery of the sermon, the hearers forget that he has any text at all, or think that the preacher must have forgotten it. Luther would have the text always kept in view, the sermon being made to set forth and apply the truths contained in the text. The text is the jewel, the sermon the setting, which exhibits it to the best advantage. — The reader will excuse the repetition of this anecdote in this place.

nimis procul discedunt a preposito, and think to speak all at once."

Preacher's Defects.

"The defects of a preacher are soon spied. Let a preacher be endued with ten virtues, and have but one fault, that one fault will eclipse and darken all his virtues and gifts, so evil is the world in these times. Dr. Justus Jonas hath all the good qualities that a man may have; yet by reason that he only often hummeth and spitteth, therefore the people cannot bear with that good and honest man."

Luther's Recommendation of Cellarius.

The senate of Nuremberg sent to Wittemberg, and called Master John Cellarius to be their preacher. Luther wrote by him letters of recommendation to the senate; then said he to Cellarius, "I will recommend and praise thee, though thou deservest not so much as I purpose to say of thee; yet thou must use diligence to reach that mark, for thou art now bound by my recommendation. In this manner God said to Moses (when Joshua was called to supply his place after his death), '*Put some of thine honour upon Joshua,*' " &c.

Qualities of a good Preacher.

"A good preacher," said Luther, "should have these properties and virtues:—

"*First,* To preach orderly.

"*Secondly,* He should have a ready wit.

"*Thirdly,* He should be eloquent.

"Fourthly, He should have a good voice.

"Fifthly, A good remembrance.

"Sixthly, He should know when to make an end.

"Seventhly, He should be sure of his things.

"Eighthly, He should venture and engage body and blood, wealth and honour, by the word.

"Ninthly, He should suffer himself to be mocked and buffeted of every one."

A Preacher to please the World.

"First, He must be learned.

"Secondly, He must have a fine delivery.

"Thirdly, He must have neat and quaint words.

"Fourthly, He must be a proper person, whom women may fancy.

"Fifthly, He must not take, but give, money.

"Sixthly, He must preach such things as people willingly hear."

How to preach before a Prince.

As Dr. Erasmus Albert was called into the Mark of Brandenburg, he desired Luther to set him down a method of preaching before the Prince Elector. Luther said, "Let all your preaching be in the most simple and plainest manner; look not to the Prince, but to the plain, simple, gross, and unlearned people, of which cloth the Prince also himself is made. If I," said Luther, "in my preaching, should have regard to Philip Melancthon and other learned doctors, then should I work but little goodness. I preach in the simplest manner to the unskilful, and that giveth content to all. Hebrew, Greek, and Latin I spare, until we learned ones come together, then we make it so curled and finical, that God Himself wondereth at us."

Luther's Preaching.

"When I am in the pulpit," said Luther, "then I resolve to preach only to men and maid-servants; I would not make a step into the pulpit for the sake of Philip Melancthon, Justus Jonas, or the whole university, for they are already well skilled in the Scripture. But when preachers will direct their sermons to the high learned, and will breathe out altogether *rabbinos* and master-pieces, then the poor unlearned people present do stand like a flock of kine."

St. Paul a plain Preacher.

"St Paul," said Luther, "never used such high and stately words as Demosthenes and Cicero did; but he spake (properly and plainly) words which signified high and stately matters: he did well, indeed, in not speaking so trim and finically; otherwise every one would speak wondrous highly."

Plain Preaching commended.

"We ought to direct ourselves in preaching according to the condition of the hearers; but all preachers commonly fail herein; they preach that which little edifieth the poor, simple people, as Bucer and Zuinglius at Marpurg, in all state and curious manner preached, thereby to bear the bell away; as though they would say, 'Behold, Luther and Melancthon, what learned fellows we are!' To preach plain and simply is a great art.: Christ Himself preacheth of tilling grounds, of mustard seed, &c., using altogether mean and simple similitudes."

"When one first cometh into the pulpit, a preacher is much perplexed. When I," said Luther, "stand in the pulpit, I look upon none, but imagine they are all blocks, which stand before me,—I utter God's word." This he spake [*] to encourage certain faint-hearted preachers, that they might not be discouraged and desist.

"I would not have preachers," said Luther, "use Hebrew, Greek, or other stange languages in their sermons; for in the churches, among the congregation, we ought to speak as we do at home in the house, the plain mother-tongue, which every one is acquainted with. It may be allowed to courtiers, lawyers, &c. to use quaint curious words, and to speak trimly, whom Osiander and Matthæus do imitate. Although Dr. Staupitz be a very well learned man, yet he is a very irksome preacher; and the people rather hear a plain brother preach, who delivereth his words plainly and simply to their understandings, than they do him. In churches no praise or extolling should be sought."

Ambitious Preaching.

"Cursed are all preachers," said Luther, "who, in the church, aim at high, hard, and neat things, and

---

[*] Here, again, the reader will observe how needful it is to make allowance for the peculiar circumstances under which Luther spoke, and the peculiar temper of the man. What great injustice may be done to his character by neglecting these considerations.

(neglecting the saving health of the poor unlearned people) seek their own honour and praise, and therewith to please one or two distinguished persons.

"When I," said Luther, "preach in this place, I sink myself deeply down. I regard neither *Doctores* nor *Magistros*, of whom above forty are here in the church; but I have an eye to the multitude of young people, children, and servants, of whom here are more than two thousand. I preach to these, and direct myself to those who have most need of instruction. Will the rest not hear me? The door standeth open unto them; they may be gone.

"I see that the ambition of preachers groweth and increaseth: this will be the greatest mischief in the Church, and will produce great disquietness and discord: for they will needs teach high things, and speak touching matters of state, thereby aiming at praise and honour; they will please the worldly wise, and, in the mean time, neglect the simple and common multitude."

"An upright, a godly, and true preacher should direct his preaching to the poor, simple, sort of people; like a mother that suckleth her child, presenting it with milk out of her breasts, and needing neither Malmsey nor Muscadine to give it. This, I say, is the way that preachers should carry themselves;— they should teach and preach plainly, so that the simple and unlearned may conceive, comprehend, and keep it. But when they come to me, to Melancthon, to Dr. Pommer, &c. then let them show their cunning, how learned they be; truly, they shall be well put to their trumps; for to sprinkle out Hebrew, Greek, and Latin in their public sermons savoureth merely of pride, which is utterly impertinent, agreeing with neither time nor place. To conclude, such preachers are untimely, ripeless, saints.

"I am heartily sorry," continued Luther, "that, even in my lifetime, I have cause to say thus much; that such proud and haughty ministers and preachers are among us, who aim at rule and government, as St. Paul saith, '*I would to God ye did reign,*' &c. The loving apostle was obliged to suffer by many of these ambitious spirits; as the Lord said concerning him, — '*I will show him how much he must suffer for my sake,*' &c. God laid very soon that *pati** upon his neck; he had great experience of it. Such sorrow of heart," said Luther, "is far greater and more heavy than dying. Thus must I also suffer in the offences and pride of my scholars: insomuch that I would rather suffer death."

How Luther would make a Preacher.

"If one would follow my advice," said Luther, "I would soon make him a preacher; for I would advise him to take the Catechism into the pulpit, and read it word by word; but on the Sunday I would have him take some part out of the Epistle and Gospel of the day, and afterwards to expound what he had read. But now they are ashamed to take this course, though I (an old doctor) do always take with me my book†, and read out of it from the pulpit.

"Dr. Jacob Schenck never preacheth out of a book, but I do," said Luther; "though not of necessity, as if it could not be otherwise; but I do it for ex-

---

* To suffer. † *i.e.* The Bible.

ample's sake. And, indeed," said he, " no one ought to be ashamed of his book in the pulpit, seeing our Saviour Christ, the highest doctor and master, was not ashamed thereof*, and hath left to us His example to preach out of the Book, as He did out of the Prophet Isaiah."

Of the Children's Catechisms.

" My advice is," said Luther, " that we dispute not much of mysteries, and hidden things; but rather cleave simply to God's word, specially the Catechism; for therein we have a very exact, right, and direct short way to the whole Christian Religion; for the chief heads and articles thereof are briefly contained in it. For God himself gave the Ten Commandments; Christ himself taught the Lord's Prayer; the Holy Ghost did most compendiously fix and comprehend the Articles of Faith.† These three pieces are set down so excellently, so comfortably, and brief, that it is impossible they could be better done. But they are slighted and contemned by us, as of small value, merely because the little children daily say and rehearse the same.

" The Catechism," continued Luther, " is the best and completest doctrine; therefore it should continually be preached, and without intermission. All other common and public preaching should be grounded

* In the synagogue of Nazareth. See Luke, iv. 16, &c.

† In every church in England these three plain and comprehensive forms of sound words are fixed up: reminding all who enter that they contain whatsoever is needful for a Christian to know and believe for his soul's health; and setting before the minister what should be the subject of his sermons: the church-walls may be his text-book.

and built thereupon. I could wish that we preached it daily, and plainly read it out of the book. But our preachers and hearers have it at their fingers' ends now; they have already swallowed it up, and are now ashamed of this slight and simple doctrine (as they hold it): they will be had in higher esteem and regard, and preach and hear of deeper learning. Our parishioners say — 'What! Our preachers fiddle only one lesson; they preach nothing but the Catechism — nothing but the Ten Commandments, the Lord's Prayer, the Creed, Baptism, and the Lord's Supper. All these we know well enough already.' So, then, our preachers now employ themselves about higher things — higher things! they preach upon such points as the people take delight in; and thereby are leaving and forsaking the strong foundation on which we all ought to build.

"He that cannot be satisfied with the preaching of the Catechism, to him may the devil preach," said Luther, " and not I."

"The common and public sermons," said Luther, " do very little edify the children: they take little notice, and learn very little by them; the more needful is it therefore that they be taught with diligence in schools, and at home in houses, and regularly heard and examined as to what they have learned. This course profiteth much; it is, indeed, very wearisome, and giveth great trouble, but, withal, it is necessary."

Luther (reproving Dr. Mayor for being fainthearted and discouraged, because, as he conceived, his preaching was so weak and simple in comparison of others,) admonished him, and said, " Loving brother, when you preach, behold not the doctors and high learned, but behold yourself and the commonest people; have regard that you teach and instruct them uprightly; for in the pulpit we ought to draw out the teats, and feed the common people with milk; for every day a new church is growing up, who stand in need of plain and sincere simple information — of the children's doctrine; therefore we ought to drive on the Catechism, and distribute the milk; but our high, subtle, and neat cogitations (and the strong wine) we will reserve for the wiselings."

"That famous painter, Albert Durer, used to say, he took no delight in such pictures as were painted with many colours, but in those that were made most plain. Even so," said Luther, "I likewise take delight in those sermons that enter fine and simply, so that they may be well understood and comprehended of the common people."

Brentius a good Preacher.

"No divine in this our time," said Luther, "handleth the Holy Scripture so well as Brentius. Very often do I admire his spirit, and despair of my own ability.[*] I verily believe there is none among us who would be able to do what he has done in the exposition of St. John's Gospel. Howsoever, he now and then

---

[*] Bishop Burnet, who was the most popular preacher of his day, says, in his "History of his own Times," that he never heard a sermon from Leighton (afterwards Archbishop of Glasgow), but he conceived such a disdain of his own powers, that he could hardly bring himself to preach for some weeks afterwards. Those who have read and studied the Archbishop's Sermons, and especially his Exposition of St. Peter, will readily believe this.

hangeth somewhat too long upon his cogitations; yet he remaineth in the true sense and meaning, and strideth not over the plain simplicity of God's word; therefore he may well be borne with touching the other, and should not be reproached with it."

Armsdorff, Osiander, &c.

"Licentiate Armsdorff," said Luther, "teacheth upright and purely; he delivereth his mind sincerely. At the princely assembly at Smalcalde, he preached a sermon, and began by saying with great earnestness, 'This Gospel belongeth to the sick, weak, and poor sinners; but here are none; for ye princes, potentates, and courtiers, live in continual pleasures, in secureness, and without tribulation, — ye feel not your sicknesses, weaknesses, poverty,' &c. It was," said Luther, "a grievous *exordium* and *captatio benevolentiæ*; for in setting out we should try to incline the hearers to a willingness to attend to what shall be preached. Nevertheless he proceedeth uprightly in all his discourses: Armsdorff is a divine by nature. Doctor Cruciger and Doctor Justus Jonas are made and conceived divines. Osiander hath eloquence, but the common man is nothing edified by his preaching. Nothing causeth Osiander's pride more than his idle life, for he preacheth but twice in the week, and hath a yearly pension of four hundred guilders."

Dr. Brucken.

"To speak deliberately and longsome becometh a preacher best, and is most fitting: for thereby he may the more diligently and with consideration deliver his sermon. Seneca writeth of Cicero that he spake deliberately from the heart, as we see Dr. George Brucken doth."

A Preacher (in Controversy more particularly) ought to keep to his Point.

"When a man standeth in fight and combat," said Luther, "then let him look to it that he remain *in statu negotii*. I never yet had an adversary," said Luther, "that remained *in ipso statu*, that kept fairly to the point in dispute, and fought with me on equal terms. They always shrunk, went aside, and flew out of the way; they would never stand their ground, and await the stroke. It is an art to stand *in statu causæ*, and say, 'We deal with this point; here let us meet:' but I must always run after them; and therefore so it is, he that hunteth will also be weary at last.

"I drove Dr. Eck into the lists," said Luther, "when he thought to prove the Pope's supremacy by this argument:— 'St. Peter,' said he, 'walked upon the sea; now the sea is the world, therefore St. Peter was chief and prince among the apostles, and consequently the Pope chief and principal bishop in the church of Christ:' but I so pressed him that every man laughed at him, because that, out of St. Bernard, he named the apostles the world. Now when he saw that I had hunted and driven him into the net, then he cried out and said to the friars at Leipsic, ' *O vos sancti fratres, videte importunitatem Lutheri, qui patris vestri Bernardi sententiam rejicit, qui tamen Spiritum Sanctum habuit.'* There did I stand *in statu causæ* (let Bernardus be Bernardus), and expounded that sentence, touching St. Peter's walking on the sea, uprightly and truly. ' St. Peter walked upon the sea; that is,' said I, ' he trod the world under his feet, and utterly contemned it.'

" In like manner, at another time, I disputed with one of my adversaries, three hours together, and confuted his opinion (which he would maintain out of the Fathers), not only by God's word, but by other sentences taken from the Fathers, insomuch that the poor fellow began to rage, and said, *' Domine Luthere, vos semper petitis principium.'* I kept to the point," said Luther, " and that is what every preacher ought to do. But my adversaries," said Luther, " have evil consciences: they will not confess their errors, as I confessed mine openly in many points, when in Popedom; and after I had forsaken Popedom, I acknowledged my error touching the opinion I held of the real presence (*corporaliter*) in the supper of the Lord. But in matters of faith (through God's grace) I always remained stedfast. We ought," said Luther, " to confess our errors, *humanum est errare;* but the wicked wretches, the Papists, will not recant their errors; they would willingly hold with us, and yet they teach quite contrary."

Ostentatious, prating, Preachers.

" There are many talking preachers," said Luther, " but there is nothing in them but words; they can talk much, but say nothing uprightly. The world hath always had such boasting *Thrasos*, boasting throat-criers.

"We read that Cicero, the best and most eloquent of heathens in the Latin tongue, having heard a notable prater speak, said, 'I never in my life heard one speak so much and with so great authority, and yet hath said nothing.'

"And when Erasmus of Rotterdam was asked, at Bononia, how he liked one who triumphed and boasted greatly in his oration, he said, 'I like him well, for he hath done far beyond my thoughts of him.' — 'How?' said the other. — 'I did not think,' said Erasmus, 'that such a fool was lurking in the man.' Therefore," said Luther, "to speak much is no art, but to speak fine, significantly, and rightly, that gift is granted to few. No man ought to undertake any thing except it be given him from above."

A good Preacher.

"A preacher," said Luther, "should be a logician and a rhetorician; that is, he must be able to teach and to admonish. When he preacheth upon any point, he must, first, distinguish it by its proper name. Secondly, he must define, describe, and show what it is. Thirdly, he must lead the texts of Scripture thereto, and by them must prove and strengthen it. Fourthly, he must explain and set it forth by examples. Fifthly, he must adorn it with similitudes; and, lastly, he must admonish and rouse up the lazy, and earnestly reprove the disobedient, together with the false doctrine, and the authors of it. Yet must he beware that these reproofs proceed not from malice and envy, but that he only seek thereby the honour of God, and the profit and saving health of the people.

"Ah!" said Luther, "what diligence used our blessed Saviour Jesus Christ, in teaching simply and plainly; he used similitudes of vines, and sheep, and trees, &c., and all to the end that the people might be able to understand, comprehend, and keep it."

The Preacher's Burden and Strength.

"If I should write of the heavy burden of a godly preacher (as I know it by my own experience), methinks," said Luther, "I should scare every man from the preacher's office. An upright and god-fearing preacher must be minded and disposed so that nothing is so acceptable and precious to him as Christ his Lord and Saviour, and the everlasting life to come. So that, although he lost his life, and all that to life belongs, it should be enough for him to know that Christ saith to him, 'Come hither to me, thou hast been my loving, true, and faithful servant.'"

Luther's Admonition to Preachers.

"Loving brethren, let us attend to our office in God's fear and reverence, with all true diligence: let us deliver the doctrine of the Gospel to the hearers in humility and calling upon God. Afterwards let us be proud* in God, whose cause we have in hand;

---

* i. e. Let us " *magnify our office,*" which cannot well be too highly esteemed, while we abase ourselves, who are utterly un-

let us not suffer ourselves to be bitten and torn from the same.

---

worthy of it, and cannot give success to any of our labours. "Who then is Paul? and who is Apollos? but ministers by whom ye believed, *even as the Lord gave to every man.*"—" We, then, as workers together with God, beseech you that ye receive not the grace of God in vain."—1 Cor. iii. 5. 2 Cor. vi. 1.

CHAPTER VI.

TOUCHING CHRISTIAN DUTIES.

Of Faith, and the Proof thereof.

"The faith of the Cross," said Luther, "doth the deed, for faith cannot subsist without the Cross. When the water runneth above the chin, as we use to say, then we see what faith's strength is, and what it is able to do. It is not a speculation, or a work of the fancy,—it is a sure and certain confidence of the heart in God, and a work of the Holy Ghost."

"No better dying," said Luther, "than as St. Stephen died, who said, '*Lord Jesus receive my spirit,*'—to lay aside the register of our sins, or of our deserts, and die relying only upon God's mere grace and mercy in Christ Jesus."

"Upright and faithful Christians," said Luther, "do always think that they do not believe and are not faithful *, and, therefore, they are diligent; they strive and wrestle continually to keep and to increase faith. It is with them as with good and ingenious workmen, who can

---

* *i. e.* They are conscious of the weakness and imperfection of their faith.

always perceive that something, yea, much, is faulty and deficient in their workmanship. Whereas the palterers and botchers think that nothing is wanting in what they do, but that every thing is well and as it should be. So the Jews think they have the Ten Commandments at their fingers' ends, when, in truth, they neither learn nor regard them."

Luther speaking in company concerning the excellent works of creation, said, " I should never have believed that the dew had been so sweet and amiable a creature, if the Scripture itself had not so highly extolled it; where God saith, *Dabo tibi de rore cœli,* ' I will give thee of the dew of heaven.' The works of creation are most excellent things, and what a help to faith, if we did rightly use them! — but," said Luther, " in this matter *balbutimus et blæsi sumus,* and we say, *cledo* for *credo,* as the little children say, *bed* for *bread;* the words are strong, but the heart is weak, and it saith *cledo: sed per hoc salvamur quod cupimus credere.* Oh! our Lord God well knows that we are poor children: if we could but acknowledge so much ourselves. The holy apostles said, ' *Lord increase our faith,*' but we will all be wiser than God, although we understand nothing, *nisi per Filium, id est, Christum.* And what was His discourse, but altogether this? ' *Per me, per me, per me:*' ye are not able to do it, though you should fret yourselves into pieces. We are brought to the Father through the Son: therefore we should get well forward, if we could but believe that God is wiser than we are."

" We must take fast hold of the Word," said Luther, " and must believe that all is true which it speaketh of God, although God, and all His creatures, should seem to us different from what the word speaketh of Him: as we see the Canaanitish woman did. The word is sure and faileth not, though heaven and earth must pass away, as Christ saith. But," said Luther, " oh! how hard and bitter is this to nature, sense, and reason, that he must strip himself naked, and forsake all that he feeleth and conceiveth, and must depend upon the bare word alone, especially when he feeleth and conceiveth quite the contrary. The Lord of His mercy help us to such a faith, in our necessities, and at our last end when we strive with death."

Of Prayer.

"No human creature can believe," said Luther, "how powerful Prayer is, and what it is able to effect; none but those who have learnt it by experience.

"It is a great matter when, in extreme need, one can lay hold on Prayer. I know that so often as I have earnestly prayed, I have been richly heard, and have obtained more than I have prayed for. Indeed, God sometimes deferred the matter, nevertheless He came.

"Oh!" said Luther, "how great an upright and godly Christian's Prayer is! how powerful with God! That a poor human creature should speak with God's high majesty in heaven, and not be affrighted, but know, on the contrary, that God smileth friendly upon him for Christ's sake, His dearly beloved Son! — What a wonder is this!"

"The heart and conscience (in this act of praying) must not fly and recoil backward by reason of sin and unworthiness; it must not stand in doubt, and be scared away. We must not do," said Luther, "as the Bavarian did, who, with great devotion, called upon St. Leonard, an idol set up in a church in Bavaria, behind which idol stood one who answered the Bavarian in all his prayers, saying, ' Fie on thee, Bavarian.' At last the Bavarian, being thus oftentimes repulsed, and seeing that he could not obtain a favourable hearing, said, ' Fie on thee, Leonard,' and so went away. We must not do so," said Luther; "we must not let it come to ' Fie on thee,' but must certainly hold, conclude, and believe firmly, that we are already heard in those things for which we pray with faith in Christ. Therefore the ancient finely describeth prayer, that it is *ascensus animi ad Deum*, a climbing up of the soul to God; that is, the heart in prayer lifteth itself up, crieth and sigheth unto God. Neither I myself," said Luther, "nor any else that I know, rightly understood the definition of this *ascensus*. We boasted, indeed, and talked much of the climbing up of the heart, but we failed in *the Syntax*, we could not bring thereunto the word *Deum*; nay, we flew from God, we were afraid to draw near to Him, and to pray through Christ, in whom prayer's strength wholly consisteth.* We always prayed in Popedom *conditionaliter*, with condition, uncertainly, and at hap-hazard.

"But let us pray in heart, sometimes also with our lips; for Prayer (by our loving God) supporteth the world; without Prayer it would stand in a far more lamentable state."

---

* John, xiv. 13, 14.

"Our Saviour Christ," said Luther, "in most excellent manner, and with very few words, comprehended in the Lord's Prayer all needs and necessities; but, without trouble, trials, and vexations, Prayer cannot rightly be made. It is well, therefore, said in David, '*Call upon me in the time of trouble,*' &c.; without need it is only a cold prattling, and goeth not from the heart. The common saying is true, 'Need teacheth to pray.'—And although the Papists have a saying that God understandeth all the words of those who pray; St. Bernard was of a different opinion, where he saith, 'God heareth not the words of one that prayeth, unless he that prayeth heareth them first himself.' The Pope," said Luther, "is a mere tormentor and hangman of the conscience. The assembly of his greased and religious crew in praying was altogether like the croaking of frogs, which edifieth nothing at all; it was mere sophistry and deceiving, fruitless and unprofitable.*

"Prayer," said Luther again, "is a strong wall and a fort of the church; it is a godly Christian's weapon, which no man knoweth or findeth but the true Christian, who hath the spirit of grace and prayer. Oh! what an excelling Master was He that penned those words in the Lord's Prayer, wherein is fastened an endless *rhetorica*, or art of speech, and in which all necessities and dealings are contained.

"The first three petitions comprehend so great and celestial things as no heart is able to search out.

* Luther here alludes to the repetitions of prayers (commonly in Latin) by the monks in their convents; where it seemed to be received as a maxim, that the more frequently certain prayers were repeated, the more acceptable those who said them became in the sight of God.

The fourth petition containeth the whole policy and economy, i.e. the civil and domestic government, and all things necessary for this life. The fifth prayer fighteth and striveth against our own devil of an evil conscience; that is, as well against original sin as against sins in practice, which give trouble to the conscience, &c. &c. Truly," said Luther, " they were penned by a man of wisdom, indeed, and are such as no earthly human creature could have done."

"I," said Luther, " have every day enough to do to pray; and when I lay me down to rest and sleep, and pray the Lord's Prayer*, and afterwards take hold of two or three sentences out of the Bible, and so take my sleep, then I am satisfied."

On the 25th of December, being Luther's birthday, he preached, and earnestly besought the people " to pray that God would preserve His word unfalsified among us, that the course thereof might not be hindered, but prosper against the raging and assaults of Satan, specially against the blood-thirsty Papists, who are the most bitter enemies to God's word ; for from them we have nothing else to expect than that without intermission they take counsel against the word of the Gospel, and to prepare for us who profess the same a bath of blood.† Therefore, loving Christian

* He who has *prayed* the Lord's Prayer has prayed indeed.

† Luther had read in the Scriptures that anti-christian Babylon should be distinguished by its blood-thirsty persecutions of the church of Christ. (Rev. xvii. 6.) He had read in history of the murders and massacres of the pious Waldenses and Albigenses, of the Lollards, of Huss and Jerome, and many other holy and harmless men, at the instigation, or under the sanction, of the Pope and his clergy. He had also great experience of their sanguinary proceedings in Germany, France, the Low Countries, &c.

brethren," said Luther, " let our prayers be poured out from our hearts, and let us repent. Let us be not hearers only of the word, but live according to it. And seeing the whole world, Papists, Sectaries, Epicures, &c. have raised such a stench in the nostrils of God, let us endeavour, by hearty Prayer, to kindle up before Him an odour of sweet incense."

Dr. Æpinus, superintendent of Hamburg, coming to Wittemberg to speak with Luther; and when he had dispatched his business, and was taking leave, " I commend myself," said he, " and our church at Hamburg, to your prayers." Luther answered him and said, " Loving Æpine, the cause is not ours, but God's. Let us join our prayers together; that is the way to help forward our cause. I will pray against the Pope and the Turk as long as I live; and I like it well that you take such course at Hamburg, and earnestly pray against Mahomet and the Pope.

" God saith, ' *Hearken unto me, O house of Jacob, and all the remnant of the house of Israel, which are carried by me from the womb: and even to your old age, I am he, and even to hoary hair will I carry and deliver you,*' &c. Therefore," said Luther, " lay it upon Him, lay it only to Him. St. Peter also saith, ' *Cast all your care upon Him,*' &c. And Psalm 55, ' *O cast thy burden upon the Lord, He will sustain thee.*' O!" said Luther, " these are comfortable sentences. But we will be doing all for ourselves, and therefore forget God, and make evil worse. ' Yea,' may one say, ' I have truly committed my prayer unto God, but He will not come, He delayeth too long.' O!" said Luther, " wait, ' *wait upon the Lord;*' we must attend and hold out, for He cometh most certainly at last.

It is far better that we wait upon the Lord, than to betake ourselves to the Pope's side, or to the Bishop of Mentz, by whom, notwithstanding, we have no hope; for they cannot help themselves, they are poor worm-sacks. I hear," said Luther, " that Eck is dead; I am sorry for that unworthy man : I well hoped that he would have acknowledged his blaspheming of God, but he did not : he allowed himself in boasting, bragging, lechery, whoredom, &c., wherein he grew old, and by continual practice they became natural to him, insomuch that he is now dead and lost."

"When Moses with the children of Israel came to the Red Sea, then he cried with trembling and quaking, yet he opened not his mouth, neither was his voice heard on earth by any of the people. Doubtless," said Luther, " he cried and sighed in his heart and said, ' Ah! Lord God, what course shall I now take? which way shall I now turn myself? How am I come to this strait? No help or counsel of man can save us. Behind us are our enemies the Egyptians; on both sides high and lofty mountains. I am the cause that all this people shall now be destroyed,' &c. Then answered God, and said, ' *Wherefore criest thou unto me?* What an alarum, what a loud and grievous cry, dost thou make, that the whole heavens must ring therewith,' &c. But, alas!" said Luther, " we read such examples as dead letters; human reason, wisdom, and understanding are not able to search this passage out. The way through the Red Sea is full as broad (if not broader) than from Wittemberg to Coburg, that is thirty of our miles at least. The people, doubtless, were obliged to stop and bait, and also to rest at night in that passage. For 600,000 men (besides women and children) would require a good time to pass through, although they went 150 rank and file. It was a passage beyond all human conception, and that outcry of Moses was but low and still in the hearing of the people, but it filled the ears of God in heaven, so that He said, 'Wherefore criest thou unto me?' *Ita Fides in infirmitate et miraculis procedit.*"

A minister of the church exhibited to Luther a petition complaining of the disobedience of his curate, whereat Luther sighed, and said, "Ah! Lord God, what an enemy is the devil unto us, in sowing discord among the servants of the Word; he kindleth always one fire or another. O! let us quench them by prayer, by reconciliation, and by mutual forbearance."

"Like as a shoemaker's trade," said Luther, "is to make shoes, and a tailor's to make a coat, even so it is the trade of a true Christian continually to pray.*

Precatio Lutheri.

"*Sum tuus in vitâ, tua sunt mea funera, Christe,
Da precor imperii sceptra tenere tui.
Cur etenim moriens tot vulnera sæva tulisti,
Si non sum regni, portio parva tui?
Cur rigido latuit tua vita inclusa sepulcro,
Si non est mea mors morte fugata tuâ!
Ergo mihi certam præstes, O Christe, salutem.*"

Of Works of Charity, &c.

"The love towards the neighbour," said Luther, "must be like a pure and chaste love between bride

* Not a bad illustration of what that meaneth, 1 Thess. v. 17., "*Pray without ceasing.*"

and bridegroom, where all faults are connived at, covered, and borne with, and only the virtues regarded."

"In ceremonies and ordinances the kingdom of love must have the precedence and govern, and not tyranny. It must be a willing love, not a halter love; it must be altogether directed and managed for the good and profit of one's neighbour; and the greater he is that doth govern," said Luther, "the more he ought to serve according to love."

"True it is," said Luther, "good works are well pleasing to God, in those who have remission of their sins through faith in Christ: the same have also their reward. But when the heart depends and trusts upon them, and thinks thereby to have a gracious God, then, instead of good works, they are in the sight of God stark naught; for confidence and trusting must look only upon God's mercy in Christ. We must beware of balancing our works with grace. O! no, they must be done as in obedience: for we are bound to make this confession to God, (who is so good, so gracious, and so merciful a Father,) ' *When we have done all that we ought to do, we are still unprofitable servants.*' "

Of the Merit of Works.

"Desert," said Luther, "is a work for the sake of which Christ rewardeth: but such a work is nowhere to be found, for Christ giveth the reward by reason of the promise. Just as if the Elector should say to me, 'Come to the court, Luther, and I will give thee one hundred guilders,' &c. Now in going to the court I should perform a work; but I should not receive the Prince's gift by reason of my work in going thither, but by reason of the promise which the Prince made me."

Luther's Exposition of Isaiah, xxx. 16.—" In quietness and in confidence shall be your strength."

This sentence was expounded by Luther in this sort:—" If thou intendest to vanquish the greatest, the most abominable and wicked, enemy, (such a one as is able, not being overcome, to injure thee both in body and soul, against whom, therefore, thou wouldest prepare thyself with all sorts of weapons, and wouldest give all thy wealth to learn this art,) then know that there is a sweet and loving herb which serveth for the same, and the name of that herb is *Patientia*,—thou must be quiet.

" But thou wilt say, ' How may I attain unto this physic?' *Answer*, Take unto thee Faith, who saith: No creature can do thee mischief, without the will of God. Now in case thou receivest hurt and mischief from thine enemy, the same is done by the sweet and gracious will of God, and in such sort that the enemy injureth himself a thousand times more than he can injure thee. From hence floweth unto me (a Christian) Love, which saith, ' I will (in return for the evil which my enemy doth unto me) do him all the good I can, *I will heap coals of fire on his head.*' This," said Luther, " is the armour and harness of a Christian, wherewith to beat down and overcome those enemies that seem to be like huge mountains. To conclude, in a word, Love teacheth to suffer and endure all things."

How necessary Patience is.

" I," said Luther, " must be patient with the Pope, I must have patience with heretics and seducers: I must have patience with the roaring courtiers: I must have patience with my servants: I must have patience with Kate my wife: to conclude, the patiences are so many, that my whole life is nothing but Patience."

On being good.

" The righteousness of works and hypocrisy are the most mischievous diseases," said Luther; " they are born in us, and not easily expelled, specially when they are confirmed and settled upon us by use and practice; for all mankind will have dealings with Almighty God, and will dispute with Him according to their human, natural understanding, and will make satisfaction to God for their sins with their own strength and self-chosen works. Therefore," said Luther, " I have, for my part, so often deceived our Lord God, by promising to be upright and good, that I will promise no more, but will only pray for a happy hour, when it shall please God to make me good."

On confessing Christ.

" Every Christian, specially those in offices, should be ready, when need requireth, boldly to stand up and confess his Saviour Christ, to maintain His faith, and to be always armed against the world, the devil, and all adversaries. But no man will do this, except he be so sure of his doctrines, that, although I myself should play the fool, and recant, and deny this my doctrine and religion (which God forbid), he would not on that account yield, but would rather say, 'If Luther, or an angel from heaven, should teach otherwise, *let him be accursed.*'"

"When kings and governors," said Luther, " are enemies to God's word, then our duty is to depart, to sell and forsake all we have, and fly from one place to another, as Christ commandeth. (Matt. x. 23.) We must raise no uproars nor tumults for the Gospel's sake, but we must suffer all things."

Of brotherly Forgiveness.

"To brotherly forgiveness belongeth this:—That the brother whom I forgive confess his fault. But," said Luther, " that fault I cannot forgive which is not acknowledged and confessed. Now, if the brother goeth on daily doing me wrong, and groweth worse and worse, then must I say unto him, ' Brother, thou hast wronged me in such and such a manner, it becomes thee to acknowledge that thou hast done me wrong.' If he contemn my remonstrance, and jeer it out, then I must endure it. But I cannot forgive him*, because he acknowledgeth not that he hath done me wrong. But when he heartily confesseth his fault, and saith, ' Brother, I have done this or that against thee and done thee wrong, I pray thee forgive it me;' then must I say unto him, 'Loving brother, I forgive thee willingly from my heart.'"

---

* *i. e.* As to the open declaration of forgiveness: for a Christian must always be of a forgiving *temper*.

Of friendly, Christian-like Reproof.

"Nothing hindereth Excommunication more at this time," said Luther, "than that no man doth what pertaineth to a Christian to do. Thou hast a neighbour whose life and conversation is well known to thee (but unknown to thy preacher or minister). Now when thou seest thy neighbour grow rich by wrongful dealing; thou seest that he liveth a lascivious kind of life, in adultery, &c.; thou seest that he governs his family negligently: is it not then Christian-like for thee to warn and earnestly to admonish him to desist from his evil courses, to have a care of his salvation, &c. Oh!" said Luther, "how holy a work hast thou performed when in this sort thou warnest thy neighbour. But, I pray, who doth this? For, first, truth is a hateful thing; he that, in these times of the world, speaketh truth, procureth hatred. Therefore thou wilt rather keep thy neighbour's friendship and good will (specially when he is rich and powerful), by holding thy peace; and conniving at his offence, than that thou wilt incur his displeasure, and make him thy adversary."

CHAPTER VII.

MISCELLANEOUS REMARKS AND OBSERVATIONS OF DR. MARTIN LUTHER TOUCHING MATTERS IN DIVINITY, AND AFFLICTIONS OF THE HEART AND CONSCIENCE.

Sundry wholesome Counsels uttered by Dr. Luther for the helping and solacing of those who are troubled in Mind, and the Subjects of spiritual Temptations.

"God delighteth in our temptations," said Luther, "and God hateth them: He delighteth in them when they drive us to prayer: again, He hates them when we despair through them. But the psalm saith, '*A broken and contrite heart is an acceptable sacrifice to God*,' &c. Therefore when it goeth well with thee, sing and praise God with a fine song, or an hymn: goeth it evil, that is, when temptation comes, then pray; for '*The Lord hath pleasure in them that fear Him:*' but that which follows is the best, namely, '*and in them that hope in His mercy.*' God indeed helpeth the poor and humble, to whom He saith, '*Thinkest thou my hand is shortened that it cannot save?*'"

"If haply it so falleth out that (apart from the article of Justification) thou hast to dispute with Jews,

Turks, or sectaries, or heretics, of God's wisdom, of His almighty power, &c., then make use of thy best art: be as sharp, pointed, and subtle as possibly thou canst; there is no danger, for then thou hast another argument.

"But," said Luther, "in this case concerning our justification; that is, when we must, in God's presence, maintain our conscience against the Law, our righteousness against sin, and our life against death and the devil; or when we seek what the satisfaction for sin is, through what means sins are forgiven, and we become reconciled to God, and eternally saved;—in this case, let us turn away our hearts, our minds, and all our thoughts in every particular, from the high, incomprehensible, majesty of God, and let us only behold and look upon That Man who presenteth Himself to be a Mediator for us, and saith, '*Come unto me all ye that labour,*' &c.

"When we do this," said Luther, "then we shall see that God's wisdom, His power and glory, will be expressed and pictured to us so lovingly and friendly, that we may well suffer, endure, and understand all things in that sweet and amiable picture, as St. Paul saith, '*That in Christ are hid all the treasures of the Godhead;—all wisdom and knowledge.*' Also, '*That in Him dwelleth all the fulness of the Godhead bodily.*'

"Hold this fast," said Luther; "suffer thyself at no time to be drawn away from this picture of Christ, in whom the angels take delight; and think not that Christ, according to His true picture, is a tormentor like Moses; for He is, indeed, a giver of righteousness. Also, He gave Himself, not by reason of our deserts and holiness, but for our sins; and although Christ now and then expoundeth the Law*, yet this is not His main office, for which the Father sent Him."

"It is an easy and light thing," said Luther, "to talk, and say that our Saviour Christ is given for our sins; but when it cometh to the upshot, and when the devil, through trials and temptations, hideth Christ, and taketh Him out of our sight, and therewith teareth out of our hearts the Word of Grace, then we find that we fail much, and that we have learned nothing. But whoso, at such seasons, can behold Christ, not as a stern and angry judge, but as the most sweet and loving Saviour, and as our High Priest, this man hath overcome all manner of adversities, and is well on his way to the heavenly kingdom. But," said Luther, "there is not a more difficult thing on earth than in times of trial and temptation to do so.

"What I say I have it from experience, for I know full well the devil's craft; he can so blow the Law into us, as to terrify and affright: he can make mountains out of molehills; that is to say, a very hell out of some small sin; and (like a wondrous juggler as he is) can make great and heavy sins of those which are no sins at all; so doth he perplex and blind the conscience. But, worst of all, he can picture Christ's person before us in such a disguised manner as we must needs be affrighted at it; for then he bringeth and layeth before us one sentence or other out of the Scripture, and, before we are aware of him, he giveth so hard a blow to our hearts (and that in a moment),

---
* The reader will find the subject fully discussed in Dr. Luther's Commentary on the Epistle to the Galatians.

that instantly we lose all light and sight, and take him to be the true Christ who possesseth us with such cogitations, whereas it is, only and alone, the envious devil."

———

"Indeed," said Luther, "although the devil be not a commenced Doctor, yet he is both deeply learned, and well experienced; he has been in the practice of his art now almost six thousand years. No human creature can prevail against him, but Christ alone; and yet he made trial of his art on our Lord Himself, as when he drily said unto Him, '*If thou wilt fall down and worship me, I will give thee all the kingdoms of the whole world,*' &c. He saith not as before, '*If thou be the Son of God,*' but saith, in plain terms, 'I am God, thou art my creature; for all the power and glory of the world is mine; I give the same to whom I please: worship me, then, and thou shalt have it.' This blaspheming of God, Christ could not endure; but calleth him by his right name, and saith, '*Get thee hence, Satan,*' &c.

"No man," said Luther, "is able to comprehend this temptation. I would willingly die on condition that I might fundamentally preach thereof. Doubtless the devil much moved Christ when he said, '*All this is mine, and to whomsoever I will I give it;*' for they are the words of the Divine Majesty, and belong to God only. True it is," said Luther, "that the devil giveth also; but let us take heed, and make a strong distinction between the true giver (who giveth all that we have and are, yea, and His only begotten Son) and between the dissembling murderer, who giveth to those that serve and worship him, for a short season; yet so that afterwards they perish everlastingly.

"Christ, ye observe, contradicteth him not, when he saith I am a lord and prince in this world; yet will He not, therefore, worship, but saith, 'Get thee hence, Satan,' &c. Even so ought we to do likewise. He must, indeed, be a most wicked, a poisoned, and a thirsty spirit, in that he durst move the Son of God to fall down and worship him. The arch-villain, doubtless, in the twinkling of an eye, laid before the Lord a delusion of all the kingdoms of the world, and showed the glory of the same (as St. Luke writeth), thereby to move and allure Him, to the end He should think — such honour might one receive, and still be the Son of God, &c. But the Lord meeteth him rightly, and saith, '*Avaunt, Satan; it is written, Thou shalt worship the Lord thy God*,' &c. The Evangelist, St. Matthew, saith clearly, '*Jesus was led by the Spirit into the wilderness to be tempted of the devil*.' The same," said Luther, "went not off without heavy tribulation and combating."

"When the envious poisoned spirit, the devil, plagueth and tormenteth us (as he useth) by reason of our sins, intending thereby to lead us to despair, then we must answer and meet him in this manner: saying unto him, 'Thou deceitful and wicked spirit, how darest thou presume to persuade me to such things? Knowest thou not that Christ Jesus, my Lord and Saviour, who crushed thy head, hath forbidden me to believe thee, yea, even when thou speakest truth; for he baptizeth and nameth thee a murderer, a liar, and a father of lies. I do not grant thee that I, as thy captive, shall be condemned to everlasting death and hellish torments, by reason of my sins, (as thou falsely dost suggest), but thou thyself, on the contrary, art, long since, by Christ, my Lord and Saviour, stripped, sentenced, and with everlasting bonds and chains of darkness, art bound, cast down, and delivered to hell, insomuch that thou art reserved to the judgment of the great day; and, finally, with all the ungodly, shalt be thrown into the bottomless pit of hell.

"'Further, I demand of thee, by what authority presumest thou to exercise such power and right against me? Forsooth, thou hast given me neither life, wife, nor child; no, not the least thing I have; neither art thou my lord, much less a creator of body and soul; neither hast thou made the members wherewith I have sinned. How, then, thou wicked and false spirit, art thou so insolent and bold as to try to domineer over that which is mine, as though thou wert God himself?'"

"Faith's tribulation is the greatest and sharpest torment; for Faith it must be which overcometh all other tribulations. Now, if Faith itself be foiled, and lieth under, then all other tribulations must needs follow upon human creatures; but if Faith hold up her head, if that be sound and in good health, then all other tribulations and vexations must grow sick, decline, and be diminished. Such tribulations was David possessed with when he made this psalm,—'*O Lord, rebuke me not in thine anger,*' &c. No doubt," said Luther, "he would rather have been stuck through and slain with a sword, than to have suffered such fearfulness of God's wrath and indignation. I am persuaded that such confessors do far excel, in the sufferings they endure, those martyrs who corporally

are plagued and pained: for when they see daily in
the world, abominable idolatry, offences, heresies,
errors, falsifying of the pure doctrine, sins, and confusion; when they see the ungodly fortunate and
their affairs prospering, while, on the contrary, the
good and godly Christians daily are plagued, banished,
hanged, drowned, and persecuted in the fiercest
manner, like so many sheep appointed to be slain;
truly, when they behold these things, their hearts
oftentimes are ready to break in pieces.

"Whoever, then," said Luther, "is possessed with
these and the like spiritual trials and temptations, he
should frequent the company of people, and in no case
be alone, nor hide himself, so to bite and torment
himself with his own and the devil's cogitations and
possessings; for the Holy Ghost saith, ' *Woe to him
that is alone.*' When I," said Luther, "am melancholy, unpleasant, and heavy minded, then I abandon
solitariness, and repair to people and talk with them.
Spiritual tribulations are far heavier and more dangerous than bodily afflictions; from hence those tribulations arose wherewith the devil touched the conscience of Judas, when he said, ' *I have betrayed the
innocent and righteous blood,*' &c. That was to him the
devil's first deadly stroke."

"The devil commonly plagues and torments us in
that part where we are most weak; he fell not upon
Adam, but upon Eve. It commonly raineth there
where it was wet enough before.

"When one is possessed with these cogitations;
namely, that although he calleth upon the Lord, he
cannot be heard, and, therefore, concludeth that the

Lord turneth the heart from him, and is angry. Let him, first, consider with himself thus:—These are thoughts which we suffer; we do not make them, but they are forced and borne in upon us. Against the same thou must arm thyself with God's word, in which He hath promised that He will hear thee. Thou must not appoint times, places, or persons, as when, how, or through whom, God shall answer thee, for that is stark naught,—thou must cleave to the promise: thou art baptized and believest in Christ, it is most certain that God heareth thee; but it is God's manner to hide His love from us, insomuch that we suffer ourselves to dream that He doth not hear us. God useth to deal with us as he saith in Moses. (Exod. xx. 21.) He will dwell in the dark; He hath his dwelling in the dark. Indeed," said Luther, "we are 'cast down,' but, in no wise, 'forsaken.' Whoso feeleth not, at times, these cogitations, knoweth not what Christ can do. Therefore, let us say, with Job, '*Though He should slay me, yet will I put my trust in Him.*' My Lord, Jesus Christ," said Luther, "hath won, conquered, and kept the field, therefore shall I well remain. This, and none other, is my comfort in tribulation. Through the Holy Ghost (who is in my heart) I say, '*I believe in Jesus Christ, God's only Son,*' &c., otherwise I could not do it. The Holy Ghost, with His finger, must write the same in our hearts, then '*With the heart we believe unto righteousness, and with the mouth make confession.*' These are the true signs that we belong to the fellowship, brotherhood, and congregation, of Christ."

How those who are in Tribulation concerning Faith are to be comforted.

" First," said Luther, " they must take heed that they be not alone, but continually among those with whom they may hold discourse touching the Psalms and Holy Scripture.

" Secondly, the chiefest physic for that disease (but very hard, indeed, to be done) is, that they firmly hold such cogitations not to be theirs, but that, most certainly, they come from the devil. They must, therefore, use the highest diligence to thrust out such thoughts from their hearts, and not undertake to dispute touching God and everlasting salvation till they be removed. But to the end thou mayest expel such cogitations and possessions of the devil," said Luther " I advise thee to hear and receive the words of some god-fearing man, as a voice sounding from heaven; in this way I have myself been oftentimes comforted and refreshed with the words of Philip Melancthon, he saying unto me, — ' Sir, what I say you must not receive as my words, but as the word of God, who speaks to you through me.' This," said Luther, " I took and believed, that it was, indeed, God's voice from heaven; and then I felt well what this meaneth, ' *Thy word hath quickened me.*' Ps. cxix.

" Thirdly, We must (as we can) diligently pray and believe, that God can and will help us, as most certainly He doth help when we believe.

" Fourthly, When Satan will not desist from tempting thee, then is the time for patience; let go neither hand nor foot, neither do thou faint, as if there would be no end to thy troubles; but rather hold out courageously, and wait the Lord's leisure: and understand that what the devil cannot bring to pass by those his assaults, by his swift and sudden power, and crafty policy, the same he thinketh to effect and gain by holding on in vexing and tempting thee; thereby to make thee faint and weary, as in the Psalm is noted, ' *Many times have they afflicted me, but have not prevailed.*' And be thou assured, in the mean time, the devil thus harassing thee, that God, our Saviour, with all his holy angels, taketh delight and joy in thee; and that the end and issue of the whole will be blessed, as thou certainly shalt both find and feel. (James, v. 10, 11.)

"Above all things," said Luther, "beware of entering into that dispute of Predestination: and, to arm thyself against it, take hold on God's word, in which God hath revealed Himself unto thee, and wherein thou acknowledgest the great benefits of Christ; that, for thy sake, He came from heaven; for thy good was made man, and thy brother; yea, thy flesh and blood; that He took from thee all thy sins, and loaded Himself with them, made satisfaction for them, and with His bitter death and sufferings made payment for them to the Father; arose again from the dead; overcame death, devil, and hell; and, by His ascending into heaven, took them captive; and all this for thy good. Hereby thou mayest perceive and know, that it is a great and unspeakable love which God the Father beareth towards thee, in that ' *He spared not His Own Son, but gave Him up* ' to death for thee. Therefore, suffer not thyself to be led away from Him by any cogitations or temptations whatever; but remain thou by Christ, lying at the breast in His mother's bosom or hanging on the cross: otherwise thou mayest be thoroughly plagued and tormented, as I have been; yea, and be tempted to blaspheme Him whom thou oughtest to praise; for all treasure lieth hid in Christ, but without Christ they are altogether locked up. The safe way in dealing with Predestination, if so thou must, is to begin low down* at Christ; all who begin at the top break their necks."

"If," said Luther, "any man will ask, Why God permitteth that men be hardened, and fall into everlasting perdition? Let him ask again, Why God did not spare His own Son, but gave Him up for us all, to die the most contemned death of the cross, which is a more certain sign of His love to us, poor people, than any thing else is of His wrath and anger against us. Such questions cannot well be answered better than by the like contrary questions. True it is," said Luther, "that the malicious devil deceived and seduced Adam; but we ought again to consider, that, immediately after the fall, Adam received the promise of the woman's seed that should crush the serpent's head, and should bless the people on earth. Therefore, we must acknowledge, lay to heart, and well contemplate, that the goodness and mercy of the Father is immeasurably great towards the wicked and ungodly world; who sent His Son to be their Saviour. Let, therefore, His good will be acceptable unto thee," said Luther,

---

* See the Seventeenth Article of the Church. The misery of man, with respect to this great doctrine, is, "that," as Luther says, "he will begin at the top instead of the bottom;" or, as Bradford the Martyr, expressed the same sentiment, "will get at once to the University of Predestination without passing through the Grammar School of Effectual Calling." St. Peter says, "Make your calling and (thus) election sure." 2 Pet. i. 10.

"and do not speculate with that devilish query, 'Why and wherefore,' touching God's words and works; for God, who is a Creator of all creatures, and ordereth all things according to His unsearchable will and wisdom, hath no pleasure in such questions, but rather abhors them.*

"That God," continued Luther, "sometimes, out of His Divine premeditated counsel, unsearchable to human reason, hath mercy on one man, and hardeneth another, as the Scripture speaks of Pharaoh, it becometh not us to search out. We must know and be assured of this," said Luther, "that He doth nothing without certain cause and premeditated counsel: and, truly, if God were to give an account to every one of His words and actions, then would He be, indeed, but a poor simple God."

"When one asked, Where God was before heaven was created? St. Austin replied, 'He was in Himself.' And as another asked him," said Luther, "the like question, he said, 'He was building of hell for such idle, presumptuous, fluttering spirits and inquisitors as thou art.' After He had created all things," said Luther, "He was every where, and yet He was nowhere; for I cannot take hold of Him (without the word) by any cogitations of mine. But He will be found there where He hath bound Himself to be. The Jews found Him at Jerusalem by the throne of grace (Exod. xxv. 21, 22.); we find Him in the word and faith, in baptism and sacraments, but in His majesty," said Luther, "He is nowhere to be found."

* Job, xxxiii. 13. Is. xlv. 9, 10.

Luther meeting a very melancholy man, whom formerly he well knew, in Wittemberg, saluted him, and said, " Ah! human creature, what doest thou? hast thou nothing else in hand, but to think on thy sins, on death and damnation? turn thine eyes quickly away, and look hither to This Man, Christ Jesus, of whom it is written, ' *He was conceived by the Holy Ghost, born of the Virgin Mary, suffered, died, was buried, the third day rose again from the dead, ascended up into heaven,*" &c. Wherefore, dost thou think, was all this done? Was it not that thou shouldest comfort thyself against death and sin? therefore surcease; be not afraid, neither do thou faint; for, truly, thou hast no cause, for Christ suffered death for thee, and prevailed for thy comfort and defence, and for that cause He sitteth at the right hand of God, His Heavenly Father, to deliver thee."

"It were a light and easy matter," said Luther, "for a Christian to suffer and overcome death, if he knew not that it were God's wrath: it is that title which makes death bitter unto us. But a heathen [*] dieth away unconcernedly, he neither seeth nor feeleth that it is God's wrath; it is the end of nature, it

[*] The most considerate and understanding men among the heathen philosophers, bent all their studies to discover arguments by which they might support themselves against the fear of death; while the unlearned and the unreflecting met it with seeming indifference. Yet has death been, in every country and in all ages, a subject of apprehension; and the Christian, regarding death as the most manifest sign of God's displeasure against sin, must needs be more than others afraid of it, but for the lively hope of pardon and peace which is given him in Christ Jesus, his Lord.

is natural. The Epicure saith, It is but to endure an evil hour."

"We read," said Luther, "of St. Vincent, that being ready to die, he saw Death standing at his feet, and said, Death! what wilt thou? Thinkest thou to gain any thing of a Christian? knowest thou not that I am a Christian? Even so," said Luther, "ought we to learn to contemn, scorn, and deride death. It is likewise written in the history of St. Martin, that being near his death, he saw the devil standing at his bed's feet, and boldly said, *Quid tu hic stas, horrenda bestia? Nihil habes in me:* that is, Why stands't thou here, thou horrible beast? Thou hast nothing to do with me. These," said Luther, "were right words of faith. Such and the like ought we to cull out of the legends of the saints, and leave other fooleries which by the Papists are foisted thereinto."

Of Adam's Fall.

"Miserable and most lamentable was the fall of Adam," said Luther, "who from the state of innocency fell into such a calamity as is not to be uttered; for during 900 years he saw God's wrath in the death of every human creature."

"After that Adam had lost the righteousness in which God created him, he was, without all doubt," said Luther, "much decayed in body, by reason of anguish and sorrow of heart. I can well believe that before the fall he could have seen further off by a thousand times, as easily as we can now see half a mile, and so proportionably with the other senses.

No doubt, after the fall, he said, 'Ah, God! How is it with me? I am both blind and deaf! Where have I been,' &c. It was a horrible fall; for he saw before that all creatures were obedient unto him, insomuch that he durst dally and play even with a serpent."

"Adam, our father," said Luther, "was doubtless a most miserable plagued man. It was a mighty solitariness for him to be alone in so wide and vast a world; but when he with Eve (his only companion and loving consort) obtained Cain their son, then there was great joy: in like manner also when Abel was born: but soon after what great misery and sorrow of heart followed, when one brother slew the other, and Adam thereby lost one son while the other was banished from his presence. This, surely, was a great cross; this murder would cause him more grief than his own fall: thus he and his loving Eve were reduced to a solitary kind of life again. Afterwards when he was 130 years old, he begat Seth. It was, surely, a great grief and woe so long a time to see God's anger. Ah! he was a perplexed man, so as no human creature can conceive. Our sufferings, in comparison of his misery and sorrow of heart, are altogether children's toys. His only comfort and refreshment was the promise of the Woman's Seed."

Adam's Judgment of Modern Luxury.

"Whereto," said Luther, "serveth such superfluity; such bravery, bragging, and extraordinary lustful kind of living as is in use now-a-days? If Adam should now come again, and see our kind of life, our food, drink, and apparel, how would he bless himself, and say, 'Surely this is not the world I belonged to! It was, doubtless, another Adam (he would say), and not I, that was here at the first.' For he drank water, ate fruit from the trees, had a house set up and supported with four wooden forks (if so good); he had no knife, nor iron tool, nor any coat but a skin one. But now is used an immeasurable cost in eating and drinking; now are raised royal and princely palaces, chargeable trimmings, apparel beyond comparison, &c. The ancients kept and maintained themselves with much more moderation and quietness, as Boaz said, '*Dip thy bread in the vinegar, and refresh thyself.*' For those countries were full of people, as we read in the book of Joshua. A great multitude of people teacheth well how to live sparingly."

Of Adam's Tribulations.

"When God, through Adam, said to Cain, '*Is it not so, if thou doest well, shalt thou not be accepted? and if thou doest not well, sin lieth at the door:*' He toucheth and showeth therewith the secureness of sinners, and He speaketh with Cain as with the greatest hypocrite, and most poisoned Capuchin friar. It was as if Adam should say, 'Thou hast heard how it went with me in Paradise. I also would willingly have hid my offence, and I wore the fig leaves, and lurked behind a tree; but know, good fellow, our Lord God will not be deceived, the fig leaves would not serve the turn,'" &c.

"Ah!" said Luther, "it was doubtless to good Adam a smarting and a sorrowful task, to be compelled to banish and proscribe his first-begotten and only son, to hunt him away from his house, and to say; 'Depart from me, and come no more in my sight: I feel still well what I have already lost in Paradise; I will lose no more for thy sake. I will now, with more diligence, take heed to my God's commandments. And, no doubt," said Luther, " Adam afterwards preached with earnest diligence."

"Adam," said Luther, " begat more children than those three which are specified in the Bible. But in that mention is made of Seth in particular, that was done on account of the lineage of our Lord Jesus Christ, who was to come of that descent. Adam, doubtless, had many sons and daughters. I am persuaded," said Luther, " he had at least 200 children, for Adam lived to be very old, 930 years. It is likely that Cain was born thirty years after the fall, as they were comforted again. I believe they were oftentimes comforted by angels, it would otherwise have been impossible for them to have lain together, so great were their sorrows and fears. Eve, at the last day, will be found to exceed all women in sorrow and misery. Never came upon the world a more sorrowful miserable woman than Eve: she saw that for her sake we were all to die. All other women may hold their peace before Eve. Some affirm," said Luther, " that Cain was conceived before the promise of the seed that should bruise the serpent's head. But I," said Luther, " am persuaded that the promise was made not full half a day after the fall."

Of David.

When Philip Melancthon was asking certain questions concerning King David and his great tribulations, though a king ordained immediately of God, Luther rendered to him his answers, and then exclaimed. " Ah, Lord God! how is it that thou sufferest such great people to fall? This David had six wives, who, no doubt, were wise and understanding women, like that wise Abigail. If they were all such, then was he, indeed, furnished with excellent surpassing wives. Moreover he had, beside them, ten concubines; yet, notwithstanding, he was an adulterer!

" Some are of opinion," said Luther, " that David did evil, when, upon his death-bed, he commanded Solomon, his son, to punish Shimei, who cursed and threw dirt at him in his flight before Absalom. But," said Luther, " I say he did well and right therein; for it is the office of a magistrate to punish the guilty and wicked malefactors. He made a vow, indeed, not to punish him, but that is to be understood of his own life-time.

" David (in so strange and confused a government, where no man knew who was cook, or who was butler, as we use to say) was constrained, much and often, to close an eye, and (according to common speech) to look through the fingers at many abuses and wrongs; but afterwards, when peace was, in Solomon's time, then, through Solomon, he punished. In time of disquiet and tumultuous governments, a ruler dareth not so to proceed as in time of peace; yet it is fit that evil be punished at last."

" Neither Cicero, Virgil, nor Demosthenes, are to be compared with David for eloquence, as we see in Psalm cxix., which he divideth into twenty-two parts (in each of which are eight verses) and yet in all there is but one kind of meaning, namely, ' Thy law (or word) is good.' He had a great gift, and was highly favoured of God. I hold that God suffered him to fall so horribly, lest he should be too haughty and proud."

Of Hezekiah.

"Hezekiah was a very good and godly king," said Luther; "full of faith; yet he fell. God cannot endure that a human creature should trust and depend upon his own works. No man entereth heaven without the remission of sins."

Of Jonah.

"An upright Christian," said Luther, " is like unto Jonah, who was cast into the sea, yea, into hell. He beheld the mouth of that monster gaping, and lay three days in his dark belly without consuming. This history should be unto us one of the greatest comforts, and a manifest sign of the resurrection from the dead.

"In such sort God useth to humble those that are His: but afterwards he went too far; would presume to master God Almighty; became a great manslayer and a murderer; for he would have had so great a city, and such a multitude of people, to be utterly destroyed, when God was resolved to spare them. This," said Luther, " was a strange saint."

Luther's Judgment concerning the Fathers.

"*Patres, quamquam sæpe errant, tamen venerandi sunt propter testimonium fidei.* We honour Jerome,

Gregory, and others," said Luther, " because, in their writings, we feel that they believed in Christ, as we do; even as the Christian church, from the beginning of the world, hath had our faith. *Bernard's* penny is of value," said Luther, " when he teacheth and preacheth; but when he falleth into dispute, then he is often against himself, and opposeth that which formerly he taught. *Non igitur valent Patres ad pugnandum; sed propter testimonium fidei omnes sunt venerandi.* When *Bernard* preacheth," said Luther, " then he is above all the doctors in the church; but when he disputeth, then he is altogether another man; *ibi nimium tribuit præcepto et libero arbitrio. Bonaventura*," said Luther, " is the best among all the School Divines and church writers. *Austin* always had the pre-eminence among the Fathers; the second in esteem was *Ambrose*, and *Bernard* the third. *Tertullian*, among the church teachers, is a right Carlestad.* *Cyril* hath the best sentences. *Cyprian*, the martyr, is a weak divine. *Theophylact* is the best expounder and interpreter of St. Paul.

" A man may read *Jerome*," said Luther, " for the history's sake; for in his writings is not so much as one word touching faith and upright true religion and doctrine. As for *Origen*, I have banished him already. *Chrysostom* I esteem nothing worth; he is only a talker. *Basil* is of no value at all; he is merely a friar; I would not give a hair for Basil. The Apology of Philip Melancthon," said Luther, " surpasseth all the Fathers of the church, yea, it surpasseth Austin. *Hilary* and *Theophylact* are good, and so is *Ambrose*,

---

* An intemperate, wrong-headed man, once a colleague of Luther's, at Wittemberg.

for he sometimes finely toucheth the remission of sins, which is the highest article; namely, that the Divine Majesty doth pardon sin."

"*Jerome*," said Luther, " should not be numbered among the teachers of the church, for he was, indeed, a heretic; nevertheless I believe that he is saved through the faith in Christ. He speaketh (in a manner) nothing of Christ, only carrying His name in his mouth. I know none among the teachers whom I hate like Jerome; for he writeth only of fasting, of victual, of virginity, &c. He teacheth nothing either of faith, of hope, or of charity, nor of the works of faith. Truly," said Luther, " I would not willingly have entertained Jerome for my chaplain."

" I much do applaud the hymns and spiritual songs of *Prudentius*; he was the best poet of the Christians. If he had been in the time of Virgil, he would have been extolled above Horace. I would wish," said Luther, " that the verses and songs of Prudentius were read in schools; but schools now become Heathenish[*], and the Holy Scriptures (upon which chiefly they stand and are built) are expelled, or else falsified and sophisticated through Philosophy.

[*] Can we say that they do not remain so to this day? The minds of youth, in most of the principal schools of our Christian land, are imbued with Heathenish mythology, history, and philosophy; while little or no pains are taken to correct the false sentiment inculcated by the Heathen writers. Hence the code of morals, in the higher classes of society amongst us, is abundantly more of a Heathenish than of a Christian character. Schoolmasters, when reading the classics with their pupils, should never allow them to forget that they are Christians.

"Among all the Fathers," said Luther, "*Austin* and *Hilary* wrote most clear and plainly: all the rest ought to be read with judgment, with circumspection, and care. *Tertullian* was harsh and superstitious, though *Cyprian* boasteth of him that he was his master. Therefore," said Luther, "let us read the Fathers with distinction, considerately. Let us lay them in the gold balance; for the Fathers stumbled oftentimes, and went astray: they mingle in their books many impertinent and monkish things. Austin had more work to screw and wind himself out of the Fathers, than he had with the heretics. *Gregory* expoundeth the five pounds (which the husbandman in the Gospel gave to his servants) to be the five senses, which the senseless beasts also do possess; but the two pounds he construeth to be the reason and understanding!"

"When God's word," said Luther, "is by the Fathers expounded, construed, and glossed, then, in my judgment, it is even like unto one that strained milk through a coal sack, which must needs spoil the milk, and make it black; even so likewise, God's word, of itself, is sufficiently pure, clean, bright, and clear; but through the doctrines, books, and writings of the Fathers, it is very sorely darkened, falsified, and spoiled."

"Truly," said Luther, "much hath been read and written without understanding: there is now risen unto us a great light; for we have not only the word but also the true understanding thereof, and (God be praised) we know what is right. No sophister was ever able to understand these words:—' *The just liveth by faith.*'

Neither did the Fathers of the church understand them; for this word '*just*', or righteous, they expounded divers ways, such blindness was in the loving Fathers.

"Therefore," said Luther, "let us, first and principally, read the Holy Scriptures, and afterwards we may read also the Fathers; yet with good heed and discretion, for the Fathers have not always judged rightly of God's causes and works: he that will leave the Bible, and will lay his study upon the comments and books of the Fathers, his study will be endless and in vain."

———

"Behold, I pray," said Luther, "what great darkness is in the books of the Fathers concerning faith? for if the article of Justification (how we are justified before God) be darkened, then may the grossest errors of mankind be smothered up. St. Jerome, indeed, wrote upon Matthew, upon the Epistles to the Galatians, and to Titus; but, alas! very coldly. Ambrose wrote six books upon the first book of Moses; but they are very slender. Augustine, till he was roused up and made a man by the Pelagians, and strove against them, wrote nothing to the purpose concerning faith. The Fathers, indeed, taught well and finely," said Luther; "but they could not openly deliver it, because they had no combating or striving. I can find no exposition upon the Epistles to the Romans and Galatians wherein any thing is taught purely and uprightly; Oh!" said Luther, "what a happy time we have now for purity of doctrines, but, alas! we little esteem it.

"The good loving Fathers," said Luther, "taught better than they wrote. After the Fathers came the Pope, and fell in with his mischievous traditions and human ordinances; and (like a breaking water cloud and deluge) overflowed the church; snared the consciences touching eating and drinking, touching friars' hoods and masses, touching his dirty laws and decrees: insomuch as he daily and continually brought abominable errors into the church of Christ, and to serve his own turn he took hold on Austin's sentence, where he saith, ' *Evangelio non crederem*,' &c.

"The ass-heads could not discern what occasioned Austin to utter that sentence, for he spake it against the Manichees, as if he should say, ' I believe you not, for I know you to be cursed heretics, but I believe and hold with the Church, the spouse of Christ, which cannot err.'"

"Epiphanius, long before Jerome, described the church histories, which are good and profitable. Separate them from matters of strife and controversial arguments," said Luther, "and they are worth the printing.

"The Fathers had a great lustre and esteem by reason of their good conversations, and strict kind of lives. Their lustre consisted in watchings and fastings, which, indeed, were surpassing, and," said Luther, " so it beseemed such people to be; for there must be either a seeming sanctity (which also the hypocrites have), or else there must be an upright essence and being, which proceedeth from the heart, as the great champions whom God awakeneth are endued withal."

"Although it becometh not me," said Luther, " to censure the holy Fathers (I being in comparison of them a little worm and of no repute,) yet, notwithstanding, the more I read their books, the more I find myself offended. They were but men, and (to speak the truth) their reputation and authority were the occasion of undervaluing and suppressing the writings of the sacred Apostles of Christ. From whence the Papists were not ashamed to blaspheme, and to say, 'What is the Scripture? We must read the holy Fathers and teachers, for they sucked the honey out of the Scriptures.' As if the Word of God were to be understood by none but themselves; whereas the Heavenly Father, touching Christ, saith, '*Hear ye Him*,' who in the Gospel spake and taught most simply, clear, and plainly, in parables and similitudes. As where he saith, '*He that believeth in me shall never die*,' also, '*Behold, the fowls of the air, and the flowers of the field*,' &c. Notwithstanding which, the Popish sophists dare presume to blaspheme the Holy Scriptures, and allege * that they are dark, and not well to be understood, unless the Fathers expound and clear them; but," said Luther, " this expounding and clearing of theirs may be much rather called overshadowing and darkening. Austin," said Luther, " pleaseth me above them all, he was a surpassing doctor and, worthy of all praise; he taught purely and uprightly, and, with Christian humility, subjected his writings to the Holy Scriptures, as where he writes, '*Noli meis scriptis*,' &c.

" The good man solemnly protesteth that we should

---

* The Third Article of the Romish Church, according to Pope Pius's Creed, is as follows : —

" I also," (after ' most steadfastly admitting and embracing apostolical and ecclesiastical traditions,') " admit the Holy Scriptures, according to that sense which our holy mother the church has held, and does hold: to which it belongs to judge of the true sense and interpretation of the Scriptures ; neither will I *ever, take and interpret them otherwise than according to the unanimous consent of the Fathers.*"

not hold his * writings comparable to the Holy Scriptures, much less give them the preference.

"I am persuaded," said Luther, "that Austin dropped that (*Noli meis scriptis*, &c.) for the sake of Chrysostom, who lived not full sixty years before Austin, and was eloquent and talkative, which brought him into great esteem among the people. Chrysostom wrote many books which had great lustre and repute, but (in truth) they were only a wild, disorderly, heap, a sackfull of windy words to little or no purpose. The same much vexed and grieved St. Austin, and induced him to drop that speech aforesaid. When Dr. Schurf bought Chrysostom and had read him, he said, 'I read much, and learn nothing.'

"Ah!" said Luther, "the Fathers were but men as we are, therefore we must well consider what it is they say; we must look to their lips. I do not contemn what is Christian-like and good in the Fathers, but they must be read with very great discretion. The best and chiefest sentences in Austin are these:—'*Sins are forgiven*,' said he, '*not that they are no more present, but in that they are not imputed.*' He likewise saith, *The law is then fulfilled, when that is pardoned which is not fulfilled.*"

"Austin knocked and offended himself on human traditions, and, oh! how pitifully doth he, now and then, torment himself, in expounding the Psalter. Nevertheless he was strong and powerful in the Holy Scriptures, and had a fine judgment and understanding in causes. He was sharpened by those heretics the

---

* It was not in vain that our Lord gave the caution, Matt. xxiii., " Call no man your master, or father, upon earth."

Pelagians; he affected the state of matrimony, spake well of good bishops, who then were ministers; but those times vexed and offended him much. If he were living now, he would doubtless be enraged to see and hear the abominations of the Pope, in boasting of St. Peter's patrimony; the same St. Austin would not endure.

"Certainly he was the most earnest, expert, and pure teacher of them all, but he was not able of himself to reduce things to their former state; for he oftentimes complaineth, that the bishops, with their traditions and ordinances, more troubled the Church than the Jews did with their laws."

Sundry Similitudes.

Once, towards evening, two birds came flying into Luther's garden, where they had made their nest, but they were oftentimes scared away by those that passed by. Luther, observing this, said, "O ye loving pretty birds, fly not away, I am heartily well contented with you, if ye could but trust me; but it is even the same with ourselves," said he; "we cannot trust in God, who, notwithstanding, showeth and wisheth us all goodness."

"When the people of Gerar saw that Isaac reaped an hundred fold from the land which Abimelech had rented to him, they came quickly and instigated the king against him, to take the ground from him again. They thought, surely the land and its increase shall be ours. They reckoned upon growing rich by the occupation of that land, little knowing or considering that *benedictio Dei* (the blessing of God) was with him, and that they were cursed. *Sic et nostri principes jam nihil agunt, quam ut fiant maledicti a Deo.* Our princes make it their only work to get the curse of God. They also hunt Isaac out of the land, but the blessing of God is very small which is left behind him."

"I saw a pretty dog at Lintz in Austria," said Luther, "that was taught to go with a basket, and with the basket he went to the butchers' shambles for meat; now when other dogs came about him to take the meat out of the basket, he set it down, and bit and fought lustily with the other dogs; but when he saw that they would be too strong for him, then he himself snatched out the first piece of meat lest he should lose all. Even so now doth our emperor Charles: he hath, for a long time, defended the spiritual livings; but seeing every prince take and rake the monasteries unto themselves, he now takes possession of bishoprics; as newly he hath snatched to himself the bishoprics of Utrecht and Luttick, to the end also he may get *partem de tunica Christi* (a share of Christ's raiment.)"

"A man," said Luther, "that dependeth upon the riches and honour of this world, and, in the mean time, forgets God and the welfare of his soul, is like a little child that holdeth in the hand a fair apple, which on the outside is pleasing to behold, and thinketh it hath also some goodness within, but it is rotten and all full of worms."

"A scorpion," said Luther, "thinketh if his head doth but be hid, and is thrust under a leaf, then he cannot be seen. Even so the hypocrites and false saints do think when they have snatched up one or two good works, then all their sins are well covered therewith."

"I am a bitter enemy to flies," said Luther, "*quia sunt imago diaboli et hereticorum*, they are the image of the devil and of heretics; for when I open a fair book, then the flies are presently upon it with their tails running about, as if they would say, 'Here will we sit, and soil this book with our excrement.' Even so doth the devil likewise; when our hearts are most pure, then cometh he and fouleth therein. When my desires are at the best, and most fitted for praise, then the devil approacheth, and carrieth my cogitations (it may be) as far as Babylon, or else I am building castles in the air."

"The clogs which the Capuchin friars wear," said Luther, "are made of the wood of that cursed fig-tree touching which Christ said, 'Cursed art thou, and henceforth never more bear fruit.'"

CONCERNING THE JEWS.

Their Sufferings and continued Obstinacy.

"Although the Jews have been punished so long," said Luther, "and still are punished to this day, yet will they not hear, but do still blaspheme. How wickedly do they blaspheme that good maid, the blessed Virgin Mary! Truly, had she been a heathen, yet were it too, too much.

"Behold," said Luther, "they have now suffered

1500 years,—what, then, will be their suffering in hell? No people on earth are so hardly punished and plagued as the Jews. I advise," said Luther, " that no man talk with a Jew of Christ being the Son of God, for he will not believe: therefore will I dispute no more with them.

" Rabbi Abida, a Jew, said once to me, ' Messias is already come; but,' said he, ' he was the son of a star, and was begotten of Jacob's star.' That poor wretched people know not what they are about; sometimes they will say, ' He is come;' at others, they deny it. For my part," said Luther, " I take the Jews to be mere Epicures, and that they have despaired of Messiah. They believe, whoso doeth good works, the same is just; whoso heareth Moses is saved, whether Messiah come or not. They allege Messiah will set up the law again; in short, they expect a temporal kingdom."

Condition of the Jews in Luther's Time.

" The Jews are the poorest people among all the nations on the earth; they are plagued every where, scattered to and fro in all countries, they have no certain place, they sit, as it were, on a wheelbarrow, have no country, people, or government; yet they wait with great desire, they cheer up themselves, and say, ' It will soon be better with us.' In such sort are they hardened, that, in the highest shame, they presume to brag and boast. But," said Luther, " I advise them to know assuredly, that there is none other Lord, nor God, but only He that sitteth on the right hand of God the Father. The Jews are not permitted to trade nor to keep cattle, they are only usurers, maintaining themselves with horse-coursing and brokerage; they eat nothing which the Christians kill and touch; they drink no wine; they have many, innumerable, superstitions; they wash the flesh most diligently, as though that were the cleansing that they needed. Such superstitions proceed out of God's anger. For they that are without faith, have laws without end, as we see by the Papists and Turks; but they are rightly served; for seeing they refused to have Christ and His Gospel, therefore instead of freedom they must have servitude."

"If I," said Luther, "were a right Jew, the Pope should never persuade me to his worshipping; rather would I suffer myself to be wheeled and racked. Popedom, with their abominations and false worshippings, has given the Jews innumerable offences. I feel persuaded if the Jews heard our preaching, and how we handle the sentences in the Old Testament, that many of them might be won; but through disputing they are made but more stiff-necked and angry, for they are too haughty and presumptuous. If but one or two of the rabbies and chief of them fell off, then we should see a falling off of one after another, for they are almost weary of expecting."

"At Frankfort on the Maine are very many Jews; they have a whole street in possession, where every house is filled with them; they are compelled to wear little yellow rings on the outsides of their coats and garments, thereby to be known; they have neither houses of their own, nor grounds; nothing but moveable and flitting goods, they dare not lend any thing on houses or lands, except at great hazard."

[illegible]

[illegible] they earnestly besought [illegible]
[illegible] that is, Jesus crucified, [illegible]
[illegible] must blaspheme [illegible]
[illegible] exceedingly that song wh[illegible]
[illegible] church. "*Christ is risen* [illegible]
[illegible] it is most wonderful that so m[illegible]
[illegible] people have been slangin[illegible]
[illegible] of them, only Jes[illegible]
[illegible] his death [illegible]

[illegible] with the Jew[illegible]

[illegible] "must be [illegible]
[illegible] this with [illegible]
[illegible]," said I[illegible]
[illegible]

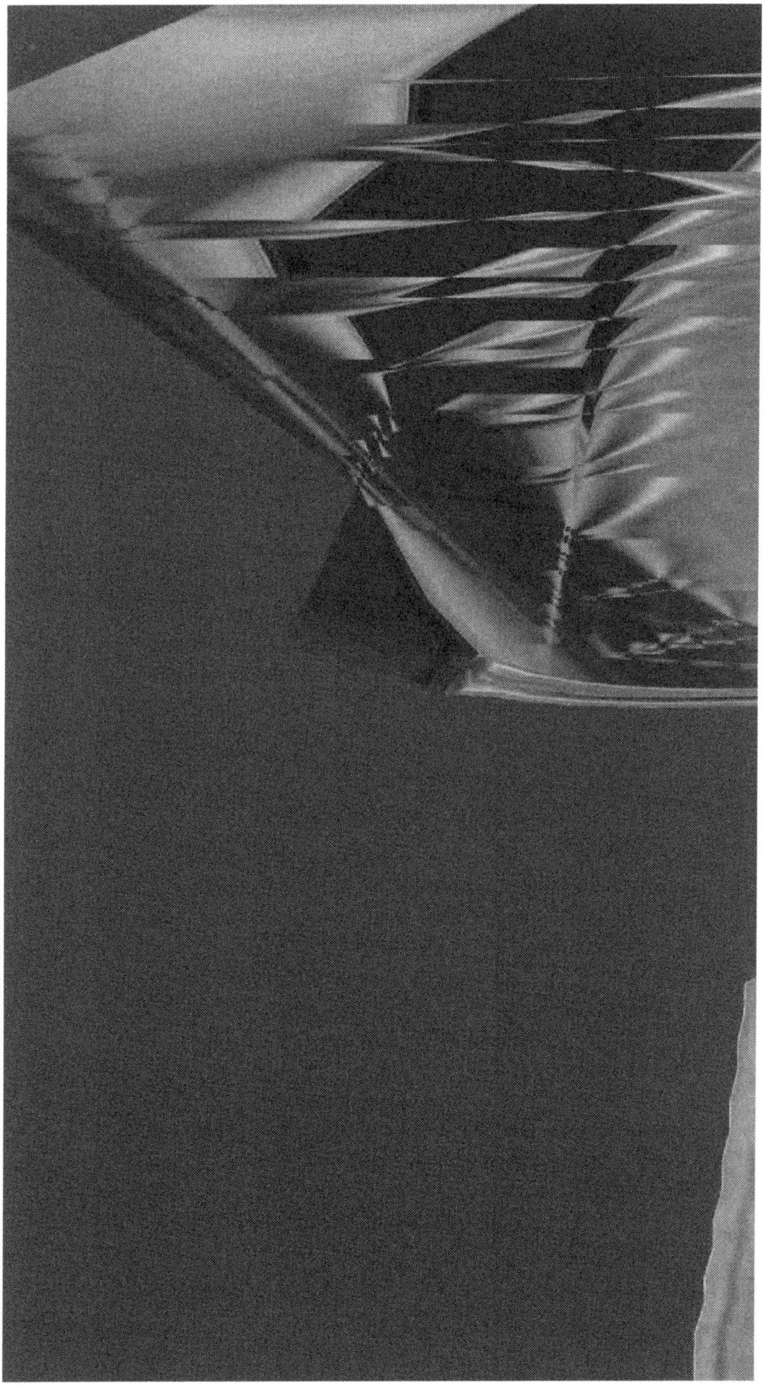

and down the whole empire, and to think that almost all the blood-kindred of Christ burn in hell. They are served rightly, and even according to their own words which they spake to Pilate, — '*His blood be on us and on our children,*' '*We have no king but Cæsar,*' &c. The Jews have haughty prayers, wherein they praise and call upon God, as though they alone were His people, and, meanwhile, curse and maledict all other nations. The poor people are not to be helped; they refuse to hear God's word, and only follow their own cogitations and conceits. They flatter themselves that they are holy by nature and kind, like as the Gentiles are of the will of the flesh. But the Papists dream of a middle way; they are neither Jews nor Christians; they will be justified neither out of the will of the flesh, nor by nature and kind, but by reason of the name and title Catholic. But all this is rejected and condemned; as St. John saith, — 'They are God's children, and justified, which are born of God."

What came of a Jew's visiting Rome.

"Another Jew repaired unto me at Wittemberg," said Luther, "and told me he was very desirous to be baptized, and made a Christian; but said, he would first go to Rome to see the chief head of Christendom. This his intention, myself, Philip Melancthon, and other divines, laboured in the strongest manner to prevent; for we feared that when he should behold the offences and knaveries at Rome, he might thereby be scared from Christianity altogether. But the Jew went to Rome; and when he had stayed long enough to witness the abominations practised there, he returned to us again, desiring to be baptized, and said, ' Now will I willingly worship the God of the Christians, for He is a patient God. Can He endure and suffer such wickedness and villany as there is at Rome? then can He suffer and endure all the vices and knaveries in the world.'"

Of the miserable state of people's lives.

"What miserable poor people we are!" said Luther; "we earn our bread with sin; for until we attain to seven years we do nothing but feed, drink, play, and sleep: afterwards, from the eighth year, we go to school, it may be, three or four hours in the day: from this time to the one-and-twentieth year, we drive on and commit all manner of folly, with playing, running, drinking, swilling, and what not; and then we begin to labour a little. When we come to fifty years, then we get done with labouring, and become children again. The half of our life we consume in sleeping, eating, &c., insomuch that scarce five years are spent in labouring. We hardly work for the tenth part of our lives. Fie upon us! we do not give to God even the tenth. What, then, are we able, with our good works, to earn of God Almighty. Yet how we brag and boast of them! Job saith, '*If God should contend with me, I cannot answer Him one thing of a thousand.*' Instead, therefore, of boasting of our good works and deservings, we should say, '*Enter not into judgment with thy servant, O Lord!*'"

A few short Sayings.

"Faith hath regard to the Word, not to the preacher.
The Gospel cometh from God; it showeth Christ, and requireth faith.

"No state or calling is of any value to make one good before God.

"A Christian's life consisteth in three points,— Faith, Love, and the Cross.

"Christ is given to those that believe, with all His benefits and works.

"Works belong to the neighbour: faith to God.

"The law is nothing but a looking-glass.

"Good works are the seals and proofs of faith. A letter must have its seal and signature, and faith must have good works.

"No man must build upon his faith.

"Where the Holy Ghost preacheth not, there is no Church."

That Women must not have the Government.

"The wives of great kings and princes have not the government; for God saith to the woman, 'Thou shalt be obedient to thy husband,' &c. The man hath the government in the house, except he be *verbum anomalum*, that is to say, a fool; or that out of love to his wife he suffers her to govern*, as sometimes the master follows his servant's counsel. Otherwise the woman must wear a kerchief, as an honest woman ought to do: she must help to bear her husband's crosses, troubles, sicknesses, &c. The law deprives

---

* It is said of the virtuous woman in Prov. xxxi., "*The heart of her husband safely trusteth in her.*" He can trust in her, both to govern, and to resign the government when called upon to do so. A very worthy and wise man, whose colloquial talents were peculiarly excellent, put the matter thus, "When my wife and I are in the gig together, I have no objection to her driving, provided she give me the reins when I ask for them."

the women of wisdom and government; therefore St. Paul saith, 1 Cor. xiv., 'they are commanded to be under obedience;' and 1 Tim. ii., 'I suffer not a woman to teach, nor to usurp authority over the man.'"

Dr. Luther's Thoughts on Domestic and Political Government.

"A mayor in a city, a father and a mother, a master and a dame, tradesmen and others," said Luther, "must now and then look through the fingers, towards their citizens, children, and servants; they must see and not see, hear and not hear, &c., if their faults and offences be not too gross and too frequent. For where we will have *summum jus*, the severest law, there followeth oftentimes *summa injuria*, so that all must go to wrack. Neither do they which are in office always hit it rightly, but do err many times in pronouncing wrong judgments, &c.; they must, therefore, seek the forgiveness of sin, and so must we all."

"*In administratione œconomiæ et politiæ*," said Luther, "there must be *lex*, where we would not have *ut aliquid peccetur. E contra*, when things are done amiss, then *remissio peccatorum* must appear, otherwise we spoil all. *Maritum oportet multa dissimulare in uxore et liberis, et tamen non amittere debet legem.* Even thus it is," said Luther, "in every state and calling: *remissio peccatorum est in omnibus creaturis.* The trees grow not all alike straight; the waters run not every where line-straight forward, neither is the earth in all places alike good. *Vera igitur est sententia: qui nescit dissimulare, nescit imperare. Hæc est ἐπιείκεια*; this is moderation,—we must bear with many things, and look through the fingers, and yet, withal, not suffer every thing to pass. It is said, '*Nec omnia, nec nihil.*'"

Difference between Parents and Magistrates.

"Parents," said Luther, "do keep their children with greater diligence and care than rulers or governors keep their subjects, from whence Moses saith, Num. xi. 12., '*Have I conceived this people?*' &c. Fathers and mothers are masters, naturally and free-willingly; it is a self-grown dominion; but that of rulers and magistrates is a forced mastery; that is, they deal by force, it is a made and prepared dominion. Therefore when father and mother can rule no more, then the hangman must do the deed, and bring them up. Therefore rulers and magistrates ought to be watchers over the Fifth Commandment."

How Governors should be qualified.

"Governors should be wise, they should be of courageous spirits, and should know how to rule without their counsellors. The princes of Anhalt are finely qualified, learned and modest princes, both in words, gestures, and actions: they are well practised in the Latin tongue, and thoroughly acquainted with the Bible, &c. I may truly say," said Luther, "I lately held with those princes a divine dinner, for at the table they had no other discourse than of God's word, with great humility, discretion, and affability. Truly they are god-fearing, understanding, and very worthy princes, who doubtless intend to gather together a treasure in heaven: which they certainly will, if they stedfastly remain by the doctrine of the Gospel."

The false reckonings of ungodly Princes.

"Potentates and princes in these days," said Luther, "when they take an enterprise in hand, do not pray before they begin; but make themselves a reckoning of this sort:—Three times three make nine, twice seven is fourteen, this faileth not, &c.; that is, in this way the business must surely take effect: therefore our Lord God saith unto them, 'For whom, then, hold ye Me? for a cipher? Do I sit here above, in vain and for no purpose? You shall therefore know that I will turn your account quite contrary, and will make them all false reckonings.'"

Concerning Pontius Pilate the Governor.

"Pilate," said Luther, "was more honest and just than, at this time, any prince of the empire, except such as are Protestants. I could name many popish princes who are not at all comparable unto Pilate, for he held stiffly to the Roman laws and rights. He would not that innocent persons, and such as were not openly convicted, should be condemned and executed, without due hearing of their cause; he, therefore, propounded all manner of civil conditions, to the end he might have released Christ; but when they threatened him with the Emperor's displeasure, then he was dazzled and forsook the Imperial Laws; thought he, 'it is but the loss of one man, who is both poor and, therewithal, contemned, no man taking his part. What hurt can I receive by his death? Better is it that one man should die, than that the whole nation should be against me.'

Dr. Matthesius, and Dr. Pommer fell into debate about this question, why Pilate scourged Jesus, and said, " *What is truth?* " for the one alleged, that Pilate did it out of compassion, but the other said, it was done out of tyranny and contempt. "Whereupon," Luther said, " Pilate was a right worldly man, he scourged Christ out of great compassion, in the hope of stilling the insatiable wrath and raging of the Jews; and in that he said to Christ ' *What is truth?*' it was as if he said, ' Wilt thou dispute concerning truth in these wicked times of the world? Truth!—truth is of no value here. But thou must think upon some other trick, upon some of the lawyers' quiddits, peradventure thou mayest in this way obtain thy release.'"

The two doctors, above named, asked Luther "What the devil intended to gain, when, through Pilate's wife, he sought to hinder the crucifying of Christ?" Luther replied, " The devil's meaning, doubtless, was this—thought he, ' I have slain and made away with many prophets, yet it groweth still worse and worse with me: they are so constant. This Jesus also is altogether unaffrighted and undiscouraged to die: therefore,' thought the devil, ' I would rather that he remained alive; it may be I shall be able to ensnare him by some other means, and overcome him with some temptation or other, and thereby I should gain much more,' &c. The devil," said Luther, " hath high cogitations. And we at this day have not to strive against Italian and Moguntian* practices, but against

---

* He refers to the agents of the Pope and the Archbishop of Mentz (*Moguntium*).

the spiritual designs and knaveries of the devil; therefore, the Holy Ghost must resist and destroy those wicked stratagems. Against those tyrants, Michael, Gabriel, and Raphael, the loving angels, must protect and defend us, otherwise we are lost."

The Prince's best Wealth.

At the Imperial Diet at Augsburg, certain Princes were speaking in praise of the riches and advantages of their countries and principalities. The Prince Elector of Saxony said, "He had in his countries store of silver mines, which brought him great revenues." The Prince Elector Palatine extolled his vineyards and wine, that were produced on the banks of the Rhine, &c. &c. Now when the turn came for Everard, Prince of Wirtemburgh to speak also, he said, "I am, indeed, but a poor prince, and no way to be compared with any of you; nevertheless, I have in my country a rich and precious jewel; namely, that if I should haply ride astray in my country, and lost myself, and were left alone in the fields, yet I could safely and securely sleep in the bosom of every one of my subjects; they are all ready, for my service, to venture body, goods, and blood."—"And, indeed," said Luther, "his people esteemed him as a *Pater patriæ*. When the other two Princes heard the same, they confessed that he was, indeed, the richest of the three."

A Great Man's Example.

"I invited Prince Ernestus of Luneburgh, and Prince William of Mecklenburgh," said Luther, " to dine with me in my house at Wittemberg; at which time they complained much of the unmeasurable swilling and drinking kind of life at courts, ' and yet,' said they, ' all will be good Christians!' Whereupon I said, 'The princes and potentates should look to these things.'—' Ah, sir,' replied then Prince Ernest, ' we princes do even so ourselves, otherwise the same would have long since gone down.' *Significans,"* said Luther, "*principis intemperantiam esse causam intemperantiæ populi;* for when the abbot throweth the dice, the whole convent will play. *Manant exempla regentum in vulgus.*"

CHAPTER VIII.

MISCELLANEOUS THOUGHTS ON POLITICS, LAW, LITERATURE, ETC.

Dr. Luther's Judgment touching Resistance to Government, or constrained Defence.

"This question (whether, with God and a safe conscience, we may defend ourselves against the Emperor, if he should take in hand to subjugate us) is to be brought before lawyers," said Luther, "and not before divines.

"If the Emperor begins a war against us, his intention is, either to destroy the office of preaching and our religion; or else, to confuse and disturb the policy and economy; *i. e.* the temporal and house government. If this be so, he is no more to be held for an elected and lawful Roman emperor, but directly for a tyrant. It is, therefore, altogether needless to demand whether we may strive for the upright, pure, doctrine and religion. We ought and must strive for wife and children, for servants and subjects; yea, we are bound to defend them from wrongful power.

"If I live," said Luther, "I will write an admonition to all the states of the Christian world touching forced defence: that every one is obliged to defend him and his against wrongful power. First, the Emperor is the head of the body in the temporal kingdom, of which body every subject and private person is a piece and member, to whom the right of forced defence is permitted, as to a civil and temporal person; for if he defend not himself, he is, in effect, a slayer of his own person.

"Secondly, the Emperor is no monarch, or sole lord, in Germany; but the Princes Electors, together with the Emperor, are temporal members: each of which is charged and commanded to take care of the Empire, to further the good thereof, and to hinder and resist what may hurt and prejudice the same. Yet not so as the principal head, the Emperor. For although the Princes Electors are with the Emperor in equal power, yet are they not in equal dignity and worth. But the Princes Electors, and other Princes of the Empire, are bound to resist the Emperor, in case he should take any thing in hand directly tending to the hurt of the Empire, or against God and legal right. Moreover, if the Emperor should proceed to depose any one of the Princes Electors, then he deposeth them all; which neither ought, nor must be permitted.

"Wherefore, before we answer conclusively to this question, whether the Emperor may depose the Princes Electors, or whether they may depose the Emperor, we must first rightly thus distinguish:—a Christian consisteth of two kinds of person; that is, a believing or spiritual person, and a civil or temporal person.*

---

* The distinction here mentioned by Luther is deserving of serious attention, not (of course) as a means of evading the force of the Saviour's command (Matt. v. 39.), but as a help to the due and conscientious discharge of duties, which may, to some, appear incompatible. The duties of the Christian, considered simply as

The believing or spiritual person ought to endure and suffer all things; he neither eateth nor drinketh; he begetteth no children, nor hath any part in such temporal doings and actions. But the temporal and civil person is subject to temporal rights and laws, and is tied to obedience; he must maintain and defend himself and his, according as the laws and rights do command.

"For instance, now, if a wicked wretch should presume to force my wife, or my maid, in my presence; then truly I would lay aside the spiritual person, and make use of the temporal; I would slay him on the spot, or call for help; for in the absence of the magistrates (and when they may not be had), then the law of the nation is in force, which alloweth to call upon the neighbour for help; for Christ and the Gospel do

---

a spiritual person, whose only concern is with the "Father of spirits," are plain: he is to endure all things; and it should be the constant tone and temper of his mind to do so; patient, forbearing, placable. But he has duties equally binding upon him, arising from his connection with civil society, and from that command which bids him "submit to every ordinance of man for the Lord's sake." It is in this capacity, as a civil and temporal person, and equally under the sanction of Divine authority, that he is to bear his part in upholding and carrying into execution the laws, according to the constitution of the state with which he is connected; and for the same reason, in resisting, in a Christian-like manner, the unconstitutional encroachments of rulers, or the perverse machinations of those who are given to change. It is from such principles that an English Christian will feel himself bound to do his part in maintaining unimpaired that excellent constitution of government, which God has bestowed upon his country;— a blessing productive of advantages, spiritual and temporal, to himself, his countrymen, and the world at large, which are absolutely incalculable.

not abolish temporal rights and ordinances, but confirm the same.

"To conclude, forasmuch as the Emperor is no absolute monarch, that governeth alone and at his will, but that the Princes Electors are in equal power with him, therefore he hath no right, nor authority, to make laws and ordinances alone: much less hath he power, right, or authority, to draw the sword, to overpower the subjects and members of the Empire, without the acknowledgment of the law, or without the knowledge and consent of the whole Empire. Therefore Emperor Otho did very wisely in ordaining seven Princes Electors, who, with and besides the Emperor, should rule and govern the Empire, which otherwise could never have endured as it has done.

"Lastly, we ought to know, that when the Emperor intendeth to make war against us, then he doth it not of and for himself (in regard of his office), but for the Pope's sake, to whom he is sworn a liegeman, and undertaketh to maintain and defend the Pope's tyranny and abominable idolatry; for the Pope regardeth the Gospel nothing at all, and intendeth only to make use of the Emperor to preserve his own power and tyranny. Therefore we ought not therein to be silent, nor to sit still.

"But," said Luther, "there may some one object, and say, 'Although David of God was chosen king, and of Samuel was anointed, yet he would not resist king Saul, nor lay his hand upon him: therefore neither ought we to resist the Emperor,' &c. To which I answer, 'David at that time had only the promise of his kingdom, he had it not in possession, he was not settled in the government.' But," said Luther, "in this cause we strive not against Saul, but against Absalom: against whom David made war, and the rebel was slain by Joab.

"I would willingly," said Luther, "have a disputation touching this case, whether we may resist the Emperor or no? And although the lawyers (with their temporal and natural rights) do approve thereof, yet by us divines it is a question of much danger, in regard of these sentences,—Matt. v. 39.; 1 Pet. ii. 18.: ' *Whoso smiteth thee on the right cheek, turn to him the other also.*' And, ' *Servants, be subject to your masters with all fear, not only to the good and gentle, but also to the froward,*' &c. We must beware," said Luther, "that we take nothing in hand against God's word. Of this, however, we are sure, that these times are not like the times of the martyrs, when Dioclesian reigned and tyrannised against the Christians; there is another manner of kingdom and government. The Emperor's authority and power without the seven Princes Electors is of no value. The lawyers have made the Emperor an evil game. He hath parted with the sword, and given us possession of that sword, *gladium traditum possessorium.* The Emperor hath over us only one sword, *gladium petitorium;* he must seek and desire it of us, when he intendeth to punish; for, by right, he can do nothing of himself alone. If his government were a Dioclesian, then would we willingly submit unto him, and suffer.

"I hope," said Luther, "that the Emperor will not make war upon us for the Pope's sake; but if he should play the part of an Arian[*], and openly fight against

---

[*] Alluding to the persecutions of the orthodox Christians by such of the Roman emperors as had fallen away to Arianism.

God's word,—not like a Chistian, but as a heathen,—then we ought to give place, to depart from him, and to suffer. To conclude: I," said Luther, "do ungird the sword from the Pope's side, not from the Emperor's and this is evident, that the Pope ought to be neither tyrant nor governor."

Luther's concluding Speech concerning forced Defence.

"*First*, Princes are no slaves.

"*Secondly*, The Emperor ruleth upon certain engagements and conditions.

"*Thirdly*, He is sworn to the Empire, to the Princes Electors, and other Princes.

"*Fourthly*, He hath by oath bound himself unto them, to preserve the Empire in its dignity, honour, royalty, and jurisdiction, and to defend every person in that which justly and rightly belongeth to him; therefore it is not to be tolerated that he should bring them into servitude and slavery.

"*Fifthly*, We may well use the benefit of the laws.

"*Sixthly*, He ought to yield to Christian laws and rights.

"*Seventhly*, Our Princes are bound to the Empire by oath, truly to maintain the privileges and jurisdictions of the same, in political and temporal cases, and not to permit any thing belonging to the same to be taken and drawn away.

They, like Emperor Charles, bore the name of Christian princes, and professed great zeal for religion, while they harassed most bitterly those that held the true faith of Christianity.

—"*Eighthly*, These cases are among equals, where one is neither more nor higher than another; therefore, if the Emperor, with tyranny, dealeth contrary to equity and justice, then he maketh himself equal with others: for thereby he layeth aside the person of a governor, and justly loseth his right over the subjects, *per naturam relativorum*, by the nature of relatives; for prince and subjects are equally bound the one to the other; and the prince is bound to perform what he hath sworn and promised, according to the common proverb, '*Faithful master, faithful servant*.'

"*Ninthly*, The laws and rights are superior to a prince and tyrant: for the laws and ordinances are not wavering, but always sure and constant. On the contrary, a human creature is of a wavering, uncertain mind, and altogether inconstant; he, for the most part, followeth his lusts and pleasures, if by the laws he be not restrained; therefore we are more bound to follow the laws and rights than to follow a tyrant.

"If," said Luther, "a robber on the highway should fall upon me, then, truly, I would be judge and prince myself; and if no one were with me and about me that were able to defend me, I would diligently use my sword. I would thereupon take the holy sacrament, that I had done a good work. But if any one fell upon me as a preacher, for the Gospel's sake, then, with folded hands, I would lift up mine eyes to heaven, and say, 'My Lord Christ, here I am; I have confessed and preached Thee, &c.; is now my time expired? so commit I my spirit into Thy hands:' and in that sort I would die," said Luther.

Luther's Discourse of Lawyers.

"Before me," said Luther, "that is, before I wrote against the abominations of the Pope, no lawyer knew what was right and just *before God;* what they have in this way, they have it of me. Before the world I will grant them to have right, but before God they shall be under me.

"I will do the lawyers no harm," said Luther; "I will but take the little catechism, and will therewith so bustle among them, and make them so afraid, that they shall not know where to remain with their laws. If the lawyers will not pray for the remission of sins, and creep to the Gospel, then will I make them err, and confused, insomuch that they shall not know which way to wind themselves. I understand not their law, but I am a master in those laws that concern the conscience. The lawyers say, 'It is a dangerous thing to define, to describe, and show a thing properly and uprightly, round and briefly.' But the divines say, 'It pertaineth to them to teach always what is sure and certain, without doubting.' Otherwise, what course should a poor, trembling conscience take, that seeketh peace and comfort, if we did not produce sure and certain doctrine out of God's word; but left a poor, trembling, quaking conscience thus between heaven and hell."

Two doctors in the law came to Luther at Wittemberg, whom having saluted, they fell into discourse, and Luther addressed them after this manner:— "O, ye canonists, I could well endure you, if you meddled only with the Imperial, and not with Popish laws. But ye, doctors of both laws, do maintain the Pope and his canons. I would give one of my hands on condition that all Papists and Canonists were compelled to *keep* the Pope's laws; I would wish them no worse devil."

" Lawyers, oftentimes, are enemies to Christ," said Luther; " as they use to say, ' a right lawyer, an evil Christian,' for such a one applaudeth the righteousness of works; as though we were justified thereby before God. But if it chance that he be enlightened and regenerate, that is, if he be a true Christian, then he is like a monster among the lawyers; he must be a beggar, and by other lawyers be held rebellious. Ye lawyers," said Luther, " take heed that ye tread not us divines under foot; if you do, be assured that we will sting your heels. If I gave attention to study in the laws but for two years, methinks I would be better learned therein than Dr. Jerome Schurf: for I would discourse of causes, as in truth they are, and ought to be understood, of themselves, as either just or unjust. But he contendeth only about words; he goeth not upon the ground of speaking the plain truth, but resteth upon a *quos*, which he may screw every way; they talk much, and make many words, but without understanding. Dr. Schurf may justly be called Dr. *Quos*. The doctrine of the lawyers is nothing but merely a *nisi*; that is, unless this or that; *nisi* must be in every case. But divinity goeth not about with *nisi*; but it is certain, and hath a constant and sure ground, which neither faileth nor deceiveth. Lawyers have need of the help of divines, but we nothing at all of their voice and assistance. A lawyer is wise according to human wisdom, but a divine is wise according to God's wisdom."

"When a lawyer knoweth no more than *terminos juris*, his law terms, so is he a mere idiot. A wise lawyer saith, 'If one be accused before a judge, and the judge know him to be innocent, yet, if he be convicted by the testimony of witnesses, he must pronounce sentence according to the testimony:' and this, their opinion, they would confirm by Scripture, because it saith, '*In the mouth of two or three witnesses every word shall be established:*' therefore, say the lawyers, the judge must condemn the innocent, because there are two or three witnesses.

"The gross asses," said Luther, "know not what the judgment of Scripture is. What must the judge do in this case? He knoweth the innocency of the accused; must he condemn the innocent party upon the evidence of witnesses, against his own conscience? In this case," said Luther, "the worldly wise lawyers do give comfort to the judge on this wise, and say, 'Forasmuch as thou knowest that wrong is done to the accused, the same thou knowest as a private person for thyself, not as a judge, who must pronounce *secundum allegata et probata*, according to the evidence and proof. Moreover, it concerneth thee, as a judge, nothing at all, in regard that thou art not called to be a witness,' &c. They cheer up, also, and comfort the innocent accused in this manner:— 'Forasmuch as thou knowest thou receivest wrong, so yield thyself to the seat of justice, and suffer wrong,' &c. But," said Luther, "were I the judge in such case, so would I open my mouth, yea, would cry out, and say, 'I bear witness that this person is innocent;' and, although ten thousand witnesses should rise against him, I, knowing his innocence for certain, neither can nor will condemn him.' Then cometh the lawyer again, with his profound wisdom, and saith, 'O judge! thou dost act herein contrary to the Emperor's laws,' &c. I answer that lawyer," said Luther, "and say, 'A sir-reverence on such law as doth a man open wrong.' — 'But,' saith the lawyer, 'there are so many witnesses against him.' — *Answer*, — 'How many false witnesses have there always been from the beginning of the world? Christ, by false witnesses, was slain, Stephen stoned, &c. Witnesses may be corrupted with money: how many are the examples of this?' To conclude," said Luther, "the lawyers have no consciences. A lawyer will take ten dollars, and serve in an evil cause under colour of right: with this they trim and trick out the matter to save their credit. The lawyers make their clients noses of wax: though the cause be lost, doubtless they have deserved the money.

"This I speak," said Luther, "to you young fellows who intend to be lawyers, not to discourage and affright you, but to admonish you that ye should deal justly, and be honest and upright lawyers. Follow not your preceptors in abuses and evil points. Flatter not in wrongful causes, nor think to make yourselves good lawyers by practising evil customs. God has not given laws for that end, to make out of right wrong, and out of wrong right, as the unchristian-like lawyers do, who study in law only for the sake of gain. Let not this dismay you; but study diligently."

Of a strange Case at Law.

Anno 1546. A case in law was related to Luther; namely, That a miller had an ass, which ran out of his yard, and came to a river's side, where he went into a fisher's boat that stood in the river, and would drink thereout. But inasmuch as the boat was not tied fast

by the fisher, it floated away with the ass, so that the miller lost his ass, and the fisher his boat. The miller thereupon complained of the fisher, that he neglected to tie his boat fast. Again, the fisher accused the miller for not keeping his ass at home, and therefore desired satisfaction for his boat. Now, it is a quære what the law is. Took the ass the boat, or the boat the ass away? Whereupon Luther said,—
" These are called *casus in jure*, cases in law; *ambo peccaverunt*, they were both in error: the fisher, in that he fastened not his boat; the miller, in not keeping his ass at home. *Culpa est in utraque parte*," said Luther; " *est casus fortuitus, uterque peccaverunt negligentid: talis casus et exempla illudunt summum jus juristarum: non enim practicandum est summum jus, sed æquitas. Omnia sunt gubernanda secundum æquitatem. Ita theologi quoque prædicare debent, ne homines omnino ligent et solvant.*"

Of Astronomy and Astrology.

" I applaud," said Luther, " *astronomiam et mathematicam*, which consist in demonstrations, or sure proofs. As for Astrology, I hold nothing at all of it. *Astronomia versatur circa materiem et genus, non circa formam et speciem;* it dealeth with matter, and what is general; not with the manner, and what is particular. God Himself shall and will be alone the Master and Creator; He only will be Lord and Governor, although He hath ordained the stars to be for signs. So long as Astronomy remaineth within her circle whereunto God hath ordained her, she is a fair gift of God; but when she will step out of her bounds,— that is, when she will prophesy, and speak of future things, how it will go with one, or what fortune or misfortune one shall have, — then is she not to be justified. But *chiromantiam* or palmistry, that is, to look in one's hand, and tell what shall happen, we ought utterly to reject.

"Philip Melancthon * hath a firm persuasion touching Astrology," said Luther; " but he was never able to bring me to his mind. He confesseth, indeed, himself, that it hath not experience or sure grounds, except they intend to call *eventum*, experience. But experience is this, — when we conclude out of particular and single points, and proceed to the general, *ex singularibus ad universalia;* as when I say, This fire burneth, that fire burneth, and so on; therefore every fire burneth. But Astrology hath not this ground of experience; it decides only according to casual events, as it happens now and then.

"I am come so far into Astrology," said Luther, "that I believe it is nothing. For Philip Melancthon, against his will, confesseth unto me that the art, indeed, exists, but there are none that understand it rightly. But they will be sure, in their almanacks, to teach and show, that we shall not have snow in summer-time, nor thunder in winter; and this the country clown knoweth as well as the astrologer. Philip Melancthon saith, that such people as are born *in ascendente Libra* (the first rising of the Scales

* It would be perfectly surprising how this wise and worthy man, with many other deeply-learned and sober-minded persons, should be infected with the belief of this vain science, did we not know the powerful effect which early impressions have upon the strongest minds. In Melancthon's early days, most of the learned were addicted to astrology. Luther's sterling good sense discovers itself very strikingly in the rejection of it.

towards the south) are unfortunate people. Ah!" said Luther, "the astrologers are simple, unhappy creatures, who dream that their crosses and mishaps proceed not from God, but from the stars. What patience can they have in troubles and adversities?"

The nativities of Luther, of Cicero, and of others (printed at Nuremberg), being brought before Luther, he said, "These things are, in my judgment, of no value, and I wish the astrologers would answer me this plain argument:—Esau and Jacob were born both together of one father and one mother, at one time, and under equal planets, and yet were altogether contrary in nature, mind, and every thing. Therefore what is done by God, and is His work, ought not to be ascribed unto the stars. The upright and true Christian religion opposeth and refuteth all such riddles and fables. The world, without religion, is Lucianical, and full of Epicurism. Well is he," said Luther, "that in faith hearkeneth unto the Word of God."

When Luther's nativity (as they call it) was shown to him, he said, " It is a fine fiction, and acceptable to natural sense and reason. The way of making nativities, and casting these accounts, is like the proceedings in Popedom, where the outward ceremonies, and pompous ordinances, are pleasing to human nature, as the holy water, torches, organs, cymbals, singing, ringing, &c.; but there is no right or certain knowledge in these tricks of theirs. Likewise such do very sorely err, who endeavour, out of these fancies, to frame a certain art or science, when, in fact, there is none; for Astrology (as they call it) proceedeth not out of the nature of Astronomy, which is a science; but it is merely a human tradition; it is altogether opposite to true philosophy; and neither Philip Melancthon, nor any man living, shall persuade me otherwise.

"Oftentimes," said Luther, " have I discoursed with Philip Melancthon, and related to him, in order, the course and manner of my whole life. ' I am,' said I, ' the son of a farmer. My father, grandfather, and great grandfather, were farmers; but my father left his farm, and went towards Mansfield, where he became a miner in the silver mines. One mile from that place (at Isliben) I was born and bred. Now, was it written in the planets that I should become a bachelor of arts, a master, a friar, &c.— was it, think you? Did not I,' said Luther, ' purchase to myself a great shame, in that I laid aside the brown beard, and became a dirty friar, which sore vexed my father, and was very grievous to him? Well, but after this, I fell to buffets with the Pope, and he again with me: I took a wife (a fled nun), and of her begat certain children. Who now, I pray you, saw these things in the stars? who told me, or could tell me, before, that thus and thus it should happen to me?'

" An astrologer, or star-peeper, is to be likened to one that selleth dice, and saith, ' Behold, here I have dice that always run upon twelve*;—the rest of the fifty casts, they run upon 2, 3, 4, 5, 6, 7, 8, 9, 10, 11.' Even thus it is with the astrologers; when, once or twice, their conceits and fancies do hit and happen,

---

* That is, they always turn up sizes, except when they do not; like a marksman who is sure to hit, if he does not miss.

then they cannot sufficietly praise and extol their art; but of their frequent failures they say not a word.

"I accept of Astronomy," said Luther, "it pleaseth me well, for the sake of her manifold profits. David, in Psalm xix., remembereth the wonderful works and creatures of God. He taketh delight in the firmament of heaven. Job also remembereth Orion, which they call Jacob's staff, the seven stars, &c. As for Astrology, it is merely a juggling trick."

A Word of Advice to Students.

"I would advise," said Luther, "that whatsoever art you study, you should betake yourself to the reading of some sure and certain sorts of books, oftentimes, over and over again; for to read many sorts of books produceth confusion, rather than any certain and exact knowledge. It is much the same as with those that dwell every where, and remain certainly in no place; such do dwell nowhere, and are nowhere at home. And like as in society, we use not the company of all friends, but of some few selected; even so likewise ought we to accustom ourselves to the best books, and to make the same familiar to us; to have them (as we use to say) at our fingers' ends."

"Wisdom, understanding, learning, and the pen,— these do govern the world," said Luther. "If God were angry, and took all the learned out of the world, then all people would become mere wild and savage beasts; for without wisdom, understanding, and laws, not even Turks or Tartars could live together and subsist."

"Before a few years are expired," said Luther; "there will be such want of learned people, that they would willingly dig them nine ells deep out of the ground, if they could but get them; but all is in vain: we provoke God too sorely to anger."

OF SUNDRY LEARNED MEN.

Of John Huss the Martyr.

"The blood of *John Huss* is cursed yearly by the Papists. Truly," said Luther, "he was an honest and a learned man, as may be seen in his Book of the Church, which I love exceeding well. There is, indeed, a weakness in him, but it is the weakness of a Christian, and God's power bestirreth itself in him, and raiseth him up again. The combat of the flesh and of the Spirit of Christ, in Huss, is sweet and delightful to behold. There remains sure and undoubted evidence of this, that *Jerome of Prague** was an eloquent, but Huss a very learned man. He accomplished

---

* There is hardly a more interesting historical document extant, than the letter of the famous Poggio Bracciolini to his friend Leonardo Aretini. These two distinguished literary characters were both secretaries to the court of Rome; the former attended the council of Constance, in A.D. 1416, and having been a witness of the whole of the proceedings connected with the condemnation of Jerome, wrote his friend, who was then at Rome, an account of what had taken place. The date of the letter is that of Jerome's martyrdom. It may be seen, at length, in Milner's Church History.

more than the whole world was able to do. From the time of the shedding of that innocent blood, Papery by degrees began to fall. Constance, since the death of Huss, is grown a miserable poor city," said Luther. "I verily believe that God's punishment struck it, because the citizens therein armed themselves, and led that holy man Huss to the fire. The Holy Ghost was powerful in Huss, who so joyfully and constantly maintained God's word against so many great and powerful nations: namely, against Germany, Spain, Italy, England, and France, then assembled, by their representatives, in the council at Constance. Against their assaults, cries, and alarum, he only stood, was constrained to bear them, and thereupon was burned to ashes. Even so," said Luther, "shall I (God willing) be more secure in death, than in this life."

Of Livy, &c.

"How pitifully," said Luther, "so many great and excellent deeds are sunk, from not being written. The Greeks and Romans only have writers of history. Of *Livius* there is only a small parcel left, the rest is darkened, lost, and destroyed. *Sabellius* intended to imitate and follow *Livius*, but fulfilled nothing. *Ovid* was an excellent poet: he excelled all the rest in fair sentences, which, masterlike, he fastened in verse, as

'*Nox, amor, vinumque, nihil moderabile suadent.*'

Virgil surpasseth all others in grandeur and sublimity, —*in heroica gravitate,*—he is, indeed, prince-like, and seriously important."

Luther, reading *Lucan*, said, "I know not whether he be a poet or a writer of histories; for they are thus distinguished:—a writer of history saith what is true; an orator, and he that is eloquent, saith what is like truth; but a poet writeth neither what is true, nor what is like to truth. Therefore Aristotle saith, 'The poets do lie much; for when they have small reason and ground, then they make it very great, stretching it high and far:—there must needs be much lying here, like a painter who pictureth a person much fairer than she is: such a painter doubtless is a liar.' *Julius Cæsar* said, 'When I read Brutus's writings, then I take myself to be eloquent; but when I read the Orations of *Cicero*, then I am ineloquent: I loll like a child.'"

Of Bucer.

"To translate my books into Latin," said Luther, "no man is better qualified than *Dr. Bucer:* he giveth my meaning so properly (if therewith he mingled not his buzzing about the sacrament), that I myself could not express my heart and mind nearer nor better."

Of Aristotle and Cicero.

"*Aristotle*," said Luther, "is altogether an Epicure; he holdeth that God meddleth not with the affairs of human-kind, but permitteth us to proceed according to our pleasure. According to him, God ruleth the world as a sleepy maid rocketh a child. But *Cicero* attained to a further scope: I believe," said Luther, "that he brought together all the good things he could find in the books of the Greek writers and teachers.

It is a good argument (which oftentimes moved me much, and went near my heart) by which he proves the being of God. 'The living creatures,' said he, 'beget on one another that which is like and agreeable, each one to himself. A cow always produceth a cow, a horse, a horse, &c. Therefore it followeth undeniably, that something is which ruleth every thing.'

"We may acknowledge God also in the regular and certain course of the stars in the heaven; in the sun likewise, which every year rises and sets in its place, that we may have winter and summer at certain times. These things, being done daily, and become common and customary to us, therefore we neither admire nor regard them; but if a child from its infancy were brought up in a dark place, and at twenty years of age were let out, how would it wonder at the sun, to think what it could be, and what a sure and certain course it held; but to us it is nothing; for what is common and done daily, the same is nothing regarded."

Discourse was held how great differences were among the learned, whereupon Luther said, "God hath very finely divided His gifts, in that the learned serve the unlearned; and, again, the unlearned must humble themselves to obtain what is needful from the learned. If all people were equal, no man would serve another, neither would there be any peace. The peacock complaineth that he wants the nightingale's voice; therefore God, with the inequality, hath made the greatest equality; for we see, when one is excellent, and hath more and greater gifts than another, then is he proud and haughty, will rule and domineer over others, and contemn them.

"God, therefore, hath very finely and well set forth the state of human society by the members of the body: one member must reach out the hand, and help the other; none can be without the other. In the face are the most honourable members; yet the nose (the house of office) is placed above the mouth and under the eyes. If only two people in the world had noses, they would be considered monsters; but forasmuch as we are all snotty and snivelling, therefore the nose humbleth us. Let us also consider the gifts of the belly and hinder parts, how necessary they be, without which we cannot live. A man or woman may live without eyes, ears, hands, feet, &c.; but (*salvâ reverentiâ*) without the tail no human creature can live; so great and necessary is the use and profit of this one member, that to it belongeth the preservation of human existence. Therefore St. Paul saith well, (1 Cor. xii.) '*Those members of the body which seem to be more feeble, are necessary; and those which we think to be less honourable, upon these we bestow more abundant honour.*'"

THE END.

London:
Printed by A. & R. Spottiswoode,
New-Street-Square.